THE KEY

STUDENT STUDY GUIDE

English 30-1

THE KEY student study guide is designed to help students achieve success in school. The content in each study guide is 100% aligned to the provincial curriculum and serves as an excellent source of material for review and practice. To create this book, teachers, curriculum specialists, and assessment experts have worked closely to develop the instructional pieces that explain each of the key concepts for the course. The practice questions and sample tests have detailed solutions that show problem-solving methods, highlight concepts that are likely to be tested, and point out potential sources of errors. **THE KEY** is a complete guide to be used by students throughout the school year for reviewing and understanding course content, and to prepare for assessments.

Publisher
Gautam Rao

Contributors
Ute Brigitte Blunck
Brigitta Braden

Rao, Gautam, 1961 –
THE KEY – English 30-1 (2010 Edition) Alberta

1. English – Juvenile Literature. I. Title

Published by
Castle Rock Research Corp.
2340 Manulife Place
10180 – 101 Street
Edmonton, AB T5J 3S4

1 2 3 FP 11 10 09

CASTLE ROCK
RESEARCH CORP

Dedicated to the memory of Dr. V. S. Rao

THE KEY—ENGLISH 30-1

THE KEY consists of the following sections:

KEY Tips for Being Successful at School gives examples of study and review strategies. It includes information about learning styles, study schedules, and note taking for test preparation.

Class Focus includes a unit on each area of the curriculum. Units are divided into sections, each focusing on one of the specific expectations, or main ideas, that students must learn about in that unit. Examples, definitions, and visuals help to explain each main idea. Practice questions on the main ideas are also included. At the end of each unit is a test on the important ideas covered. The practice questions and unit tests help students identify areas they know and those they need to study more. They can also be used as preparation for tests and quizzes. Each unit is prefaced by a ***Table of Correlations***, which correlates questions in the unit (and in the practice tests at the end of the book) to the specific curriculum expectations. Answers and solutions are found at the end of each unit.

KEY Strategies for Success on Tests helps students get ready for tests. It shows students different types of questions they might see, word clues to look for when reading them, and hints for answering them.

Practice Tests includes one to three tests based on the entire course. They are very similar to the format and level of difficulty that students may encounter on final tests. In some regions, these tests may be reprinted versions of official tests, or reflect the same difficulty levels and formats as official versions. This gives students the chance to practice using real-world examples. Answers and complete solutions are provided at the end of the section.

For the complete curriculum document (including specific expectations along with examples and sample problems), visit http://education.alberta.ca/teachers/program/english/programs.aspx.

THE KEY *Study Guides* are available for many courses. Check www.castlerockresearch.com for a complete listing of books available for your area.

For information about any of our resources or services, please call Castle Rock Research at 780.448.9619 or visit our website at http://www.castlerockresearch.com.

At Castle Rock Research, we strive to produce an error-free resource. If you should find an error, please contact us so that future editions can be corrected.

TABLE OF CONTENTS

NOTES

KEY Tips for Being Successful at School

KEY TIPS FOR BEING SUCCESSFUL AT SCHOOL

KEY FACTORS CONTRIBUTING TO SCHOOL SUCCESS

In addition to learning the content of your courses, there are some other things that you can do to help you do your best at school. Some of these strategies are listed below.

- **KEEP A POSITIVE ATTITUDE**—always reflect on what you can already do and what you already know.

- **BE PREPARED TO LEARN**—have ready the necessary pencils, pens, notebooks, and other required materials for participating in class.

- **COMPLETE ALL OF YOUR ASSIGNMENTS**—do your best to finish all of your assignments. Even if you know the material well, practice will reinforce your knowledge. If an assignment or question is difficult for you, work through it as far as you can so that your teacher can see exactly where you are having difficulty.

- **SET SMALL GOALS FOR YOURSELF WHEN YOU ARE LEARNING NEW MATERIAL**— for example, when learning the parts of speech, do not try to learn everything in one night. Work on only one part or section each study session. When you have memorized one particular part of speech and understand it, then move on to another one, continue this process until you have memorized and learned all the parts of speech.

- **REVIEW YOUR CLASSROOM WORK REGULARLY AT HOME**—Review to be sure that you understand the material that you learned in class.

- **ASK YOUR TEACHER FOR HELP**—your teacher will help you if you do not understand something or if you are having a difficult time completing your assignments.

- **GET PLENTY OF REST AND EXERCISE**—concentrating in class is hard work. It is important to be well-rested and have time to relax and socialize with your friends. This helps you to keep your positive attitude about your school work.

- **EAT HEALTHY MEALS**—a balanced diet keeps you healthy and gives you the energy that you need for studying at school and at home.

How to Find Your Learning Style

Every student learns differently. The manner in which you learn best is called your learning style. By knowing your learning style, you can increase your success at school. Most students use a combination of learning styles. Do you know what type of learner you are? Read the following descriptions. Which of these common learning styles do you use most often?

- **Linguistic Learner**: You may learn best by saying, hearing, and seeing words. You are probably really good at memorizing things such as dates, places, names, and facts. You may need **to write and then say out loud** the steps in a process, a formula, or the actions that lead up to a significant event.

- **Spatial Learner**: You may learn best by looking at and working with pictures. You are probably really good at puzzles, imagining things, and reading maps and charts. You may need to use strategies like **mind mapping and webbing** to organize your information and study notes.

- **Kinaesthetic Learner**: You may learn best by touching, moving, and figuring things out using manipulative. You are probably really good at physical activities and learning through movement. You may need to **draw your finger over a diagram** to remember it, **"tap out" the steps** needed to solve a problem, or **"feel" yourself writing** or typing a formula.

SCHEDULING STUDY TIME

You should review your class notes regularly to ensure that you have a clear understanding of all the new material you learned. Reviewing your lessons on a regular basis helps you to learn and remember ideas and concepts. It also reduces the quantity of material that you need to study prior to a test. Establishing a study schedule will help you to make the best use of your time.

Regardless of the type of study schedule you use, you may want to consider the following suggestions to maximize your study time and effort:

• Organize your work so that you begin with the most challenging material first.

• Divide the subject's content into small, manageable chunks.

• Alternate regularly between your different subjects and types of study activities in order to maintain your interest and motivation.

• Make a daily list with headings like "Must Do," "Should Do," and "Could Do."

• Begin each study session by quickly reviewing what you studied the day before.

• Maintain your usual routine of eating, sleeping, and exercising to help you concentrate better for extended periods of time.

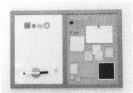

CREATING STUDY NOTES

MIND-MAPPING OR WEBBING

- Use the key words, ideas, or concepts from your reading or class notes to create a *mind map* or *web* (a diagram or visual representation of the given information). A mind map or web is sometimes referred to as a knowledge map.

- Write the key word, concept, theory, or formula in the centre of your page.

- Write down related facts, ideas, events, and information and then link them to the central concept with lines.

- Use coloured markers, underlining, or other symbols to emphasize things such as relationships, time lines, and important information.

The following mind map is an example of one that could help you develop an essay:

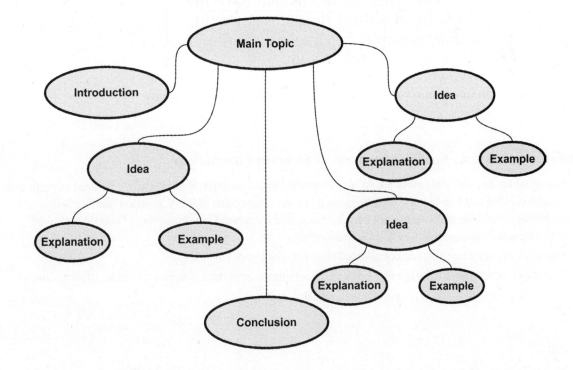

INDEX CARDS

To use index cards while studying, follow these steps:

• Write a key word or question on one side of an index card.

• On the reverse side, write the definition of the word, answer to the question, or any other important information that you want to remember.

```
┌─────────────────────────────────────┐
│                                       │
│                                       │
│         What are                      │
│         synonyms?                     │
│                                       │
│                                       │
│                                       │
└─────────────────────────────────────┘
```

```
┌─────────────────────────────────────┐
│                                       │
│         What are synonyms?            │
│                                       │
│   Synonyms are words that have the    │
│   same or almost the same meaning.    │
│   For example, "coarse" is a synonym  │
│            for "rough."               │
│                                       │
└─────────────────────────────────────┘
```

SYMBOLS AND STICKY NOTES—IDENTIFYING IMPORTANT INFORMATION

• Use symbols to mark your class notes. For example, an exclamation mark (!) might be used to point out something that must be learned well because it is a very important idea. A question mark (?) may highlight something that you are not certain about, and a diamond (◊) or asterisk (*) could highlight interesting information that you want to remember.

• Use sticky notes when you are not allowed to put marks in books.

• Use sticky notes to mark a page in a book that contains an important diagram, formula, explanation, etc.

• Use sticky notes to mark important facts in research books.

MEMORIZATION TECHNIQUES

- **ASSOCIATION** relates new learning to something you already know. For example, to remember the spelling difference between dessert and desert, recall that the word sand has only one s. So, because there is sand in a desert, the word desert only has on s.

- **MNEMONIC DEVICES** are sentences that you create to remember a list or group of items. For example, the first letter of each word in the phrase "Every Good Boy Deserves Fudge" helps you to remember the names of the lines on the treble clef staff (E, G, B, D, and F) in music.

- **ACRONYMS** are words that are formed from the first letters or parts of the words in a group. For example, RADAR is actually an acronym for radio detecting and ranging, and MASH is an acronym for mobile army surgical hospital.

- **VISUALIZING** requires you to use your mind's eye to "see" a chart, list, map, diagram, or sentence as it is in your textbook or notes, on the chalk board or computer screen, or in a display.

- **INITIALISMS** are abbreviations that are formed from the first letters or parts of the words in a group. Unlike acronyms, initialisms cannot be pronounced as a word themselves. For example, BEDMAS is an initialism for the order of operations in math (Brackets, Exponents, Divide, Multiply, Add, Subtract), and HOMES helps you to remember the names of the five Great Lakes (Huron, Ontario, Michigan, Erie, and Superior).

KEY STRATEGIES FOR REVIEWING

Reviewing textbook material, class notes, and handouts should be an ongoing activity. Spending time reviewing becomes more critical when you are preparing for tests. You may find some of the following review strategies useful when studying during your scheduled study time.

- Before reading a selection, preview it by noting the headings, charts, graphs, and chapter questions.

- Read the complete introduction to identify the key information that is addressed in the selection.

- Read the first sentence of the next paragraph for the main idea.

- Skim the paragraph and note the key words, phrases, and information.

- Read the last sentence of the paragraph.

- Repeat this process for each paragraph and section until you have skimmed the entire selection.

KEY STRATEGIES FOR SUCCESS: A CHECKLIST

Review, review, review: review is a huge part of doing well at school and preparing for tests. Here is a checklist for you to keep track of how many suggested strategies for success you are using. Read each question and then put a check mark (✓) in the correct column. Look at the questions where you have checked the "No" column. Think about how you might try using some of these strategies to help you do your best at school.

KEY Strategies for Success	Yes	No
Do you attend school regularly?		
Do you know your personal learning style—how you learn best?		
Do you spend 15 to 30 minutes a day reviewing your notes?		
Do you study in a quiet place at home?		
Do you clearly mark the most important ideas in your study notes?		
Do you use sticky notes to mark texts and research books?		
Do you practise answering multiple-choice and written-response questions?		
Do you ask your teacher for help when you need it?		
Are you maintaining a healthy diet and sleep routine?		
Are you participating in regular physical activity?		

Comprehend and Respond

COMPREHEND AND RESPOND

2.1.1a   *explain the text creator's purpose, including implicit purpose when applicable; describe whether or not the purpose was achieved*

2.1.1b   *analyze elements or causes present in the communication situation surrounding a text that contribute to the creation of the text*

DETERMINING WRITER'S PURPOSE AND ANALYZING WRITER'S CRAFT

Reading may seem like a passive activity: you sit down and absorb what someone else has written. This could not be further from the truth because good readers read actively. Imagine, for example, that someone is writing a biography of your life and the writer has asked you to review it before it is published. Since you know all of the facts of your life quite well, you would probably be quite critical in analyzing the writer's work. You would probably ask a lot of questions about where the writer got his or her information and about how the writer reached certain conclusions about who you are. Because you know so much about yourself, it is easy to be critical of a text that is about something in which you have expertise. You should apply this same level of analysis to all texts you read. Reading requires an active, critical mind, no matter how much you may know about a text.

Reading should be an ongoing interaction between your thoughts and the text. As a natural part of your reading process, questions should be formulated, images of descriptions should be conjured, and the meaning of the text should be analyzed. The strategies in this section of your KEY will help you to be as observant, critical, and curious as possible when reading.

What you do before starting to read can make or break your reading experience. First, decide what purpose your reading is going to serve. Are you researching information for an essay? Answering questions for an assignment? Getting instructions for assembling a new bicycle? Escaping into the latest best-selling novel? Reading an advertisement for a product you are interested in purchasing? Deciding your purpose for reading will determine your attitude toward the text you read, the time you take to read it, the strategies you use to interpret it, and what you do with the information you have taken from it. Having a purpose when reading is like having a road map when driving: once you know your destination, you can make use of a number of signposts along the way to help you reach your destination.

STEP-BY-STEP CRITICAL READING

The following steps are useful as a guide to reading carefully. You may find that you already perform some of these steps without even thinking about them.

• Without studying the details, quickly scan the text to determine the:

  – intended audience

  – type of text (for example, play, essay, report, short story, informal letter, formal letter, article, advertisement)

  – writer's purpose (for example, to describe, to inform, to explain, to instruct, to persuade)

  – general contents of the text

- Take the time to look for information about the writer and the text. The front or back covers sometimes give information, or you can refer to outside sources, such as other books or online sources. The writer's country of origin or dates of birth and death, for instance, can be useful information. Knowing when and where a writer lived can help you interpret his or her meaning and purpose.

- As you read, make note of significant words in the text. Highlighting, underlining, circling words, or writing notes in the margin are all effective methods of documenting your observations.

- Use the features of the text to help you to determine meaning and purpose. Text features include:

  – titles or thesis statements

  – organization of ideas

  – punctuation

  – fonts and type faces

In nonfiction works, the thesis statement is usually stated in the first paragraph. Sometimes, it is also stated in the title and the conclusion. Make particular note of titles and endings when you read. Titles often give clues about or reinforce purpose. Your interpretation of a text must take into account the ending. If it does not, you could end up with an incomplete interpretation.

Observe the organization of the text. If there is a lot of dialogue in a text, the writer may be using indirect characterization to achieve his or her purpose. If there are charts or diagrams, the writer could be trying to persuade the reader with statistics. By questioning how a text is organized, you can find out more about the writer's intent.

- Consider the intended audience. Who was originally meant to read the text?

  – A poet might write for a small circle of friends—or for the whole world and for the coming centuries.

  – A novel is generally written with the hope that it will be read by as many people as possible.

  – Diaries are usually private, but some writers will journal their experiences with one eye on a potential future audience.

  – Emails and letters are usually written only for their recipients. Letters to the editor of a newspaper are written with the intention of a larger audience.

  – Shakespeare wrote for the Londoners who attended theatre productions. It seems that the publication of his plays was an afterthought. His purpose for writing plays was to attract more people to the theatre.

  – Leonardo da Vinci wrote his famous notebooks for himself. He even wrote using a mirror, so that it would be more difficult for someone else to read what he wrote.

- What was the writer's intent?

  – Some writers intend to persuade, spread ideas, or instruct.

  – The writer's purpose may be to move people to action.

  – Some writers want to share personal thoughts and feelings.

  – Sometimes, a writer writes simply for entertainment purposes.

2.1.1c explain how understanding the interplay between text and context can influence an audience to appreciate a text from multiple perspectives (for example, an audience can appreciate how historical and societal forces present in the context in which a text is set can affect the style, diction and point of view chosen by the text creator)

CONTEXT AND BACKGROUND

Context includes background information, knowledge, ideas—anything that adds to the understanding of a text. Writers frequently draw on the experiences of their lives when they write. It makes sense, then, that finding out more about a writer's life will give you added insight into the themes and main ideas of his or her text. The following section touches on aspects of a text to consider when trying to understand the relationship between context and the writer.

Context provides perspective. A better understanding of the context of even a single word can help you to better understand an entire text. For example, imagine that you were reading a book from the time of your great-grandparents. Most likely, you would be puzzled by some words and phrases.

Example

> "Ah, poor Smythe. Both of his sons killed at Arras, you know. And he lost his wife in the last Zeppelin raid."

You might find this bit of dialogue hard to follow at first. Words and phrases like "Arras" and "Zeppelin raid" are probably not familiar to you. At this stage, it is a good idea to slow down your reading. Take some time to analyze the text in smaller pieces. Among the unfamiliar phrases, you should find some phrases that you can understand, such as "poor Smythe." You can understand that someone is being referred to, and in this case, being pitied, so you also infer from the context that the speaker is expressing sympathy. In addition, the use of dialogue suggests that the book is a story.

If you read that the story takes place in the 1920s—not long after the First World War—you can use your general knowledge of that time to better understand this dialogue. The context now suggests that the sons were soldiers and that Arras was a battle. The Zeppelin raids would have had something to do with civilian casualties, since Smythe's wife, as a woman in the time of the First World War, would not have been fighting. You can infer that she probably died as an innocent civilian. The context of only two sentences allows you to make numerous inferences. While these inferences do not give you a complete understanding, they do give you a basic understanding, especially if the unfamiliar words initially confused you.

Why would a writer refer to details that might confuse the reader in the first place? Usually, a writer provides detail to make the story realistic—to provide a believable context to lend effect to the work. If a writer sets his or her story in a particular time and place, he or she will often refer to details that were part of the reality for that setting. Zeppelin raids would have been a reality for people living in Europe at the time of the First World War. When a writer refers to details of the world he or she is creating to make that world more realistic, the writer is using a technique referred to as verisimilitude. For example, if a writer wanted to employ verisimilitude in a novel set in Canada in 2008, he or she might mention Prime Minister Harper or the war in Afghanistan, or the writer might describe the most common types of cars.

A writer will also often use allusions to make a story seem real or to make a connection to a context that the reader might understand and relate to. An allusion is a reference to something that is familiar to both the writer and the readers. Allusions bring to mind people, events, stories, or things. Allusions are often Biblical, mythological, historical, or literary; they are deliberate reminders of context. They can connect characters in fiction to the events of the real world.

Pay Careful Attention to the Following Aspects of Context:

Time

When was the work produced?

- Writers working during periods of war or upheaval may be influenced by those conditions. For example, many people living in the 1930s shared a sense of insecurity and fear that resulted from the economic instability of the time.

- Similarly, times of peace and prosperity can also shape a writer's ideas and purpose.

- A work written when a writer is young may have marked differences than a work written when the writer is more mature.

Place

Where did the writer live?

- Place can be just as relevant to a writer's life as the time in which the writer lived because the surroundings help to shape the writer and can also give the material a setting.

- During the Depression, people in countries such as the Soviet Union and the Ukraine suffered greatly from poverty and famine.

- North Americans of the past two generations have been shaped by years of peace and prosperity; around the world, however, people in countries plagued by poverty and war probably have a very different perspective on life. Because of Canada's relative stability and wealth, people living here sometimes ignore or forget about the suffering of people in other countries. Writers who tell stories of hardship in other countries bring to light the suffering that exists outside of North America.

Point of View

What lies behind the character?

Writers sometimes give fictional characters a kind of "real" life with thoughts, feelings, and opinions of their own.

- Writers choose to create characters in different ways. Some characters are totally unique creations that do not express the viewpoints of the writer at all. Some characters are vehicles for the writer to make a point about something. When a writer feels strongly about something, he or she may create a character to express his or her opinion.

- It is important to separate the writer from the characters he or she creates. The characters are not always reflections of the writer, and characters in a text do not always express the opinions of the writer.

- Research about the writer's life and beliefs can sometimes help you figure out which type of character a writer has created in a given text.

- Writers often reveal themselves in their writing, but it is the reader's job to pay attention to the whole context of the work and decide when the writer is speaking and when the characters are speaking.

Style and Diction

A writer's style and choice of words can affect the meaning and impact of communication. The following definitions deal with different aspects of language that a writer may change depending on the effect he or she wants to achieve in the writing.

- **Diction** is the choice of words and phrases.

- **Register** refers to the special features of speech or writing used by a particular group or that used for a particular purpose. For example, newspaper reporters have a certain register, a common vocabulary, and established patterns of organization that they use in writing news stories.

- **Jargon** refers to specialized language that is used by the members of a trade or some other group. Jargon has the advantage (for those who understand it) of shortening communication and sometimes of making communication more accurate. Jargon is like a set of tools. People who do not know the jargon are lost, but those who do understand it can communicate quickly.

The control of diction, the use of a particular register, and the use of jargon depend entirely on the intended audience. However, to help you understand a work more fully, it is important to recognize who the target audience is.

Intention and Connotation

Diction also depends on intention. Consider the following pairs of questions. Although sentences seem to be communicating the same meaning, there are slight differences in intention between them.

Example

> *So you claim* that you handed in your assignment?
>
> *Did you say* that you handed in your assignment?

How does the word "claim" change the question? Which sentence seems more accusatory?

> *Do you admit* that you were present?
>
> *Do you agree* that you were present?

The word "admit" makes it seem as though the person who may have been present needs to somehow confess their presence. All words have special connotations that have developed over time. Writers are aware of these connotations and choose words carefully to meet their precise intentions.

Here are two more examples showing how word choices can have a strong effect on what is communicated.

Example

> Did the prices *rise*? Did they just *increase*, or did they *skyrocket*?
>
> Did the prime ministerial candidate *admit, state, assert*, or *proclaim* a change in policy?

Look at the nuances (subtle and slight differences in their expression and meaning) of the above words. In each case, there is a slight difference in what the words mean.

Context gives life to the skeletons of structure and organization. Context requires understanding—you cannot read, write, or speak about something without understanding it—and understanding requires context.

2.1.1d   identify the impact that personal context—experience, prior knowledge—has on constructing meaning from a text.

BROADEN YOUR OWN LITERARY CONTEXT

Nearly every form of communication requires context. Until the last century, anyone writing in the English-speaking world could assume that an audience that had at least some knowledge of the Bible, Shakespeare's plays, Greek and Roman mythology, some poetry, a few classic works of prose like *Pilgrim's Progress*, and a basic knowledge of history.

If you want to do as well as possible in your study of English and especially if you will be going on to university, experience in reading a wide variety of texts is necessary. Each new text that you read offers a new perspective and widens your overall knowledge of literature. The more general knowledge you have, the better.

Connect the words on the page to what you already know. For example, if you like a sport, reading the sports page is easy because you already have a framework for reading, understanding, and analyzing the language that is used in sports articles. When you read any text, think about what you already know about the subject and connect it with what you are reading.

Look at the context and structure of unfamiliar words to figure out their meaning if the definitions are not given at the bottom of the page. Using roots, prefixes, and endings to find the relationship between unfamiliar words and familiar words is as a good strategy for finding meaning. The context of a passage in which the word is used can sometimes help you to figure out the meaning of the unfamiliar word. Read the following short passage and see if there are any words you do not recognize. Can you guess at the meaning of these words?

Example

> The committee members left the boardroom close to midnight. Although they were exhausted after the sederunt, they agreed that we would meet again in the morning to complete the discussion.

You may not know the meaning of an unusual word like sederunt, but the context supplies the clues: words and phrases such as "committee," "boardroom," "midnight," "exhausted," and "complete the discussion" contribute to a solid context. You can guess with reasonable confidence that a sederunt is a long meeting or discussion.

2.1.2a   use a variety of strategies to comprehend literature and other texts, and develop strategies for close reading of literature in order to understand contextual elements

ESTABLISHING A PURPOSE FOR READING

Unlike non-literary informational texts, which typically serve a practical purpose, the reading of literature is a leisure activity and as such is a vehicle of entertainment and recreation. Mindful of this, some people argue that reading literature (fiction) is an impractical and time-consuming task. Of course, the same thing can be said of listening to music, watching television, looking at art, playing sports, viewing movies, or even sleeping. For what reason do people pursue any of these activities? The answer is simple. By participating in these supposed "useless activities," you are in one way or another recreating yourself and the world around you. Like most forms of recreation, the arts satisfy several basic human needs. They satisfy a hunger for self-expression, give a framework for ordering a seemingly random and confusing world, and often provide insight into what it means to be a human being. However, not all activities are equally beneficial, as there is a great difference between what you can gain from active as opposed to passive involvement. Just as the sports enthusiast derives a variety of physical, emotional, and intellectual rewards from playing the game he or she loves, the individual who chooses to read fiction rather than simply viewing it (in movies) derives similar tangible benefits. The same cannot be said of the fan that sits on the sidelines and watches others play the game. Similarly, those who watch stories unfold on a television or movie screen restrict the imaginative process and in doing so, rob themselves of significant growth and satisfaction.

INFERRING IDEAS FROM TEXTS

Often, many of the main ideas in a piece of writing are not stated directly, so you should apply various strategies when you read. One strategy that readers use is to make assumptions or *inferences*. To make an inference, you need to draw a conclusion about the meaning of a text using all the given information. It is also useful to think about your own experiences with the subject in order to understand the writer's meaning.

Read Laurie Halse Anderson's short story "Sanctuary." Then, read the possible inferences that a student drew from evidence in the story. The student's points are not explicitly given, but they can be inferred from the text. When you read, remember to consider what is implied as well as what is actually stated. Anderson explicitly states how Mr. Freeman looks (ugly, big, old, nose sunk between eyes) but does not tell us about Mr. Freeman's character. To get to know the real Mr. Freeman, you have to observe his words and actions in the story.

SANCTUARY

Art follows lunch, like dream follows nightmare. The classroom is at the far end of the building and has long, south-facing windows. The sun doesn't shine much in Syracuse, so the art room is designed to get every bit of light it can. It is dusty in a clean-dirt kind of way. The floor is layered with dry splotches of paint, the walls plastered with sketches of tormented teenagers and fat puppies, the shelves crowded with clay pots. A radio plays my favorite station.

Mr. Freeman is ugly. Big old grasshopper body, like a stilt-walking circus guy. Nose like a credit card sunk between his eyes. But he smiles at us as we file into class.

He is hunched over a spinning pot, his hands muddy red. "Welcome to the only class that will teach you how to survive," he says. "Welcome to Art."

I sit at a table close to his desk. Ivy is in this class. She sits by the door. I keep staring at her, trying to make her look at me. That happens in movies—people can feel it when other people stare at them and they just have to turn around and say something. Either Ivy has a great force field, or my laser vision isn't very strong. She won't look back at me. I wish I could sit with her. She knows art.

Mr. Freeman turns off the wheel and grabs a piece of chalk without washing his hands. "SOUL," he writes on the board. The clay streaks the word like dried blood. "This is where you can find your soul, if you dare. Where you can touch that part of you that you've never dared look at before. Do not come here and ask me to show you how to draw a face. Ask me to help you find the wind."

I sneak a peek behind me. The eyebrow telegraph is flashing fast. This guy is weird. He must see it; he must know what we are thinking. He keeps on talking. He says we will graduate knowing how to read and write because we'll spend a million hours learning how to read and write. (I could argue that point.)

Mr. Freeman: "Why not spend that time on art; painting, sculpting, charcoal, pastel, oils? Are words or numbers more important than images? Who decided this? Does algebra move you to tears?" (Hands raise, thinking he wants answers.) "Can the plural possessive express the feelings in your heart? If you don't learn art now, you will never learn to breathe!!!"

There is more. For someone who questions the value of words, he sure uses a lot of them. I tune out for a while and come back when he holds up a huge globe that is missing half of the Northern Hemisphere. "Can anyone tell me what this is?" he asks. "A globe?" ventures a voice in the back. Mr. Freeman rolls his eyes. "Was it an expensive sculpture that some kid dropped and he had to pay for it out of his own money or they didn't let him graduate?" asks another.

Mr. Freeman sighs. "No imagination. What are you, thirteen? Fourteen? You've already let them beat your creativity out of you! This is an old globe I used to let my daughters kick around my studio when it was too wet to play outside. One day Jenny put her foot right through Texas, and the United States crumbled into the sea. And voilà—an idea! This broken ball could be used to express such powerful visions—you could paint a picture of it with people fleeing from the hole, with a wet-muzzled dog chewing Alaska—the opportunities are endless. It's almost too much, but you are important enough to give it to."

Huh?

"You will each pick a piece of paper out of the globe." He walks around the room so we can pull red scraps from the center of the earth. "On the paper you will find one word, the name of an object. I hope you like it. You will spend the rest of the year learning how to turn that object into a piece of art. You will sculpt it. You will sketch it, papier-mâché it, carve it. If the computer teacher is talking to me this year, you can use the lab for computer-aided designs. But there's a catch—by the end of the year, you must figure out how to make your object say something, express an emotion, speak to every person who looks at it."

Some people groan. My stomach flutters. Can he really let us do this? It sounds like too much fun. He stops at my table. I plunge my hand into the bottom of the globe and fish out my paper. "Tree." Tree? It's too easy. I learned how to draw a tree in second grade. I reach in for another piece of paper. Mr. Freeman shakes his head. "Ah-ah-ah," he says. "You just chose your destiny, you can't change that."

He pulls a bucket of clay from under the pottery wheel, breaks off fist-sized balls and tosses one to each of us. Then he turns up the radio and laughs. "Welcome to the journey."

—*by* Laurie Halse Anderson

Inferences are assumptions. You have probably made many assumptions about this story after reading it only once. For example, what is the narrator's character like? How does he feel about art? What are his feelings toward Ivy? How does he approach school? Do you think he is a good student?

The answers you have to these questions are inferences you have made from the text. Think of some more inferences about the teacher in the story, Mr. Freeman. What kind of man is he? What does he seem to value? Do you think he has a sense of humour?

Read the following example of a student's inferences about the narrator of the story and the teacher.

Possible Inferences from "Sanctuary"

The Narrator:

- likes art

- likes Ivy

- is not a particularly academic student—he does not see himself doing a lot of reading before he graduates

- does not realize the extent of the assignment

Mr. Freeman:

- believes art is part of the soul

- believes art infuses great emotions

- believes art is more important than the "core" subjects

- is imaginative

- has a sense of humour

- enjoys teaching the students

Thinking more about inferences will help you write essays, too. Finding evidence from the text to support your thesis statement begins with something you already do when you read: making inferences. You already make inferences about texts you read, and being able to pinpoint exactly what part of the text caused those inferences is important. Backing up your thesis statement by using evidence from the text is extremely important. To help your reading and writing skills, start thinking more about the inferences that you already make when you read.

VOCABULARY

When you read, it is important to pay attention to the meaning of words, the writer's styles, nuances (the subtle and slight differences in expressions and tone), and the diction used to describe characters and events. Here are some strategies that you can use to help you extend your own vocabulary usage.

Before reaching for the dictionary to find the definition of an unfamiliar word, try to figure out the meaning from the context. If a writer's style is unfamiliar, read carefully and focus your attention on the style. Are there patterns in the style? For example, if the style makes frequent use of appositives, then look for restatements of unfamiliar nouns.

Example

> She insisted on bringing her *Pomeranian*, a yappy, irritating little dog.
>
> Alcazar immediately *absconded*, slipping out of town one step ahead of the detectives.

Try reading slowly. Adjust your speed to the difficulty of the content and the complexity of the style. Reading out loud is often helpful, especially with poetry and plays, since they are usually meant to be heard, not read.

When reading a play, try to see the actors and hear the words. Read the directions and watch the characters move around the stage; hear and see their emotions. Reading out loud is helpful, but if that is not possible, try subvocalizing, or going through all the motions of speech without actually making any sounds.

Be prepared to reread several times. Remember that reading for information and understanding is different from reading for amusement and pleasure, although serious reading can often be both pleasant and amusing.

It is a good idea to start asking questions internally. It will soon become a natural part of your reading process. Questions such as "What is this about? Why did she do that? What will happen next? Will his words come back to haunt him? Why was this setting chosen?" can assist you in making inferences and in analyzing the text on different levels.

TECHNOLOGY TERMINOLOGY

Technological vocabulary is easier to understand if you are familiar with the meaning of the root words and affixes. The following prefixes and words are just a few examples of components of words that combine to form terms that relate to computers and technology.

Example

Common Prefixes

kilo = a thousand = 1 000 = 10^3
mega = a million = 1 000 000 = 10^6
giga = a billion = 1 000 000 000 = 10^9

Common Root Words

byte = unit of measurement of information storage = 8 bits
hertz = unit of frequency = 1 per second
watt = unit of power = 1 per second

Technological terms that can be formed from these root words and prefixes are gigabyte, gigahertz, gigawatt, megabyte, megahertz, megawatt, kilobyte, kilohertz, and kilowatt. From the definitions of the parts of the word, you can determine the meaning of the whole word.

Example

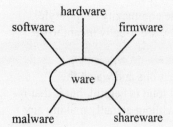

When you come across technical terms with which you are unfamiliar, remember to break them down into meaningful parts and look for the origins of the words.

GENERAL SCIENTIFIC TERMINOLOGY

Analysis of the affixes and root words in scientific terms can help you can find the meaning of the word.

Example

photo = light

synthesis = putting together (to synthesize is to create something new out of different parts)

photo + *synthesis* = photosynthesis = the process by which plants and some bacteria use chlorophyll to trap sunlight energy

Taking into consideration the meaning of the different components of the word *photosynthesis*, you could take a guess at what the word *chemosynthesis* means if you are told that the prefix *chemo* refers to chemicals.

Chemosynthesis refers to the formation of carbohydrates from energy resulting from the breakdown of inorganic substances. Was your guess at a definition close to the exact definition?

Here are some prefixes commonly found in scientific terminology and words that are formed using them.

Bio– = life (Greek)	biology biotechnology biomass biosphere biography biome biologist biotic biological
Hydro– = water (Greek)	hydrogen hydrothermal hydrosphere hydrologic hydroponic hydroelectricity hydropower hydroxide
Trans– = across (Latin)	transmission translucence transverse transcription transpiration transmission transforming transposons

Understanding components of words gives you access to understanding many more words you might not understand if you did not know the exact meaning. By paying attention to the different affixes that appear in words, you can make educated guesses at the meanings of words.

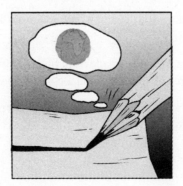

2.1.2b analyze the relationships among controlling ideas, supporting ideas and supporting details in a variety of texts.

CONTROLLING IDEAS AND SUPPORTING IDEAS

All texts share basic elements. In general, a writer states an idea and then supports it with details that lead to a logical conclusion. To better understand the writing, you must first be able to define the writer's idea. You should be able to clearly interpret the intent of the work from the supporting information that has been included in the text. You should also be able to make reasonable inferences from the conclusions that the writer has drawn.

You are often asked to identify the main or controlling idea of a text. You should also be able to find details and supporting information in the text. From the conclusions that you draw, you should be able to make a logical extension of the writer's ideas. Here is a good method for identifying a main idea in a text and expanding on that idea using support from the text.

FINDING THE CONTROLLING IDEA

To begin defining the main idea of a passage, poem, or dramatic piece, first ask yourself the following basic questions.

- What is the title of this work, and why was it chosen? The answer to this question may immediately point to the main idea of the passage.

- Why did the writer write this piece? By understanding the writer's purpose, you may see where the passage is heading.

- What main idea is the writer conveying directly or through characters, dialogue, imagery, etc? If the writer does not speak directly to the reader, then one of the characters may be the writer's mouthpiece.

- What is the topic sentence of the paragraph, subject of the stanza, or interest of the characters? Sometimes, the main idea is not explicitly stated but can be found by interpreting dialogue or deciphering verse.

Ask yourself these questions either during reading or after you have finished reading the passage. The answers you form will help expand your knowledge of the main ideas in a text.

Next, find clues that support the main idea through additional details or developments. When applicable to a text, ask yourself the following questions.

- Does the writer provide proof or information to support the argument? Use any supporting information to reinforce your interpretation of the writer's ideas.

- What specifics are given to expand on the general idea? A general idea needs specific details in order to advance an argument or a position.

- Is a comparison with related or parallel ideas made? An indirect writing style will require you to sift through rhetorical devices or figures of speech to find a coherent position.

- What information conforms to this position, and what information presents a contrasting view? A writer may consider opposing views and illustrate his or her own central idea by discussing such opposing views.

Finally, connect the information that is directly stated with the information that is implied in order to reach a conclusion that is a logical extension of these ideas. While watching a movie, you may find yourself wondering or guessing what will happen next. When you speculate like this, you are using your interpretative skills to infer possible outcomes. Reading can be approached in the same way. The following questions can help you find the main idea at this stage in the process.

• From the information that has been presented, what outcomes or results can be expected?

• What is implied or suggested by the writer, narrator, or characters?

• What else would fit within the framework of the writer's position?

• How can someone apply the information contained in this passage?

All of these questions can help you to make logical conclusions from the information provided by the writer directly and through dialogue and actions.

The three steps outlined in this section can help improve reading comprehension of poetry and prose. Some of the questions are useful to think about while you are reading, while others may be best answered after you have had a chance to read the whole selection. Being as curious as possible about a text can help you discover different layers of meaning and will help you to form ideas about the meaning of a text for assignments and tests.

2.1.2c assess the contributions of setting, plot, character and atmosphere to the development of theme when studying a narrative

THE DEVELOPMENT OF THEME

You develop your analytical skills when you explore and assess ideas, themes, concepts, and arguments in print and electronic texts. The intent of literature is to present the reader with values, perspectives, and world views in a way that invites engagement, interpretation, discussion, and comparison. While values are invisible, they are based on beliefs and principles that influence your perspective or point of view on the experiences of your life, on the issues you encounter, and, consequently, the way you view the world. Your world view influences your judgements as well as your feelings toward and treatment of others. Consequently, literature is an wide spectrum of values, perspectives, and world views revealed through the narration of writers, description of settings, and motivation of characters. Characters in literature often become a "voice" for beliefs, perspectives, and world views, and their stories offer you the opportunity to explore your own actions, thoughts, and feelings while reading about others. Your own analytic skills will develop as you explore and assess ideas, themes, concepts, and arguments. However, it is worth noting at the outset that all elements of a narrative contribute to its theme or the controlling idea, as is indicated on the following page.

MULTIPLE PERSPECTIVES AND THEME IN THE NOVEL

Theme can be defined as the controlling or core idea of a narrative. All elements of a narrative contribute to its theme, as illustrated in the following diagram:

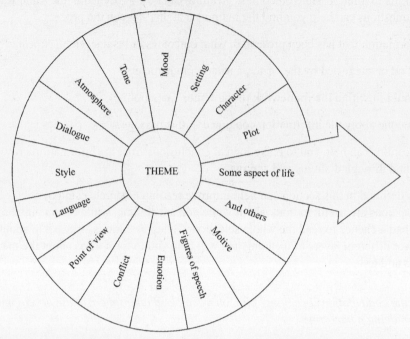

It is important to recognize universal themes in literature, many of which have existed in various time periods and various cultures. Some frequently encountered universal themes include the:

- fear of the unknown

- struggle between good and evil

- struggle to meet challenges or overcome adversity

- desire for meaningful relationships

- desire for understanding and search for meaning or truth

- desire to control our environment

- desire to be understood

The fact that some themes recur—are universal—contributes to the enduring appeal of cross-cultural literature and classical literature. Charles Dickens' novel *Oliver Twist*, for example, addresses the theme of good struggling against evil. In the novel, written approximately 200 years ago, various aspects contribute to the theme.

Consider this novel in relation to the following aspects.

Setting

The dark, dank workhouse environment, the dark, closed casket where Oliver hides at Sowerberry's undertaking establishment, and the dark, seamy underbelly of criminal London contrast sharply with the airy open windows of Mr. Brownlow's home looking out over the sunny square bustling with legitimate human endeavours and business.

Character

The novel is filled with contrasting good and evil characters, most notably Bill Sikes, who represents the very epitome of evil, and Oliver's gracious and benevolent grandfather, Mr. Brownlow.

Mood

The mood of suspense and foreboding created by the deep shadows of the London Bridge at night contrasts with the mood of salvation and anticipation evident in Mr. Brownlow's hurrying steps as he hastens toward his fateful meeting with Nancy.

Conflict

In the climactic struggle under the bridge, evil seems to temporarily triumph over good, as Bill Sikes takes Nancy's life in a fit of rage.

Plot

Many of the episodes comprising the rising action of the novel reflect the theme of good versus evil: the old nurse stealing the locket from Oliver's mother, the struggle for fair treatment in the workhouse that climaxes in Oliver asking for more food, the struggles at the undertaker's, and Fagin's constant vacillation between good intentions and his profitable but evil lifestyle.

Point of View

The omniscient narrative viewpoint allows the ongoing struggle between good and evil to be revealed through character perspectives, including Nancy's gradual transformation from cynical exploiter (evil) to heroic saviour (good).

Foreshadowing

Bill Sikes' threats against Nancy foreshadow the evil outcome that will result from her courageous choice, while the ironic surrender of a small gold locket to Mr. Brownlow by the greedy Bumbles foreshadows the golden outcome that lies ahead for Oliver.

If you refer back to the theme diagram, you will see that other elements of the narrative also contribute to the universal theme underlying the novel.

THEME

Theme is the central idea that is dramatized through the conflicts of characters, plot, and even the atmosphere of the play. Theme can be developed in many ways. For example, the theme of *The Firstborn* reflects on how individuals can be torn between their upbringing and their ancestry. Specifically, Moses is in conflict with his nature and his destiny and what it means to be seized by a purpose greater than oneself. In the following example, the setting contributes greatly to the development of this theme.

Example

From Act I Scene II

MOSES: Egypt and Israel both in me together!
How would that be managed? I should wolf
Myself to keep myself nourished. I could play
With wars, oh God, very pleasantly. You know
I prosper in a cloud of dust—you're wise
To offer me that. And Egypt would still be,
In spite of my fathers, a sufficient cause…

Splendid, then.
What armour shall I wear? What ancestral metal
Above my heart? Rib, thighbone and skull:
Bones from the mines of Egypt. I will clank
To Egypt's victory in Israel's bones.
Does this please you? Does it not? Admire
How when preparing a campaign I become
Oblivious to day and night, and in
The action, obsessed. How will that do? I make
My future, put glory into Egypt, enjoy myself
Into your father's confidence—yes, that,
I know; and being there, perhaps I coax
Little concessions for the Hebrew cause
To justify me.—Idiot, idiot!
I should have lost them, Aaron, and be lost,
More than when in Midian I sat
Over my food and let them trudge in my bowels.

From Act I, Scene III

I am here to appease the unconsummated
Resourceless dead, to join life to the living.
Is that not underwritten by nature? Is that
Not a law? Do not ask me why I do it!
I live. I do this thing. I was born this action.
Who can say for whom, for what ultimate region
Of life? A deed is what it becomes.
Despite you, through you, upon you,
I am compelled

[*A distant long cracking sound of thunder.* **MOSES** *jerks back his head to listen*]

Are we overheard? Behind
The door that shuts us into life, there is
An ear.

PLOT

Plot is the main action of the play. The protagonist faces a problem from which conflict arises that must be resolved. The manner in which the plot evolves from act to act or scene to scene is often driven by a central theme. Observe the connected themes of *love*, *passion*, and *violence* as they are played out in the significant plot points of Shakespeare's *Romeo and Juliet* in the following chart.

Example

These main plot points are all linked through and serve to develop the central themes.

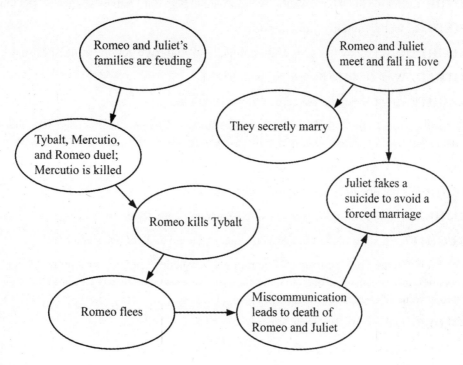

CHARACTER

Characters in a play should have interesting and memorable personalities. Such characters aid in the development of the theme. The most effective way to reveal the personalities and traits of characters is through actions and dialogue. In their dialogue, characters must come alive and speak in a manner that would make them believable to the audience. Whatever they say must be consistent with their character.

In George Bernard Shaw's play *Pygmalion*, one of the central themes is class and class distinctions. Through dialogue, the characters are immediately brought to life and their social class is made evident, thus developing this theme. The audience can recognize the mother's and daughter's bossiness, selfishness, and lack of concern for Freddy, who is desperately trying to please them. The flower girl's social class is immediately made evident by her Cockney accent in lines such as "Theres mnnersf'yer! Tee-oo banches o voylets trod into the mad."

Example

THE DAUGHTER: [*in the space between the central pillars, close to the one on her left*] I'm getting chilled to the bone. What can Freddy be doing all this time? He's been gone twenty minutes.

THE MOTHER: [*on her daughter's right*] Not so long. But her ought to have got us a cab by this.

A BYSTANDER: [*on the lady's right*] He wont get no cab not until half-past eleven, missus, when they come back after dropping their theater fares.

THE MOTHER: But we must have a cab. We can't stand here until half-past eleven. It's too bad.

A BYSTANDER: Well, it aint my fault, missus.

THE DAUGHTER: If Freddy has a bit of gumption, he would have got one at the theatre door.

THE MOTHER: What could he have done, poor boy?

THE DAUGHTER: Other people got cabs. Why couldn't he?

FREDDY rushes in out of the rain from Southampton Street side, and comes between them closing a dripping umbrella. He is a young man of twenty, in evening dress, very wet round the ankles.

THE DAUGHTER: Well, haven't you got a cab?

FREDDY: There's not one to be had for love or money.

THE MOTHER: Oh, Freddy, there must be one. You can't have tried.

THE DAUGHTER: It's too tiresome. Do you expect us to go and get one ourselves?

FREDDY: I tell you they're all engaged. The rain was so sudden: nobody was prepared; and everybody had to take a cab. I've been to Charing Cross one way and nearly to Ludgate Circus the other; and they were all engaged.

THE MOTHER: Did you try Trafalgar Square?

FREDDY: I tried as far as Charing Cross Station. Did you expect me to walk to Hammersmith?

THE DAUGHTER: You haven't tried at all.

THE MOTHER: You really are very helpless, Freddy. Go again; and don't come back until you have found a cab.

FREDDY: I shall simply get soaked for nothing.

THE DAUGHTER: And what about us? Are we to stay here all night in this draught, with next to nothing on? You selfish pig—

FREDDY: Oh, very well: I'll go, I'll go.

[*He opens his umbrella and dashes off Strandwards, but comes into collision with a flower girl, who is hurrying in for shelter, knocking her basket out of her hands. A blinding flash of lightning, followed instantly by a rattling peal of thunder, orchestrates the incident*].

THE FLOWER GIRL: Nah then, Freddy: look wh'y' gowin, deah.

FREDDY: Sorry [*he rushes off*].

THE FLOWER GIRL: [*picking up her scattered flowers and replacing them in the basket*] There's menners f'yer! Te-oo banches o voylets trod into the mad.

ATMOSPHERE

Writers use a variety of techniques and tools to create atmosphere, and one of the best ways to create vivid sensory details in the minds of the audience is through imagery. For example, in Shakespeare's tragedy play Macbeth, Shakespeare uses the word "blood" over one hundred times in order to strengthen the image of violence and death. This goes a long way in helping to develop the theme of corrupt power and ambition.

Example

Act I Scene V

LADY MACBETH: …make thick my blood;
Stop up the access and passage to remorse,
That no compunctious visiting of nature
Shake my fell purpose, nor keep peace between
The effect and it!

The following passage describes Lady Macbeth's resolve to kill Duncan the King so that her husband can seize power.

Act II Scene I

MACBETH: I see thee still,
And on thy blade and dudgeon gouts of blood,
Which was not so before. There's no such thing.
It is the bloody business which informs
Thus to mine eyes.

The following passage reveals Macbeth's guilt at killing the King. Here, blood figures again as the imagery that develops the theme of corruption and power.

Act V Scene I

LADY MACBETH: Yet who would have thought the old man
to have had so much blood in him?...
Here's the smell of the blood still.

Lady Macbeth's guilt causes her to walk and talk in her sleep, thus revealing details of the murder of Duncan. As you can see, the blood that represents the tragedy and hatred caused by their corrupt action will not be washed away. Similarly, Macbeth's and Lady Macbeth's guilt and memories are permanent.

The image of darkness represents evil, portrays an ominous atmosphere, and arouses emotions in the audience that help to contribute to the overall tragic theme in Macbeth. All the remarkable scenes take place at night or in darkness.

Act I Scene I

FIRST WITCH: When shall we three meet again
In thunder, lightning, or in rain?

In Act II Scene I, Banquo's remarks that the night is especially dark reflects Macbeth's dark desires to kill King Duncan.

BANQUO: How goes the night, boy?

FLEANCE: The moon is down; I have not heard the clock.

BANQUO: And she goes down at twelve.

FLEANCE: I take't, 'tis later, sir.

BANQUO: Hold, take my sword.
There's husbandry in heaven;
Their candles are all out. Take thee that too.
A heavy summons lies like lead upon me,
And yet I would not sleep.

In Act V Scene I, it is discovered that Lady Macbeth had been sleepwalking and talking for several nights. The darkness of the night enhances the dark evil of her actions.

Act V Scene I

DOCTOR: I have two nights watched with you, but can perceive
no truth in your report. When was it she last walked?

GENTLEWOMAN: Since his majesty went into the field,
I have seen her rise from her bed, throw her night-gown
upon her, unlock her closet, take forth paper, fold it,
write upon't, read it, afterwards seal it, and again
return to bed; yet all this while in a most fast sleep.

DOCTOR: A great perturbation in nature, to receive at once
the benefit of sleep, and do the effects of
watching! In this slumbery agitation, besides her
walking and other actual performances, what, at any
time, have you heard her say?

GENTLEWOMAN: That, sir, which I will not report after her.

DOCTOR: You may to me: and 'tis most meet you should.

GENTLEWOMAN: Neither to you nor any one; having no witness to
confirm my speech.
   Enter **LADY MACBETH***, with a taper*
Lo you, here she comes! This is her very guise;
and, upon my life, fast asleep. Observe her; stand close.

DOCTOR: How came she by that light?

GENTLEWOMAN: Why, it stood by her: she has light by her
continually; 'tis her command.

Lady Macbeth demands the light to be near her in order to assuage the fear and terror she feels due to the evil in which she has taken part. Finally, in Act III Scene II, Macbeth calls upon night to hide his evil deeds.

Act III Scene II

MACBETH: Come, seeling night,
Scarf up the tender eye of pitiful day;
And with thy bloody and invisible hand
Cancel and tear to pieces that great bond
Which keeps me pale! …
Good things of day begin to droop and drowse;
While night's black agents to their preys do rouse.

The foregoing examples illustrate clearly how atmosphere (and the imagery used to create it) play a large part in developing a theme.

SETTING

The setting of a piece of literature also contributes to the development of theme.

In the short story "To Build a Fire," by Jack London, one of the central themes revolves around the vast power of nature. Here, the circumstances of the setting establish the mood because the cold and the snow serve as antagonists. Nature is not in man's control: nature will not change because of humanity, and humans must simply learn to cope with whatever hardship Nature brings.

In the story, a man and a dog set off against the advice of others on the Yukon Trail at the time of the gold rush in the late 1800s. This part of Canada does not receive any sun for several days in winter and temperatures can drop to –60°C. The cold, dark environment emphasizes the mood. The man is alone in the cold with only a fire as protection from the cold. The dog is not concerned with the man; it cares only for its own survival. When the man steps into the creek and becomes wet, he knows the urgency with which he must build another fire in order to stay alive. However, high up in a tree, a bough laden with snow capsizes. Because his fingers are so badly frozen that he cannot build another fire, the man eventually dies.

Example

FROM "TO BUILD FIRE"

But all this—the mysterious, far-reaching hairline trail, the absence of sun from the sky, the tremendous cold, and the strangeness and weirdness of it all—made no impression on the man. It was not because he was long used to it. He was a newcomer in the land, a cheechako, and this was his first winter. The trouble with him was that he was without imagination. He was quick and alert in the things of life, but only in the things, and not in the significances. Fifty degrees below zero meant eighty-odd degrees of frost. Such fact impressed him as being cold and uncomfortable, and that was all. It did not lead him to meditate upon his frailty as a creature of temperature, and upon man's frailty in general, able only to live within certain narrow limits of heat and cold, and from there on it did not lead him to the conjectural field of immortality and man's place in the universe. Fifty degrees below zero stood for a bite of frost that hurt and that must be guarded against by the use of mittens, ear flaps, warm moccasins, and thick socks. Fifty degrees below zero was to him just precisely fifty degrees below zero. That there should be anything more to it than that was a thought that never entered his head.

This man did not know cold. Possibly all the generations of his ancestry had been ignorant of cold, of cold one hundred and seven degrees below the freezing point. But the dog knew; all its ancestry knew, and it had inherited the knowledge. And it knew that it was not good to walk abroad in such fearful cold. It was the time to lie snug in a hole in the snow and wait for a curtain of cloud to be drawn across the face of outer space whence this cold came. On the other hand, there was no keen intimacy between the dog and the man. The one was the toil-slave of the other, and the only caresses it had ever received were the caresses of the whiplash and of harsh and menacing throat sounds that threatened the whiplash. So the dog made no effort to communicate its apprehension to the man. It was not concerned in the welfare of the man; it was for its own sake that it yearned back toward the fire.

He knew there must be no failure. When it is seventy-five below zero a man must not fail in his first attempt to build a fire—that is, if his feet are wet. If his feet are dry, and he fails, he can run along the trail for half a mile and restore his circulation. But the circulation of wet and freezing feet cannot be restored by running when it is seventy-five below. No matter how fast he runs, the wet feet will freeze the harder.

There was the fire, snapping and crackling and promising life with every dancing flame. He started to untie his moccasins. They were coated with ice; the thick German socks were like sheaths of iron halfway to the knees; and the moccasin strings were like rods of steel all twisted and knotted as by some conflagration. For a moment he tugged with his numb fingers, then, realizing the folly of it, he drew his sheath knife.

But before he could cut the strings it happened. It was his own fault, or, rather, his mistake. He should not have built the fire under the spruce tree. He should have built it in the open. But it had been easier to pull the twigs from the bush and drop them directly on the fire. Now the tree under which he had done this carried a weight of snow on its boughs. No wind had blown for weeks, and each bough was fully freighted. Each time he had pulled a twig he had communicated a slight agitation to the tree—an imperceptible agitation, so far as he was concerned, but an agitation sufficient to bring about the disaster. High up in the tree one bough capsized its load of snow. This fell on the boughs beneath, capsizing them. This process continued, spreading out and involving the whole tree. It grew like an avalanche, and the fire was blotted out! Where it had burned was a mantle of fresh and disordered snow.

—*by* Jack London

In this story, the setting is important because the protagonist is at odds with his environment. The protagonist is in continual struggle with nature in order to survive. The theme of the story and this conflict between the protagonist and nature emphasizes that humans require an awareness of survival techniques because people are ultimately at the whimsy of nature and survival is dependent on human initiative.

MOOD AND THEME

In "Another Solution" by Gilbert Highet, four young people are plunged into the Mediterranean Sea when their boat capsizes. The protagonist, Victor, is the only one left alive. In this passage, the reader can feel Victor's relief and happiness when his feet touch a rock jutting out of the sea. He was going to be okay.

Take a look at the following analysis of an excerpt from "Another Solution." The underlined words work to convey a certain mood. Examining mood can help you determine possible themes for texts. The following analysis is also an example of a strategy you can use when you are analyzing mood.

Example

words and
phrases
that show
discomfort
and urgency.

It seemed that he was hardly under water before his back felt a pain. There was something firm and sharp beneath him. It was a rock.

Victor sprang into movement—his lungs wee still full of air. In his struggles, he ground his shoulder on the rock with a welcome pang, and his first gasp after he reached the surface was choked by his splashing. He swallowed a great deal of water, which made him shiver and *＊change in mood＊* cough with nausea. But he was happy, breathing in great gulps of air. Escape was found, a solution was found. It was only one tall thin wedge of rock rising from the seafloor, or from some deep-sunken buttress of the cliff. If there had been a wide shelf, he would have touched it long before as he swam about; but it was easy enough to miss this—he felt it now with his feet—this blade six inches wide. After swimming over and over this place, he had thought of it only as a chasm of deep sea, with his friends buried far below. The boat was sunk, and he had never thought of the rock which had sunk it.

words and
phrases
that show
relief.

As he cautiously put his weight on his feet, he felt ill with relief and hope and horror to think that he might have drowned two fathoms away from his safety. Here was the seventh, the unexpected solution. Now he had a firm foothold, his head and shoulders were out of the water, and there were no waves, so that he could stand still and rest. The tide would not rise more than an inch. He could stand all night on this rock, and bear the chill—never so dreadful. And in the morning there would be fishermen, in the morning at the earliest moment of dawn. Night was long. For a moment the whole scene was friendly, and the stars were companions. He felt the solid grateful rock with his feet, bent his strained muscles. This night was a terrible adventure; but he would live to tell about it.

From the quick change in mood from terror and pain to relief, you can make some inferences as to a possible theme for this story. A possible theme is how humans are always at odds with their environment. Nature is unforgiving, and Victor's tumultuous experience reflects that.

2.1.2d   analyze the personality traits, roles, relationships, motivations, attitudes and values of characters developed/persons represented in literature and other texts; and explain how the use of archetypes can contribute to the development of other textual elements, such as theme.

CHARACTER DEVELOPMENT

Literary characters that are developed by a writer are motivated by their attitudes, values, and perspectives. Because they are not static, their world views tend to evolve through conflict and experience; this is especially true of characters in novels. Consider Nancy, the tragic character in *Oliver Twist*.

Early in the Novel

Nancy, who is bawdy, self-mocking, and irreverent, survives by working as a hardened prostitute in London. Street life is all she has known since her earliest association with Fagin, who exhibits the same fancy and superficial airs of the "gentlemen" she despises. The closest emotion to love that Nancy has encountered is her love–hate relationship with the violent and unpredictable Bill Sikes, a professional thief who verbally and physically abuses her.

Later in the Novel

Nancy meets young Oliver when he is brought into Fagin's gang by the Artful Dodger. Although she sneeringly teases the new recruit, some long-dead softness in her heart is awakened by the vulnerability and innocence of the young orphan. Nancy's world view opens to admit a ray of generosity, hope, and optimism. At this point, however, Nancy's world view is still opportunistic and cynical enough that she participates in kidnapping Oliver back from Mr. Brownlow.

Near the End of the Novel

Nancy's world view has changed dramatically. The opportunistic, cynical view that has influenced Nancy to submit to a violent life of criminal activity has been replaced by hope, not for herself, but for the disarming child, Oliver. Although it is too late for her, Nancy realizes that the world represented by Mr. Brownlow truly is a good place, full of opportunities for Oliver if he can escape the criminal slums of London. So completely has Nancy embraced her moral, philanthropic, and optimistic world view that she is willing to sacrifice everything, even her life, to return the child she has stolen to his grandfather. Nancy does indeed sacrifice her life for her new world view.

As you study literature, connect the changes you observe in characters to evolving world views. These are the memorable connections that link characters in a work of fiction to the ever-evolving complexities of our real lives.

COMPARING ATTITUDES AND MOTIVATION

You can also make connections between characters in different literary worlds by examining their attitudes or the motivations for their actions. Consider, for instance, two female characters from two different plays, Ophelia from Hamlet and Lady Macbeth from Macbeth. The following chart shows similarities and differences in their perceptions of their respective worlds.

Ophelia (Unique traits)	Similarities	Lady Macbeth (Unique traits)
young, innocent, inexperienced	women in love loved men who had fatal flaws	older, shrewd, experienced
viewed life as a rosy dream, probably with a loving husband, and a happy family life	Neither women has built coping mechanisms for rejection	viewed life as a plot to be manipulated—"the end justifies the means"
viewed men (her father, brother, Hamlet) as gallant protectors	both women probably viewed suicide as a viable solution to thwarted dreams	viewed men as equals (Macbeth) or as adversaries and obstacles

Are there any similarities or differences you could add to this chart? The comparison of two characters can help define attributes of each character individually. The more comparisons you add, the more depth you can find about each individual character. This type of chart is an alternative approach to character analysis. This analysis reflects the values, perspectives, and world views that appear to have motivated characters' judgments and actions.

2.1.2e relate a text creator's tone and register to the moral and ethical stance explicitly or implicitly communicated by a text.

TONE

The tone of a piece of literature conveys the writer's emotions or attitude with respect to a topic. It might be ironic, scornful, sorrowful, or any other from a wide range of attitudes. Consider how the meaning of the phrase, "That's just great!" can change just by the tone with which it is expressed. Tone evokes the reader's emotion and enhances the effect of the message or theme.

Tone is created in a variety of ways, perhaps through choice of diction, the structure of the piece, imagery, or extended metaphor. To determine tone, it is important to "listen" to the passage and apply your own experience to it.

The following poem communicates the writer's anger and disdain for what she perceives as an exaggerated demand by modern society that women be thin if they are to be considered beautiful. The tone is achieved through numerous allusions to religion and the sacrifices and prohibitions sometimes connected to it.

THE HYMN OF A FAT WOMAN

All of the saints starved themselves.
Not a single fat one.
The words "deity" and "diet" must have come from the same
Latin root.

Those saints must have been thin as knucklebones
or shards of stained
glass or Christ carved
on his cross.

Hard
as pew seats. Brittle
as hair shirts. Women
made from bone, like the ribs that protrude from his wasted
wooden chest. Women consumed
by fervor.

They must have been able to walk three or four abreast
down that straight and oh-so-narrow path.
They must have slipped with ease through the eye
of the needle, leaving the weighty
camels stranded at the city gate.

Within that spare city's walls,
I do not think I would find anyone like me.

I imagine I will find my kind outside
lolling in the garden
munching on the apples.

—*by* Joyce Huff

The poem concludes with a derisive, mocking tone that suggests that the writer is happy to be excluded from the ranks of the "thin and beautiful."

2.1.2f   assess the contributions of figurative language, symbol, imagery and allusion to the meaning and significance of texts; and appreciate the text creator's craft.

WRITER'S CRAFT

In literature, you will find a broad range of figurative language, symbolism, and imagery meant to help the reader look through the obvious meaning and content of a piece to infer an implied meaning. Symbols and imagery tend to appeal more to the senses than to reason and intelligence. In this manner, they add just as much to the effect of a piece as the meaning of the words do.

The following poem by Steven Heighton shows skillful use of many different types of figurative language. Alliteration and onomatopoeia help the reader to hear the sounds of a runner's steps and the vaulting pole's swish as it slices the air and even the "boing" as it bends and straightens. Allusions to space through words like "orbit," "thinning air," "earth," and "sky" develop the image of the athlete escaping the bonds of gravity to make his leap. Through metaphor, the athlete is likened to a "dolphin," a "diver," and a "gull"—all images that help us to imagine the movements of the jumper.

HIGH JUMP

Four strides the legs compass, close,
burst gravity's shell and vault

as sunrise at the pole bends
back, sickles the sun-

sleek arc of dolphin, diver, gull,
his skull at noon and hovering. There

the body contends with higher things—
sharp light, thinning air; the eclipse

and setting of records; a fixed
orbit he believes he frames. At his height

he wavers, reels like a lover and prays
his lunging survives him

in a perfect act; feels time
tug at his second hand

as the earth draws breath, pole
and body into ground. Hear it:

a hissing of wind in the high
arena, and his spikes

rattle, raised like knuckles at the sky.

Even the structure of the poem is critical. Observe where the writer breaks his lines for emphasis and effect. Why do you think the last line introduces a change in the two-line format?

Jane Urquart's poem "Shadow" uses personification to describe sunlight as a somewhat curious, possibly interfering visitor. By imbuing the sun's presence with human characteristics, she develops the theme of loneliness and isolation. Symbols like mirrors, crystal, and shadows allude to the speaker's introspection and self-absorption. The pain of loneliness and old memories, where the only regular visitor is sunlight, is symbolized by expressions like "bright incisions" and "burning at the flesh." Take note of the verbs chosen by the writer to add extra dimension to the poem.

SHADOW

The sun decides to
enter from the garden

moving on the carpet
he touches all your furniture
crawls under your closet door
investigates your wardrobe

moves his arm across
your memories
substituting light
heat and silence

he erases last year's
conversations with the stars
changes the contents of your mirrors
invents an alternative
palette for your crystal

scrapes his nails across brocade
revealing tangled threads
like contours on a map

he polished your tables
his brilliance clings to cutlery
till spoons become large
bright incisions
all across the grain

a weight of gold and heat
he stops   burning
at the flesh of your neck

you are the only shadow in the room.

2.1.2g   assess the contributions that visual and aural elements make to the meaning of texts

VISUAL AND AURAL ELEMENTS IN TEXT

The imagery used to convey sights and even sounds help a writer to create the mood in a piece of writing. Layering these images over the message in the work enhances the effect on the reader. Often, the sounds evoked by the words mirror the emotion of the work. The following poem by Wilfred Owen, a poet known for his poems about the futility of war, voices the sounds of battle. The title suggests a musical composition sung in honour of something. In this case, it is in honour of the youth that would never have the chance to grow old.

In the first stanza of this poem, Owen includes elements such as "bells," "guns," "rifles," "choirs," and "bugles" that suggest sounds. The imagery is intensified through his use of onomatopoeia. The line "Only the monstrous anger of the guns" evokes the deep, booming sounds of cannons. Similarly, the phrase "stuttering rifles' rapid rattle" allows the listener to hear the deadly fire of machine guns.

ANTHEM FOR DOOMED YOUTH

> What passing-bells for these who die as cattle?
>   - Only the monstrous anger of the guns.
>   Only the stuttering rifles' rapid rattle
> Can patter out their hasty orisons.
> No mockeries now for them; no prayers nor bells;
>   Nor any voice of mourning save the choirs, -
> The shrill, demented choirs of wailing shells;
>   And bugles calling for them from sad shires.
>
> What candles may be held to speed them all?
>   Not in the hands of boys, but in their eyes
> Shall shine the holy glimmers of good-byes.
>   The pallor of girls' brows shall be their pall;
> Their flowers the tenderness of patient minds,
> And each slow dusk a drawing-down of blinds.
>
> —by Wilfred Owen

The second stanza contains words such as "candles," "eyes," "shine," "glimmers," "pallor," "dusk," and "blinds" that suggest images. Together, they evoke the atmosphere of a funeral or a dimly lit church. The dark sounds of the final line, combined with the image of blinds being drawn to dim the light. Combined, the visual and aural imagery reinforces the theme of untimely death and the meaning of the words.

2.1.3a   reflect on and describe strategies used to engage prior knowledge as a means of assisting
*   comprehension of new texts; and select, monitor and modify strategies as needed.*

WORD AND STRUCTURAL ANALYSIS

Word analysis refers to the process of decoding unfamiliar words. It includes the ability to recognize spelling patterns of words, the knowledge and the meanings of root words, prefixes, and suffixes, using word parts to determine pronunciation and meaning, and being able to use word attack skills. If you are able to analyze everyday words, you will find it easier to attack unfamiliar technical and scientific terms.

Structural analysis is the process of using word parts to determine the meaning and pronunciation of unknown words. When you examine a compound word, for example, focus on each part of the word and how each part contributes to the meaning of the word. Many scientific and technical English words consist of compound words composed from Latin or Greek root words; for example *thermometer*, *kilogram*, *centimetre*, and *astronaut*.

Medical terminology is the scientific vocabulary used to describe the human body and its components, conditions, and processes. Nearly all medical terminology is derived from Greek and Latin and is made up of two or more parts taken from root words, prefixes, and suffixes. You will understand medical terminology more easily if you understand the main ideas of how words are formed and the meanings of the various affixes used.

When the root of a word has been taken from another language, as is often the case in medical terms, the root is not usually capable of standing on its own and is meaningless without an affix. Consider the following two examples.

• Cardia comes is Greek for "heart." To have meaning in English, cardia requires a suffix: cardiology, cardiac, cardiovascular.

• Haemat/hemat/haem/hem comes from the Latin word for "blood." To have meaning in English, an affix is required with the root word: hematology, hematoma, hemoglobin, hemorrhage, hemophiliac.

By understanding the common medical prefixes, suffixes, and root words, and how they are put together, you will be able to understand many medical terms.

The following chart shows how two or more affixes are combined to form different medical terms.

Prefixes		Suffixes	
physio–	nature	–al	pertaining to
bio–	life	–tom	cutting
ante–	in front of	–y	process of
post–	behind	–tomy	process of cutting
super–	above	–ology	study of
crani–	skull	–pathy	disease/feeling
dors–	back	–ologist	one who studies
neuro–	nerve	–itis	inflammation of

Example

Pathology = path/ology = the study of diseases
Neuropathologist = neuro/path/ologist = one who studies nerves
Appendectomy = append(ix)/tomy = process of cutting out the appendix
Neuritis = neuron/itis = inflammation of the nerves

EXTENDING UNDERSTANDING OF TEXTS

To better understand what you read, you should connect, compare, and contrast.

Connect

As you read different things about a subject, look for connections between the ideas, themes, and issues that are presented. First, are there connections? Is the subject the same? Do the writers feel the same way about the subject? Even when two pieces of writing seem to be about different subjects, you can often find connections.

Compare

When you compare pieces of writing, think about how they are similar to one another. Maybe they are very different in style, but they give the same basic information. When you compare, the similarities are your focus.

Contrast

When you contrast pieces of writing, you think about how they are different or stand apart from one another. Perhaps the writers give the same information, but the way they go about it is very different. When you contrast, the differences are your focus.

2.2.1a analyze a variety of text forms, explain the relationship of form to purpose and content, and assess the effects of these relationships on audience

TYPES OF TEXTS

Since individuals communicate for different reasons—to inform, to persuade, or to entertain, for example—the form and style of text will differ according to the writer's purpose. The following categories are the usual forms of informational text, and each has its unique characteristics.

Exposition is writing designed to explain, and it is used wherever individuals wish to impart information. Magazine articles, newspaper articles, essays, and technical reports are common types of expository writing. In form, expository writing begins by stating its thesis or topic, and then, through a series of supporting ideas, develops the central thesis in subsequent related paragraphs. This type of text is very likely to use evidence and logic.

Persuasion, which is writing designed to "win over" or convince, is used wherever differences in ideas or feelings compete. Political speeches, critical essays, letters to the editor, and advertisements are common examples of persuasive writing. In form, persuasion, like exposition, begins by establishing a thesis or position and then develops that thesis by providing supportive arguments. This type of text is likely to include a combination of logic, analogy, statistics, satire, and emotional appeals, which come in the form of loaded language.

Narration is writing designed to tell a story. Narration can be used like exposition to inform people of a series of events and may also be used either to entertain or teach. Essays, newspaper articles, historical accounts, and travelogues are typical forms of narration. Unlike exposition or persuasion, narration follows a plot that is structured by time and typically involves characters who bring the plot to life. Paragraph structure in this type of writing is controlled by shifts in point of view, time, and plot occurrences.

Description is writing designed to tell how something looks—to freeze it in time. Although all forms of writing usually contain descriptive details, the purpose of description is to have the reader see and/or feel what the writer has experienced. It can be either clinical or factual, as one might find in a scientific report describing the Moon's surface, or it could be a far more artful description of a beautiful scene whereby the writer attempts to translate his or her impressions and create a mood through the use of imagery. Unlike narration, it is organized by space rather than time and makes use of a variety of rhetorical techniques. Paragraph structure is more likely controlled by shifts in spatial point of view.

Graphic text is writing combined with some type of graphic. At one level, it can be a simple form, such as a table, chart, or graph, designed to group information in order to facilitate quick comprehension of factual information. At a more sophisticated level, graphic text adds cartoons, diagrams, drawings, and photographs to written text as aids in communicating both thoughts and feelings. Since pictures can suggest a variety of interpretations, the reading of this type of graphic text requires the reader to interpret connotative language and implicit suggestions associated with the picture or diagram.

FORM

Form describes the structure and style of a text. A writer will choose the form best suited to the purpose of the piece of writing. A short story, for example, might have a purpose of entertaining or of gaining the reader's interest. A memorandum, on the other hand, is meant to inform and transmit accounts and descriptions. Each form has particular characteristics that make it best suited to a particular purpose. The following chart contains examples and definitions of common text forms.

Examples of Forms	Characteristics
letter	Generally begins with an inside address and date; uses conventional greeting and closings like *Dear——* and *Yours sincerely*
memorandum	Often brief and addressed to a limited group, such as the employees of a company; limited to essential information
short story	Usually 20 000 words or less; usually few characters, one main character; a single plot
novella	Between 20 000 and 50 000 words; a shorter version of a novel
novel	Over 50 000 words; usually 90 000 to 100 000 or more; may contain many characters and multiple plots within the main story
screenplay	Contains mainly dialogue and directions for the action; special rules for margins and font size give a standard length of approximately one page to one minute of screen-time

GENRE

Genre refers to content or subject matter of a work. Works that are categorized in the same literary genre share certain characteristic elements. A western, for example, usually includes a gunfight. Science fiction often includes imaginary scientific developments like spaceships. A romance is often characterized by an emphasis on romance between two leading characters.

Forms and genres can be combined in various ways. For example, an epistolary novel, which is a novel that is told through letters, uses the novel and the letter as forms. Such a novel could be written in any genre. Genres can also be combined in a work. A science fiction story might also be a romance, and an historical novel might also be a detective story. Also, elements of one genre are sometimes used in different genres.

There are many possible combinations of form and genre. The following chart contains examples of common text forms and genres.

Examples of Forms			Examples of Genres
fiction	poetry	metrical free verse sonnet	epic ballad lyric
	prose	play musical motion picture Shakespearean modern	tragedy comedy
		novel novella short story	historical detective fantasy science fiction realistic
non-fiction		history	political social military
		biography autobiography memoir	
		documentary film	
		essay	expository persuasive research
		letter	personal business letter to the editor
		diary	
		references	encyclopedia dictionary thesaurus atlas
		textbook manual	

The choice of form depends on the writer's purpose and on the intended audience. Examples of the forms of poetry, short stories, and the essay are given below. Each section offers explanations and analysis of the examples, according to the characteristics and elements of their particular form.

POETRY

Every part of a poem is carefully chosen to create a particular message, experience, or idea. The words, the sounds of the words, the line breaks, the stanzas, and the spaces are all aspects of a poem that are deliberately chosen by a poet. There are many different styles of poetry, but all poems contain some or all of these elements: form, sound, a speaker, figurative language, and imagery.

Observe how John Masefield uses these elements to enhance meaning in his poem "Sea-Fever." Even though it seems to be a simple poem, there are a variety of poetic elements. An analysis of the poetic elements in "Sea-Fever" follows the poem.

SEA-FEVER

> I must go down to the seas again, to the lonely sea and the sky,
> And all I ask is a tall ship, and a star to steer her by;
> And the wheel's kick and the wind's song and the white sails shaking,
> And the grey mist on the sea's face, and a grey dawn breaking.
>
> I must go down to the seas again, for the call of the running tide
> Is a wild call and a clear call that may not be denied;
> And all I ask is a windy day with the white clouds flying,
> And the flung spray and the blown spume, and the sea-gulls crying.
>
> I must go down to the seas again, to the vagrant gypsy life,
> To the gull's way and the whale's way where the wind's like a whetted knife;
> And all I ask is a merry yarn from a laughing fellow rover,
> And quiet sleep and a sweet dream when the long trick's over.
>
> —*by* John Masefield

Form

Poems can be written in a wide variety of forms. Many poems are written in stanzas. Each stanza is like a paragraph in prose that contributes to the whole meaning of the poem.

Example

"Sea-Fever" is composed in three stanzas, each stanza comprising four lines:

I must go down to the seas again, to the lonely sea and the sky,	
And all I ask is a tall ship, and a star to steer her by;	Stanza 1
And the wheel's kick and the wind's song and the white sails shaking,	(4 lines with *aabb*
And the grey mist on the sea's face, and a grey dawn breaking.	rhyming pattern)
I must go down to the seas again, for the call of the running tide	Stanza 2
Is a wild call and a clear call that may not be denied;	(4 lines with *aabb*
And all I ask is a windy day with the white clouds flying,	rhyming pattern)
And the flung spray and the blown spume, and the sea-gulls crying.	

Sound

How a poem sounds consists of the following elements.

- Rhyme: Internal rhyme occurs when the words in the poem rhyme within a line, and external rhyme occurs when the words at the end of each line rhyme. Masefield has used an *aabb* rhyming pattern for the external rhyme.

- Rhythm: The pattern of sound created by the arrangement of stressed and unstressed syllables in a line is referred to as rhythm. "Sea-Fever" has a definite rhythm that you can discover as you read the poem aloud.

- Alliteration: the repetition of the consonant sound at the beginning of words in close proximity. Masefield has deliberately repeated the "s" sound in his poem because it represents the sound of the sea. *Example*: "the flung spray and the blown spume, and the sea-gulls crying."

- Assonance: the repetition of a vowel sound in words
  Example: "the wheel's kick and the wind's song and the white sails shaking."

- Consonance: the repetition of the consonant sound in words
  Example: "wild call and a clear call"

Speaker

The speaker is the voice that conveys the ideas or tells the story. As with fiction, voice can be first person and is not necessarily the voice of the poet. In "Sea-Fever," it is not known if Masefield himself had any longing to be on a ship at sea, but his poem is written in the first person.

Figurative Language

Figurative language is the use of figures of speech. Figurative language works to create a more vivid image in the mind of the reader.

In "Sea-Fever," Masefield uses the following figurative language.

- Simile: the comparison of unlike objects using the words like or as
  Example: "where the wind's like a whetted knife"

- Metaphor: a comparison without using the words like or as
  Example: "and the wind's song"

- Personification: the attribution of human qualities to inanimate objects
  Example: "for the call of the running tide / Is a wild call and a clear call"

Most poems contain at least some figurative language because it makes descriptions come alive for readers.

Metrical or Traditional Poetry

Consider elements of the rhythm of metrical poetry, such as sonnets. Recall how dictionary words are divided into syllables and how the stressed syllables are marked with accents: *re·mem'·ber*, *com'·men·tar'·y*. The second example has a primary stress and a secondary stress. Both may be regarded simply as stressed syllables. In metrical poetry, the regular alternation of stressed and unstressed syllables produces the regular rhythm. The rhythm of poetry is called *metre*, and a unit of rhythm is called a *foot*.

Certain metrical feet have names. Two of the most common metrical feet and some single-word examples for each follow.

- iambic foot: unstressed, stressed (to day′, ab stain′, re cruit′, re turn′)

- trochaic foot: stressed, unstressed (coun′ ter, chem′ ist, wick′ er, sim′ ple)

A line of metrical poetry is usually made up of a fixed number of feet. Thus, a poem written in iambic pentameter has lines made up of five iambs. (Recall that *penta* means five and that an iamb has two syllables. Thus, each line usually has ten syllables.) Because poets pattern words into a regular rhythm, that rhythm can be indicated with stress marks above syllables: a "—" above an unaccented syllable (weak stress) and a " / " above an accented syllable (strong stress). Such a careful examination of the rhythm of a poem is called *scansion*.

Here are two lines of Shakespeare's blank verse (unrhymed iambic pentameter).

> Why, what a candy deal of courtesy
> This fawning greyhound then did proffer me!
>
> from *Henry IV Part I*

Notice the use of candy as an adjective to modify *deal* (quantity, amount). This is an example of how Shakespeare freely used parts of speech.

Here are the same lines scanned (marked to show the metrical feet).

```
 —    /  — /—    /  — /—
Why what a candy deal of courtesy
 1    2    3  4–5   6   7  8–9–10

 —    /—      /—       /  — /—    /
This fawning greyhound then did proffer me!
 1   2–3      4–5       6   7  8–9   10
```

SHORT STORY

The elements of a short story, such as character, plot, theme, and setting, are related to each other in such a way that the reader is left with a definite impression. In order to examine how the elements of a *short story* are connected to one another, the following section contains several examples of short stories and how elements in those stories connect. The following analysis of the short story "The Sniper" by Liam O'Flaherty contains examples of how theme, character, and action are connected.

Setting

Setting is the time and place in which the text takes place. O'Flaherty introduces the setting in the first paragraph of his story.

Example

> The long June twilight faded into night. Dublin lay enveloped in darkness but for the dim light of the moon that shone through fleecy clouds, casting a pale light as of approaching dawn over the streets and the dark waters of the Liffey. Around the beleaguered Four Courts the heavy guns roared. Here and there through the city, machine guns and rifles broke the silence of the night, spasmodically, like dogs barking on lone farms. Republicans and Free Staters were waging civil war.
>
> On a roof top near O'Connell Bridge, a Republican sniper lay watching. Beside him lay his rifle and over his shoulders were slung a pair of field glasses.

Many texts begin with a detailed description of the setting so the reader has a foundation for imagining the environment in which the action between characters takes place.

Character, Action, and Setting

Character and action are two essential elements in all stories. Without characters, there would be no story. Setting plays an important role in both these elements.

In the following example, setting and character contribute to the reader's understanding of a text. In "The Sniper," the setting reveals the central character's feelings and actions as he engages in this battle during the Irish civil war. The reader is not told anything about the character's background or of the circumstances that brought him to the rooftop. As you read the story, you discover the main character's excitement ("his eyes had the cold gleam of the fanatic"), his need to satisfy his hunger, and the fact that he is also a risk-taker.

In the following excerpts, it is through the description of setting that readers learn that the character has violent behaviours because he is very comfortable in a war-torn area. He is so comfortable and confident that he will risk alerting the enemy to his existence by lighting a cigarette.

Example

> He was eating a sandwich hungrily. He had eaten nothing since morning. He finished the sandwich, and, taking a flask of whisky from his pocket, he took a short draught. Then he returned the flask to his pocket. He paused for a moment, considering whether he should risk a smoke. It was dangerous. The flash might be seen in the darkness, and there were enemies watching. He decided to take the risk.
>
> Placing a cigarette between his lips, he struck a match, inhaled the smoke hurriedly and put out the light. Almost immediately, a bullet flattened itself against the parapet of the roof. The sniper took another whiff and put out the cigarette. Then he swore softly and crawled away to the left.

The action in the following excerpt demonstrates the character's ability to shoot and kill, even if it means killing innocent civilians.

Example

> The turret opened. A man's head and shoulders appeared, looking toward the sniper. The sniper raised his rifle and fired. The head fell heavily on the turret wall. The woman darted toward the side street. The sniper fired again. The woman whirled round and fell with a shriek into the gutter.

The action and setting in the following excerpt provides readers with evidence that the character is able to plan and think clearly even while wounded.

Example

> The sniper lay still for a long time nursing his wounded arm and planning escape. Morning must not find him wounded on the roof. The enemy on the opposite roof covered his escape. He must kill that enemy and he could not use his rifle. He had only a revolver to do it. Then he thought of a plan.

The action and setting in the following excerpt demonstrates the remorseful and more humane side of the character.

Example

The sniper looked at his enemy falling and he shuddered. The lust of battle died in him. He became bitten by remorse. The sweat stood out in beads on his forehead. Weakened by his wound and the long summer day of fasting and watching on the roof, he revolted from the sight of the shattered mass of his dead enemy. His teeth chattered, he began to gibber to himself, cursing the war, cursing himself, cursing everybody.

Mood is the feeling the reader has when reading a story. For example, the setting in "The Sniper" helps to create the mood by the words and phrases used by the writer. The mood the writer creates seems to instill a feeling of anticipation and then jubilation as the sniper shoots his enemy.

Example

Then when the smoke cleared he peered across and uttered a cry of joy. His enemy had been hit. He was reeling over the parapet in his death agony. He struggled to keep his feet, but he was slowly falling forward, as if in a dream. The rifle fell from his grasp, hit the parapet, fell over, bounded off the pole of a barber's shop beneath and then clattered on the pavement.

Then the dying man on the roof crumpled up and fell forward. The body turned over and over in space and hit the ground with a dull thud. Then it lay still.

The feeling of fear as an armoured car comes across the bridge is also portrayed.

Example

Just then an armored car came across the bridge and advanced slowly up the street. It stopped on the opposite side of the street, fifty yards ahead. The sniper could hear the dull panting of the motor. His heart beat faster. It was an enemy car. He wanted to fire, but he knew it was useless. His bullets would never pierce the steel that covered the gray monster.

ESSAY

Essays are compositions of several paragraphs in which a writer writes in detail about a certain subject. Essayists have a purpose for writing, organize their ideas clearly, and come up with creative and original details in order to support their theme.

Elements of an Essay

The Introduction

- must grab the reader's attention and be creative and imaginative

- must introduce the main idea and provide a preview of supporting details that will be discussed

The Body

- defines key terms and elaborates on them

- explores similarities and differences between things

- considers causes for events and behaviours and discusses their results

- states a problem giving details that emphasize its severity and offers solutions supported with evidence and facts that will address the problem

Conclusion

- short, precise ending

- brief summary of main points

- should not include new information

There are many different types of essays. Examine a few different essays to see how the organization strengthens the writer's argument.

Descriptive Essays

Descriptive essays are essays in which the writer gives concrete details to describe people, places, experiences, or ideas. Observe how J. B. Priestley and J. Hawkes provide rich detail in their descriptions of the dance in the following excerpt from their essay "Dance at Santo Domingo."

Example

I began to distinguish the larger pattern of the dance. The lines of men and women seemed to repeat the same series of joining and partings four times, and at the end of each movement the men raised and lowered their rattles with a fierce vibration that made a dying fall, a weird yet heart-affecting sound which is said to symbolize the fall of raindrops. After each movement the leaders, the dancers, the drummer and chanters all advanced several yards down the plaza before renewing the fourfold pattern of the dance. It was indeed a pattern of four times four; when the movements had been repeated for this number of times the drumming and chanting were worked up to an intense though never wild crescendo, and the final dying fall of the rattles was louder, more rending than before. Then the four lines of men and women fell into a single column which wound out of the plaza through one of the gaps between the houses and turned into the doorway of a two-storey house on the alleyway beyond. As the whole company tripped, still softly dancing, into so small a space, it seemed a miracle that the walls did not fall outwards; yet after the last chanter had entered, the sound of the drum and a glimpse through the doorway of moving head-dresses showed that the dance was being continued within. Soon the sense of confined activity, energy and heat, was like that of a wasp's nest humming below ground.

After a spell inside the house the compact mass reshaped itself into a column, and returned along the same route back to the plaza where the pattern of four times four was to be repeated; probably, though I am not certain, the whole dance would be complete when this largest pattern had itself been re-enacted four times. Some western people find this monotonous repetition unbearable; if they do, perhaps it is because they cannot rid themselves of the idea that a dance must be either a spectacle or an entertainment. Instead, these Pueblo dances are enactments, celebrations, no more to be censured for monotony than the perpetual celebration of the Catholic Mass.

One small but most happy change I did notice when the lines re-formed: a small girl and boy had now taken their place at the lower end. Both wore clothes identical in every detail with those of their elders and performed the steps and movements with equal perfection; indeed, the little boy in his eagerness and pride seemed even to outdo them in exactness and force. From afar the two miniature figures, their heads reaching only up to the waists of their companions, had the appearance of animated dolls drawn into the human dance. It was a glad as well as an enchanting sight, for it meant that an intricate ritual which had passed from generation to generation through the centuries was to reach yet another. In twenty years' time, it was possible to hope, these dolls might be leading the same dance in the plaza of Santo Domingo, maintaining at least one of those unique forms, peculiar to their own place, which are now fading so fast and leaving us so much the poorer.

As you can see, these writers use descriptive essays to allow readers to have a full, sensory experience of the dance. The main focus of a descriptive essay is to make readers feel as though they are really experiencing what the writer described.

Narrative Essays

Narrative essays allow the writer to present real or imagined events in the first person perspective. Writers use their essays to comment about life or to present ideas about a situation.

In "How Mr. Dewey Decimal Saved My Life," writer Barbara Kingsolver discusses how, while in high school, a librarian recognized potential in her and set her on the path to become a writer.

FROM "HOW MR. DEWEY DECIMAL SAVED MY LIFE"

A librarian named Miss Truman Richey snatched me from the jaws of ruin, and it's too late now to thank her. I'm not the first person to notice that we rarely get around to thanking those who've helped us most. But now that I see the wreck that could have been, without Miss Richey, I'm of a fearsome mind to throw my arms around every living librarian who crosses my path, on behalf of the souls they never knew they saved.

I reached high school at the close of the sixties, in the Commonwealth of Kentucky, whose ranking on educational spending was I think around fifty-first. Many a dedicated teacher served out earnest missions in our halls, but it was hard to spin silk purses out of a sow's ear budget. We didn't get anything fancy like Latin or Calculus. Apart from English, the only two courses of study that ran for four consecutive years, each one building upon the last, were segregated: Home Ec for girls and Shop for boys. And so I stand today, a woman who knows how to upholster, colour-coordinate a table setting, and plan a traditional wedding—valuable skills I'm still waiting to put to good use in my life.

I found myself beginning a third year of high school in a state of unrest, certain I already knew what there was to know, academically speaking—all wised up and no place to go. I had gone right ahead and used the science and math classes up, like a reckless hiker gobbling up all the rations on day one of a long march. Now I faced years of Study Hall, with brief interludes of Home Ec III and IV as the bright spots. I was developing a lean and hungry outlook.

We did have a school library, and a librarian who was surely paid inadequately to do the work she did. Yet there she was, every afternoon, presiding over the study hall, and she noticed me. For reasons I can't fathom, she discerned potential. I expect she saw my future, or at least the one I craved so hard it must have materialized in the air above me, connected to my head by little cartoon bubbles. If that's the future she saw, it was riding down the road on the back of a motorcycle, wearing a black leather jacket with the name of our county's motorcycle gang stitched in a solemn arc across the back.

There is no way on earth I really would have ended up on a motorcycle—I could only dream of such a thrilling fate. But I was set hard upon wrecking my reputation in the limited ways available to skinny, unsought-after girls. They consisted mainly of cutting up in class, pretending to be surly, and making up shocking, entirely untrue stories about my home life. I wonder now that my parents continued to feed me. I clawed like a cat in a gunnysack against the doom I feared: staying home to reupholster my mother's couch one hundred thousand weekends in a row until some tolerant myopic farm boy came along to rescue me from sewing machine slavery.

Miss Richey had something else in mind. She took me by the arm in study hall one day and said, "Barbara, I'm going to teach you Dewey Decimal."

One more valuable skill in my life.

She launched me on the project of cataloging and shelving every one of the, probably, thousand books in the Nicholas County High School library. And since it beat Home Ec III by a mile, I spent my study-hall hours this way without audible complaint, so long as I could look plenty surly while I did it. Though it was hard to see the real point of organizing books nobody ever looked at. And since it was my God-given duty in those days to be frank as a plank, I said as much to Miss Richey.

She just smiled. She with her hidden agenda. And gradually, in the process of handling every book in the room, I made some discoveries. I found *Gone With the Wind*, and I found Edgar Allan Poe, who scared me witless. I found William Saroyan's *Human Comedy*, down there on the shelf between Human Anatomy and Human Physiology, where probably no one had touched it since 1943. But I read it, and it spoke to me. In spite of myself, I imagined the life of an immigrant son who believed human kindness was a tangible and glorious thing. I began to think about words like *tangible* and *glorious*. I read on. After I'd read all the good ones, I went back and read Human Anatomy and Human Physiology and found that I liked those pretty well too.

It came to pass in two short years that the walls of my high school dropped down, and I caught the scent of a world. I started to dream up intoxicating lives for myself that I could not have conceived without the books. So I didn't end up on a motorcycle. I ended up roaring hell-for-leather down the backroads of transcendent, reeling sentences. A writer. Imagine that.

—*by* Barbara Kingsolver

Expository Essays

Expository essays give information about events, issues, or ideas. The purpose of expository essays is to expose, explain, analyze, or clarify a topic. The writer does this by using comparison and contrast, cause and effect, logical reasoning, or definition. Expository essays are informative; a writer will try to remain objective and avoid emotional language.

Persuasive or Argumentative Essays

The main purpose of a persuasive or argumentative essay is to convince readers to agree with the writer's point of view or ideas on a topic. The writer presents his or her arguments and uses factual examples to support and convince readers. The basic text is expository because it uses definition, examples, and comparison and contrast to present the arguments. Persuasive, emotional language can also be used in order to sway readers to agree with the writer's ideas.

Consider the following excerpt from G. K. Chesterson's essay "A Defense of Detective Stories." Chesterton speaks with a voice of authority in his defense of the detective story. He also lives up to his reputation as a man who likes to play devil's advocate on a variety of issues. Instead of defending the detective story in the usual way as harmless escape reading, he defends it as the only form of popular literature that expresses the mystery and poetry of modern city life.

Example

In attempting to reach the genuine psychological reason for the popularity of detective stories, it is necessary to rid ourselves of many mere phrases. It is not true, for example, that the populace prefer bad literature to good, and accept detective stories because they are bad literature. The mere absence of artistic subtlety does not make a book popular. Bradshaw's Railway Guide contains few gleams of psychological comedy, yet it is not read aloud uproariously on winter evenings. If detective stories are read with more exuberance than railway guides, it is certainly because they are more artistic. Many good books have fortunately been popular; many bad books, still more fortunately, have been unpopular. A good detective story would probably be even more popular than a bad one. The trouble in this matter is that many people do not realize that there is such a thing as a good detective story; it is to them like speaking of a good devil. To write a story about a burglary is, in their eyes, a sort of spiritual manner of committing it. To persons of somewhat weak sensibility this is natural enough; it must be confessed that many detective stories are as full of sensational crime as one of Shakespeare's plays.

There is, however, between a good detective story and a bad detective story as much, or, rather more, difference than there is between a good epic and a bad one. Not only is a detective story a perfectly legitimate form of art, but it has certain definite and real advantages as an agent of the public weal.[1]

The first essential value of the detective story lies in this, that it is the earliest and only form of popular literature in which is expressed some sense of the poetry of modern life. Men lived among mighty mountains and eternal forests for ages before they realized that they were poetical; it may reasonably be inferred that some of our descendants may see the chimney-pots as rich a purple as the mountain-peaks, and find the lamp-posts as old and natural as the trees. Of this realization of a great city itself as something wild and obvious the detective story is certainly the 'Iliad.'[2] No one can have failed to notice that in these stories the hero or the investigator crosses London with something of the loneliness and liberty of a prince in a tale of elfland, that in the course of that incalculable journey the casual omnibus assumes the primal colours of a fairy ship. The lights of the city begin to glow like innumerable goblin eyes, since they are the guardians of some secret, however crude, which the writer knows and the reader does not. Every twist of the road is like a finger pointing to it; every fantastic skyline of chimney-pots seems wildly and derisively signalling the meaning of the mystery.

There is, however, another good work that is done by detective stories. While it is the constant tendency of the Old Adam[3] to rebel against so universal and automatic a thing as civilization, to preach departure and rebellion, the romance of police activity keeps in some sense before the mind the fact that civilization itself is the most sensational of departures and the most romantic of rebellions. By dealing with the unsleeping sentinels who guard the outposts of society, it tends to remind us that we live in an armed camp, making war with a chaotic world, and that the criminals, the children of chaos, are nothing but the traitors within our gates. When the detective in a police romance stands alone, and somewhat fatuously fearless amid the knives and fists of a thieves' kitchen, it does certainly serve to make us remember that it is the agent of social justice who is the original and poetic figure; while the burglars and footpads are merely placid old cosmic conservatives, happy in the immemorial respectability of apes and wolves. The romance of the police force is thus the whole romance of man. It is based on the fact that morality is the most dark and daring of conspiracies. It reminds us that the whole noiseless and unnoticeable police management by which we are ruled and protected is only a successful knight-errantry.

[1] weal – welfare

[2] Iliad – a Greek epic poem about the Trojan War

[3] Old Adam – human, tendency to sin

What kind of assumptions did you initially have about the genre of mystery or detective stories? After reading this passage, have your assumptions changed? How was the passage persuasive? Were there any arguments in particular that may have altered how you think about the mystery genre? Which arguments or statements were effective? It is important not only to understand that a text has persuaded you but how that text has persuaded you. When you are trying to write a persuasive essay, think about other essays or texts that have persuaded you into adopting an idea. Try to analyze how you can use the same persuasive techniques that you have read in your own writing.

2.2.1c   apply knowledge of organizational patterns and structural features to understand purpose and content, and assess the effectiveness of a text's organizational structure

ORGANIZATIONAL PATTERNS AND STRUCTURAL FEATURES

Structural features are evident in many forms and genres of texts, from poetry to informational texts. Through organizational patterns or throught text features such as font, layout, and graphics, the purpose and content of the piece of writing may be enhanced.

E. E. Cummings experimented with innovative text and style with a disregard for correct syntax in his writing. Cummings seems to construct his poetry to play with the page. He had a passion for painting and a belief that poetry should be both a visual and a verbal experience. The visual qualities of the poem's words should complement the content.

i have found what you are like

i have found what you are like
the rain,

    (Who feathers frightened fields
with the superior dust-of-sleep. wields

easily the pale club of the wind
and swirled justly souls of flower strike

the air in utterable coolness

deeds of green thrilling light
                    with thinned

new fragile yellows

                  lurch and.press

–in the woods
      which
        stutter
          and
            sing
And the coolness of your smile is
stirringofbirds between my arms;but
i should rather than anything
have(almost when hugeness will shut
quietly)almost,

              your kiss

           —by ee cummings

Notice how some of the words are jammed together and others are scattered across the page. There is no regard for punctuation or capitalization, and Cummings did not left justify the poem. This makes the poem difficult to read quickly, which is exactly what Cummings intended. By forcing the reader to slow down and consider the words written, the poem's emotional effects are more likely to be absorbed. The design, spacing, and disregard for punctuation conventions are published as Cummings wanted them to be presented.

In Tennyson's poem "Morte d'Arthur," the shape is more conventional. However, the stanzas are of different lengths (from twenty-six lines to two lines) depending on the description and/or dialogue within the poem. Tennyson's poem is full of imagery and has been laid out so that the reader can have a better understanding and, at the same time, come to fully appreciate the artistry of the text. Look at the following short excerpt from "Morte d'Arthur" and notice the stanzas and the length of the lines. As you read, you will appreciate why Tennyson shaped this poem the way he did.

MORTE D'ARTHUR

Then spoke King Arthur, breathing heavily:
"What is it thou hast seen? or what hast heard?"
And answer made the bold Sir Bedivere:
"I heard the water lapping on the crag,
And the long ripple washing in the reeds."

To whom replied King Arthur, much in wrath:
"Ah, miserable and unkind, untrue,
Unknightly, traitor-hearted! Woe is me!
Authority forgets a dying king,
Laid widowed of the power in his eye
That bowed the will. I see thee what thou art,
For thou, the latest-left of all my knights,
In whom should meet the offices of all,
Thou wouldst betray me for the precious hilt;
Either from lust of gold, or like a girl
Valuing the giddy pleasure of the eyes.
Yet, for a man may fail in duty twice,
And the third time may prosper, get thee hence:
But, if thou spare to fling Excalibur,
I will arise and slay thee with my hands."

Then quickly rose Sir Bedivere, and ran,
And, leaping down the ridges lightly, plunged
Among the bulrush-beds, and clutched the sword,
And strongly wheeled and threw it. The great brand
Made lightnings in the splendour of the moon,
And flashing round and round, and whirled in an arch,
Shot like a streamer of the northern morn,
Seen where the moving isles of winter shock
By night, with noises of the northern sea.
So flashed and fell the brand Excalibur:
But ere he dipped the surface, rose and arm
Clothed in white samite, mystic, wonderful,
And caught him by the hilt, and brandished him
Three times, and drew him under in the mere.

—*by* Alfred Lord Tennyson

The previous examples show how organization and structural patterns enhance a work of fiction to maximize the effect that imagery and emotional effects. Other types of texts, especially non-fiction rely heavily on organization and text features, too.

TEXT FEATURES

Text features are elements of a text like titles, a table of contents, diagrams or labels, captions, and glossaries that facilitate understanding for the reader. Often, text features are included in a non-fiction text to assist the reader with information that may not actually be written in the text itself. Text features are found in text books, news articles, magazines, and web pages.

Scanning text features and evaluating them before reading can enhance comprehension and retention considerably.

Read the following text without the benefit of text features. Then, compare it with the same text with text features incorporated.

I would like to buy a car—but how?

Our Automobile experts will help you through the process.

Wait—I have questions

Do I need money for a downpayment?

No, a downpayment is not necessary.

What is the average interest rate?

We give everyone 0.5%

I am living on a single income, and do not know my credit rating.

Don't worry. At Big Joe's we will take anyone with any kind of credit.

Where are you located?

How long until I am driving my new car?

Come in for an appointment, and we will get you set up as quickly as we can! We value efficiency.

This will be my first vehicle, do you have any insurance providers?

We are affiliated with Wickywich Insurance.

Above—Information without text features

Next—Same information presented in brochure with text features

Textbooks exemplify the importance of effective text features. Textbooks are written for the specific purpose of imparting information that must be learned and retained. For such books, the font style, the layout of the text, and the spacing are all taken into consideration in order to enhance meaning and strengthen the impact of the text on the reader.

In textbooks, different sizes and types of font are used in order to help clarify their explanations and to organize content clearly. Textbooks contain diagrams that are labelled and pictures or photographs that have captions. Italics are frequently used to set apart subject-specific words or to refer to figures rather than the text.

Make note of the font, use of capitals, bolded text, italics, and font size in the following Biology text. Notice how the writers have maximized the use of varying font and have designed the layout of the pages in order to promote maximum understanding of the information presented. The following text is reader-friendly in layout and word choice.

2.2.2a *assess the contributions of rhetorical devices and stylistic techniques to the clarity and coherence of print and non-print texts, and assess the various means by which devices and techniques are used to emphasize aspects or portions of a text*

ELEMENTS OF STYLE

Language and syntax are used by writers in creative ways to manipulate mood, tone, suspense, and other elements of a text. You have probably noticed how short, staccato sentences in the middle of a narrative denote rapid action. A series of references related to blood and death in a story like the "Most Dangerous Game" help to add suspense and a sense of danger to the text. Through the use of such stylistic techniques as specific word choices and syntax, a writer can create the desired response in readers. Consider, for example, how language is used to create pathos in a play.

LANGUAGE USED TO CREATE PATHOS

Pathos refers to an aspect of a work that arouses the reader's feelings of pity, sorrow, or compassion for a character. It is a Greek term and is an element that is a part of the genre of tragedy. Pathos can be present in comedies as well.

For example, pathos is present throughout Shakespeare's tragedy *King Lear*. The depths of human suffering become almost exaggerated in the broken ramblings of the aging, senile King, beleaguered by the heartless attitudes of two of his daughters, Regan and Goneril. The reader feels pathos when King Lear's third and least hostile daughter, Cordelia, admits that her efforts to sway her two sisters have been futile:

> "We are not the first
> Who with best meaning have incurred the worst."

The harsh words of Regan and Goneril toward their father evoke more pathos: "Prescribe not us our duties." The daughters show scorn and disrespect as they defy Lear's plea that they be dutiful daughters. Their hatred of any advice related to doing what is right intensifies the pathos the audience feels for the helpless old King as he falls victim to mistreatment.

As the incompetency of Lear's advancing years descends into insanity, pathos can be felt from King Lear's perspective, a perspective that has eroded Lear's speech into a bitterness that leads him to scream at Goneril.

> "That these hot tears, which break from me perforce
> Should make thee worth them—Blasts and fog upon thee!
> … old fond eyes,
> Beweep this cause again, I'll pluck you out;
> … Ha! is it come to this?
> Let it be so—yet have I left a daughter (Cordelia),
> Who, I am sure, is kind and comfortable;
> When she shall hear of thee, with her nails
> She'll flay thy Wolfish visage. Thou shalt find
> That I'll resume the shape, which thou dost think
> I have cast off forever."

Lear warns that his faculties will return and that Goneril will live to regret her unnatural cruelty and insensitive words.

In Shakespeare's *Hamlet*, Hamlet's famous soliloquy in Act 3, Scene 1, creates pathos for his character as the heir to the throne of Denmark, deprived of his father and his rightful inheritance by a lecherous and avaricious uncle. Hamlet expresses his anguish by contemplating the meaning of his own existence.

> To be, or not to be: that is the question:
> Whether 'tis nobler in the mind to suffer
> The slings and arrows of outrageous fortune,
> Or to take arms against a sea of troubles,
> And by opposing end them? To die: to sleep;
> No more; and by a sleep to say we end
> The heart-ache and the thousand natural shocks
> That flesh is heir to, 'tis a consummation
> Devoutly to be wish'd. To die, to sleep;
> To sleep: perchance to dream: ay, there's the rub;
> For in that sleep of death what dreams may come
> When we have shuffled off this mortal coil,
> Must give us pause: there's the respect
> That makes calamity of so long life;
> For who would bear the whips and scorns of time,
> The oppressor's wrong, the proud man's contumely,
> The pangs of despised love, the law's delay,
> The insolence of office and the spurns
> That patient merit of the unworthy takes,
> When he himself might his quietus make
> With a bare bodkin? who would fardels bear,
> To grunt and sweat under a weary life,
> But that the dread of something after death,
> The undiscover'd country from whose bourn
> No traveller returns, puzzles the will
> And makes us rather bear those ills we have
> Than fly to others that we know not of?
> Thus conscience does make cowards of us all;
> And thus the native hue of resolution
> Is sicklied o'er with the pale cast of thought,
> And enterprises of great pith and moment
> With this regard their currents turn awry,
> And lose the name of action.—Soft you now!
> The fair Ophelia! Nymph, in thy orisons
> Be all my sins remember'd.

Even Claudius, the villain of the play, generates some pathos for the spiritual darkness that has come from his selfish choices as he tries without success to pray in the chapel:

> "My prayers fly up to heaven,
> My thoughts remain below."

The *Rime of the Ancient Mariner*, a long narrative poem by Samuel Taylor Coleridge, relates the tale of the lone survivor of a sailing mishap who has been lost at sea for many days. The pathos of the sailor's lonely vigil and quest for survival are captured in the echoing repetition and assonance of lines "Alone, alone, all, all alone, Alone on a wide, wide sea."

Finally, a more contemporary example of pathos is evident in American writer Arthur Miller's play *Death of a Salesman*. The play revolves around the strained relationship between the main character, Willy Loman, and his oldest son, Biff. Willy Loman carries the underlying pathos of a son hating his father, never feeling good enough to meet his own father's approval, and believing he has let his father down.

Pity is felt when Linda, Willy's wife, cries, "Attention must be paid," as she helplessly witnesses the downward spiral of her husband's depression. That pathos, however, is tempered by the audience's recognition that Willy is a philandering, dishonest spouse who has let himself go physically, spiritually, and emotionally, and who has stopped making enough money to support his family. The language of the play creates pathos that highlights the emptiness of the American Dream, in the sense that the "dream" only points men like Willy toward a path of material wealth at the expense of more genuine components of life, like family and personal relationships. Finally, Willy's spiritual and emotional blindness are echoed in the pathos generated by Biff's words, "The man didn't know who he was."

EVALUATING STYLE

When you are reading literature, you need to be aware of how mood, tone, and theme are influenced by diction and figurative language. These will be a part of the writer's unique style. What makes a particular poem such a pleasant reading experience? What makes a story memorable? Why do people still quote from Martin Luther King's speech "I Have a Dream" or from John F. Kennedy's Inaugural Address, both of which were written so many years ago? Most memorable speeches and essays have a mood and tone manipulated by the writer to have an impact on the reader.

Mood is the atmosphere or feeling conveyed by a piece of work. The mood the writer creates might be one of sadness, fear, happiness, anger, contentment, excitement, or optimism. Writers create mood through their diction and use of figurative language. Understanding the mood will help you to understand the work as a whole.

Tone is best described as the attitude the author takes toward the subject, character, or reader. There are many possible tones, such as serious, formal, informal, sympathetic, passionate, respectful, or disgusted. To find the tone, you will have to search for clues in the words, phrases, and images the author uses.

2.2.2b   assess the contributions of textual elements and stylistic techniques to the creation of atmosphere, tone and voice

TEXTUAL ELEMENTS AND STYLISTIC TECHNIQUES

To create atmosphere in a piece of writing, a writer has many techniques at his or her disposal. In addition to figurative language such as metaphors, symbolism, or allusions that can be used to develop themes through imagery, writers may use a broad range of sentence varieties and structures.

SENTENCE VARIETY AND STRUCTURE

The term "sentence variety" can refer to any of the following aspects of sentences.

• Sentence length: Longer sentences provide the reader with more information and particulars than do shorter sentences. Longer sentences allow a writer to investigate an idea more thoroughly or provide a powerful description. Shorter sentences focus on critical points. Too many sentences with similar structure and length can cause the reader to lose interest. A succession of short sentences might be used for strong effect after a series of longer sentences.

- Sentence type: Simple, compound, complex, and compound-complex sentences can be used for variety or to control the development of ideas (transitional devices can be useful for this purpose).

- Sentence order: The most important part of a sentence can be emphasized by putting it first. NASA might note that "A meteorite hit a man in Whitehorse," while the *Whitehorse Star* might report, "Local Man Hit by Meteorite."

- Word order is closely related to sentence order.

Example

> "accused mass murderer Goneril Brocadie"
>
> "Goneril Brocadie, who is accused of mass murder,"
>
> At first glance, the meaning of these two sentences appears to be the same, but the first phrase subtly suggests that Brocadie is actually guilty, not merely accused. The adjectives closest to the noun clearly imply the message *mass-murderer-Brocadie*.

The term "sentence structure" refers to aspects of sentences such as anaphora, parallelism, and rhetorical questions.

- Anaphora: This term refers to the stylistic technique of employing the same phrase or word to begin a succession of sentences or clauses. Far from achieving the effect of monotony, this technique focuses attention on the message.

This famous example is from a speech by Winston Churchill.

> We shall not flag or fail. We shall go on to the end. We shall fight in France, we shall fight on the seas and oceans, we shall fight with growing confidence and growing strength in the air, we shall defend our island, whatever the cost may be, we shall fight on the beaches, we shall fight on the landing grounds, we shall fight in the fields and in the streets, we shall fight in the hills. We shall never surrender.

- Parallelism: This is another technique that is used to emphasize the message. It is similar to anaphora, but it reflects structure, rather than word choice as the element that is repeated in a succession of sentences or clauses. Consider the following example by Margaret Atwood.

VARIATION ON THE WORD SLEEP

I would like to watch you sleeping,
which may not happen.
I would like to watch you,
sleeping. I would like to sleep
with you, to enter
your sleep as its smooth dark wave
slides over my head

and walk with you through that lucent
wavering forest of bluegreen leaves
with its watery sun & three moons
towards the cave where you must descend,
towards your worst fear

I would like to give you the silver
branch, the small white flower, the one
word that will protect you
from the grief at the centre
of your dream, from the grief
at the center I would like to follow
you up the long stairway
again & become
the boat that would row you back
carefully, a flame
in two cupped hands
to where your body lies
beside me, and as you enter
it as easily as breathing in

I would like to be the air
that inhabits you for a moment
only. I would like to be that unnoticed
& that necessary.

In this poem, Atwood repeats the structures "I would like." She also repeated uses "you" as the object of verbs that denote yearning, as in the phrases "watch you," "sleep with you," "give you," "protect you," "follow you," "inhabits you." These structures emphasize the message that the speaker yearns to be close to the person to whom the poem is directed. In addition, it underlines the sincere and urgent tone of the message.

- Rhetorical questions: This variation of structure asks a question, but does not expect an answer. Rhetorical questions might be used to indicate that the answer is obvious, which is an effective technique in arguments or to provide immediate emphasis. Read the following lyrics to a song, based on a Quebec folk song, by Leonard Cohen and consider his repeated question. It requires no answer, thus suggesting the answer is clear.

THE FAITH

The sea so deep and blind
The sun, the wild regret
The club, the wheel, the mind,
O love, aren't you tired yet?
The club, the wheel, the mind
O love, aren't you tired yet?
The blood, the soil, the faith
These words you can't forget
Your vow, your holy place
O love, aren't you tired yet?
The blood, the soil, the faith
O love, aren't you tired yet?
A cross on every hill
A star, a minaret
So many graves to fill
O love, aren't you tired yet?
So many graves to fill
O love, aren't you tired yet?
The sea so deep and blind
Where still the sun must set
And time itself unwind
O love, aren't you tired yet?
And time itself unwind
O love, aren't you tired yet?

PERCEPTION AND REALITY IN LITERATURE

In literature, there are often deliberate discrepancies between textual statements and what is actually happening with the characters and plot. As a reader, being able to interpret and evaluate ambiguities, subtleties, contradictions, ironies, and incongruities in a text enriches your reading experience by allowing you to interact with the text on several different levels. In order to illustrate this, consider "The Weapon," a short story by Frederic Brown. This story has found its place in literature as a powerful parable about the fragility of world peace, the survival of the planet, and the dangers inherent in the twin follies of rationalization and complacency.

The story itself is brief and relatively simple. A famous scientist is relaxing at home when a stranger, Mr. Niemand (*niemand* is German for "no one") rings the doorbell. Mildly irritated, Dr. Graham interrupts his thoughts of his mentally handicapped son to answer the door. Because he is caught off guard, the scientist invites Mr. Niemand, who appears to be non-descript and harmless, inside and leads him to an armchair. Without a preamble, the stranger leans forward and challenges Dr. Graham to stop working on his current project, telling him that he was "the man whose scientific work is more likely than that of any other man to end the human race's chance for survival." The visitor then warmly greets the scientist's 15-year-old son, who has entered the room to ask his father for a bedtime story. The obvious limitations of Dr. Graham's son, who speaks with the words and inflection of a four-year-old boy, are not lost on the guest, who seems to be aware of the family situation. The scientist, Dr. Graham, politely but firmly refuses to consider abandoning his project as he rises to dismiss his guest. The guest suddenly asks for the drink he had been offered earlier. While Dr. Graham is in the kitchen, the guest slips into the boy's bedroom to bid him goodnight. Shortly after, he departs, mentioning that he had presented Dr. Graham's son with a small gift, which is actually a loaded gun. After safely retrieving the gun from his son's hands, Dr. Graham examines the gun with shaking hands, while thinking "only a madman would give a loaded revolver to an idiot."

Consider some of the techniques that the writer deliberately uses to enhance the impact of the parable and increase its complexity. The story raises emotions, identifies disparities in point of view, and raises controversial issues. That is what good stories do—they engage the reader on more than one level.

Ambiguity in a story is deliberate vagueness or a lack of directly stated information. The main ambiguity in "The Weapon" lies in the identity of the uninvited visitor. His purpose, to dissuade the scientist from continuing dangerous research, seems clear, but who is he? Has he been sent by a government, and if so, whom does he represent? How does he know so much about Dr. Graham and his family situation? This ambiguity heightens the mystery surrounding the visit.

Subtleties are pieces of information that a writer includes in a text for a reason. For example, one subtlety frequently used by mystery writers is to introduce the culprit or murderer quite early in a mystery story. Readers hopefully miss the initial implications of guilt and are surprised when the identity of the culprit is revealed. In "The Weapon," the following subtleties foreshadow the end of the story:

- That the scientist's son is mentally handicapped seems to be an innocent bit of information at the beginning of the story.

- The stranger appears "nondescript, obviously harmless," when in fact he is quite lethal.

Contradictions, which are pieces of information that do not make sense when placed together, create contrast and irony. Consider the following examples:

- It seems like a character contradiction that a polite, unassuming, soft-spoken, and protective father could be designing and developing a weapon of mass destruction.

- When the stranger says, "Dr. Graham, you are the man whose scientific work is more likely than that of any other man to end the human race's chance for survival," Dr. Graham views him as a "crackpot." Such a judgement is a contradiction, considering the sensible concern for world peace that has just been expressed.

Irony in literature involves discrepancies between the imagined and the actual. For instance, Dr. Graham deceives himself, through rationalization, into believing that he is morally off the hook because he is only a scientist doing scientific research. He says, "Yes, it is public knowledge that I am working on a weapon, a rather ultimate one. But for me personally, that is only a by-product of the fact that I am advancing science." The irony of his self-deception, and the truth of his foolhardy project, is revealed at the end of the story, when Dr. Graham discovers that the stranger has placed a loaded revolver in the hand of his mentally handicapped son. It is also ironic that the son's favourite bedtime story is "Chicken Little," the story about a character making irrational statements about the end of the world.

Incongruities are things that fail to add up logically and disturb the overall pattern in the story. The incongruities of this story—a "mad" scientist who seems unpretentious and logical; a caring and protective father who allows a total stranger into his living room and leaves him alone long enough to pass a handgun to his child—come together by the end of the story to present the theme that rationalization allows people to accept dangerous or immoral concepts, such as the possibility of the destruction of the entire human race. The incongruities of the story expose the incongruities of human nature.

2.2.2c   analyze the use of irony and satire to create effects in print and non-print texts [for example, dramatic irony to create suspense, verbal irony to create humour and satire to evoke response]

LANGUAGE AND TECHNIQUES USED TO CREATE IRONIC TONE

Irony is used in literature to indicate, either through character or plot, an attitude that is opposite to what is actually stated. Often, the use of irony implies the writer's opinion that there is a gap between the way things are and how he or she feels they ought to be. Writers employ a variety of techniques to create this tone in their work.

- **Dramatic irony**: a situation in which the audience is aware of something of which the characters are not aware; for example, in the play Oedipus Rex, the audience knows that Oedipus is marrying his mother, but the characters do not

History produces dramatic irony. For example, in 1938, Prime Minister Neville Chamberlain proclaimed to the British nation, "I believe it is peace in our time." In reality, Chamberlain's actions were factors that contributed to the Second World War.

Life produces dramatic irony. For example, for over fifty years after the end of the First World War, the bodies of men killed in the fighting in France would be recovered from excavations made for construction. It was not uncommon to find the last letter home perfectly preserved. In fact, it was common enough that there was a rule about handling them: letters to sweethearts were to be destroyed, letters to families were to be delivered. Imagine the bitter irony of receiving such a letter, written in the youthful voice and the forgotten slang of a time as dead as the writer—*Dear All, I hope this finds you in the pink, as it leaves me.*

- **Verbal irony**: occurs when the true meaning of words is different from their surface meaning; for example, if a politician praises his opponents for their honesty and integrity when he knows quite well that they are corrupt, then he is speaking ironically

- **Sarcasm**: similar to irony, except that it is directed at someone—usually in a sarcastic tone of voice—who knows that what is meant is the opposite of what is said; for example, the question "Well, you really are clever, aren't you?" stated in a sarcastic way actually means the contrary. A person may sometimes use sarcasm as a way of attacking someone else without appearing completely nasty.

- **Satire**: occurs when failings of individuals, institutions, or societies are ridiculed or scorned. The purpose of satire is to correct or expose some evil or wrongdoing. George Orwell's Animal Farm is a satire about life in Russia during the rise of Communism.

Shakespeare was a master of dramatic irony, using verbal and situational irony to enhance comedy, as in *Midsummer Night's Dream*, or to deepen tragedy, as in *Romeo and Juliet*. If only Romeo and Juliet had arrived at the designated meeting place at the same time! If only Romeo had checked more closely to discover that his beloved was drugged, not dead!

"A Modest Proposal," written by Jonathan Swift in 1729, is perhaps the greatest example in literature of an essay written with an ironic tone. As a social critic, much like Charles Dickens a hundred years later, Swift was appalled by the wretched poverty of Ireland. Absentee landlords lived luxuriously abroad (usually in England) and were interested only in collecting rent. Impoverished tenants eked what they could out of the land, often surviving near starvation. With no incentive to work for themselves, frequent famines, and large families to support, there seemed to be no way out for the poor of Ireland.

Jonathan Swift exposed and attacked the social and political injustices of his time in a scathing and witty essay in which he proposed, in jest, the cannibalism of Ireland's children. The proposal is ironic in tone, dripping with sarcasm, and is a clever satire that follows the rules and structures of Latin satires. Far from mocking the poor, Swift was appealing to his educated countrymen, who would be familiar with the satires of Horace and Juvenal.

The ironic tone continues throughout the entire essay, and it can be clearly recognized in the following examples. Near the beginning of the essay, Swift looks for a "national hero" to step forward with a solution for the poor children of Ireland:

> therefore, whoever could find out a fair, cheap, and easy method of making these children sound, useful members of the commonwealth, would deserve so well of the public as to have his statue set up for a preserver of the nation.

He then proposes that instead of being a millstone of responsibility to parents and the Church (the welfare providers of his time), that children could "give back." The irony here is that they would contribute by becoming a source of food and clothing:

> provide for them in such a manner as instead of being a charge upon their parents or the parish, or wanting food and raiment for the rest of their lives, they shall on the contrary contribute to the feeding, and partly to the clothing, of many thousands.

The following two examples of ironic tone are located a few lines apart and refer to children stealing, probably because of hunger or parental neglect. The notion that stealing would be a livelihood is a sarcastic thrust at the politicians who have failed to provide either sustenance or hope for the poor:

> they can very seldom pick up a livelihood by stealing, till they arrive at six years old, as I have been informed by a principal gentleman in the county of Cavan, who protested to me that he never knew above one or two instances under the age of six, even in a part of the kingdom so renowned for the quickest proficiency in that art.

Shortly thereafter, Swift makes a shocking, ironic proposal: since the resources of Ireland are already being devoured by the greedy landlords, why not devour the children of the land as well?

> I have been assured by a very knowing American of my acquaintance in London, that a young healthy child well nursed is at a year a most delicious, nourishing, and wholesome food, whether stewed, roasted, baked, or boiled; and I make no doubt that it will equally serve in a fricassee or a ragout.

In the following excerpt, Jonathan Swift seems to be mocking the poor as savages who do not bother with the institution of marriage. In reality, he is savaging the so-called "persons of quality and fortune" who exploit the poor to support their lavish lifestyles. Because the wealthy entertain frequently, often with decadent dinner parties, the meal provides a satirical extension of the cannibalism metaphor:

> my reason is, that these children are seldom the fruits of marriage, a circumstance not much regarded by our savages, therefore one male will be sufficient to serve four females. That the remaining hundred thousand may, at a year old, be offered in the fortune through the kingdom; always advising the mother to let them suck plentifully in the last month, so as to render them plump and fat for a good table. A child will make two dishes at an entertainment for friends; and when the family dines alone, the fore or hind quarter will make a reasonable dish, and seasoned with a little pepper or salt will be very good boiled on the fourth day, especially in winter.

Swift sarcastically adds:

> I grant this food will be somewhat dear, and therefore very proper for landlords, who, as they have already devoured most of the parents, seem to have the best title to the children.

Swift then takes another jab at wealthy landlords, labelling them as self-righteous and sanctimonious hypocrites who would claim to abhor any practice bordering on cruelty while blind to the insensitive, politically sanctioned practices that have kept the Irish farmers poor and wretched:

> some scrupulous people might be apt to censure such a practice (although indeed very unjustly), as a little bordering upon cruelty; which, I confess, hath always been with me the strongest objection against any project, however so well intended.

Swift begins to list the advantages in creating a new and trendy menu item out of Ireland's disadvantaged children. Once again, the ironic tone "borrows" Ireland's economic goals of increasing domestic production:

> Thirdly, whereas the maintenance of an hundred thousand children, from two years old and upward, cannot be computed at less than ten shillings a-piece per annum, the nation's stock will be thereby increased fifty thousand pounds per annum, beside the profit of a new dish introduced to the tables of all gentlemen of fortune in the kingdom who have any refinement in taste. And the money will circulate among ourselves, the goods being entirely of our own growth and manufacture.

In the next example, Swift comments on some of the unfortunate side effects of poverty, namely, domestic violence and unwanted pregnancies because pregnancy meant "one more mouth to feed" in homes where families were already going hungry:

> Men would become as fond of their wives during the time of their pregnancy as they are now of their mares in foal, their cows in calf, their sows when (as is too frequent a practice) for fear of a miscarriage.

At this point in the essay, Jonathan Swift finally introduces some reforms that could alleviate the alarming social and economic conditions of Ireland. However, the ironic tone continues, because Swift seems to be deriding the ideas with his introduction:

> Therefore let no man talk to me of other expedients: Of taxing our absentees at five shillings a pound: Of using neither cloths, nor household furniture, except what is of our own growth and manufacture: Of utterly rejecting the materials and instruments that promote foreign luxury: Of curing the expensiveness of pride, vanity, idleness gaming in our women: Of introducing a vein of parsimony, prudence and temperance: Of learning to love our country, wherein we differ even from Laplanders and the inhabitants of Topinamboo: Of being a little cautious not to sell our country and consciences for nothing: Of teaching landlords to have at least one degree of mercy towards their tenants. Lastly, of putting a spirit of honesty, industry, and skill into our shop-keepers, who, if a resolution could now be taken to buy only our native goods, would immediately unite to cheat and exact upon us in the price, the measure, and the goodness.

The ironic tone of the essay is sustained to the end, where Swift invites his "opposition" to actually check with the victims of the Irish system. He implies, ironically, that many are so miserable as to wish they had never been born:

> wives and children who are beggars in effect: I desire those politicians who dislike my overture, and may perhaps be so bold as to attempt an answer, that they will first ask the parents of these mortals, whether they would not at this day think it a great happiness to have been sold for food, at a year old in the manner I prescribe, and thereby have avoided such a perpetual scene of misfortunes as they have since gone through by the oppression of landlords, the impossibility of paying rent without money or trade, the want of common sustenance, with neither house nor clothes to cover them from the inclemencies of the weather, and the most inevitable prospect of entailing the like or greater miseries upon their breed forever.

Jonathan Swift quite breezily signs off on his cutting satire, claiming that he would not stand to gain a "single penny" from his shocking proposal, his youngest child being nine years of age and his wife "past child-bearing."

IRONY IN POETRY

Andrew Marvell's "To His Coy Mistress," written in the 17th century, is an example of ironic insincerity. Because of an inheritance, the poet was able to spend much of his youth wandering around Europe, impressing young ladies. Responsibility and commitment were not high priorities for this youthful adventurer. Read the poem through a few times to enjoy the easy flow of language and the vivid imagery. Following the poem is an analysis of the irony and the poet's methods of creating irony.

TO HIS COY MISTRESS

> Had we but world enough, and time,
> This coyness, lady, were no crime.
> We would sit down, and think which way
> To walk, and pass our long love's day.
> Thou by the Indian Ganges' side
> Shouldst rubies find; I by the tide
> Of Humber would complain. I would
> Love you ten years before the flood,
> And you should, if you please, refuse
> Till the conversion of the Jews.
> My vegetable love should grow
> Vaster than empires and more slow;
> An hundred years should go to praise
> Thine eyes, and on thy forehead gaze;
> Two hundred to adore each breast,
> But thirty thousand to the rest;
> An age at least to every part,
> And the last age should show your heart.
> For lady, you deserve this state,
> Nor would I love at lower rate.

But at my back I always hear
Time's wingèd chariot hurrying near;
And yonder all before us lie
Deserts of vast eternity.
Thy beauty shall no more be found,
Nor, in thy marble vault, shall sound
My echoing song; then worms shall try
That long-preserved virginity,
And your quaint honor turn to dust,
And into ashes all my lust:
The grave's a fine and private place,
But none, I think, do there embrace.
    Now therefore, while the youthful hue
Sits on the skin like morning dew,
And while thy willing soul transpires
At every pore with instant fires,
Now let us sport us while we may,
And now, like amorous birds of prey,
Rather at once our time devour
Than languish in his slow-chapped power.
Let us roll all our strength and all
Our sweetness up into one ball,
And tear our pleasures with rough strife
Thorough the iron gates of life:
Thus, though we cannot make our sun
Stand still, yet we will make him run.

—*by* Andrew Marvell

Analysis of the Poem

Behind the quaint phrases, vows of undying devotion, and romantic exaggerations, the poet's real message to his current love can be interpreted. Put bluntly and in modern terms, a summary of the poet's main idea might be, "Life's too short to waste time dating when we just want to be together."

What the poet appears to be professing and what he is actually proposing are two very different things. That is what makes the tone and mood ironic throughout the poem. Why, then, does Marvell extend such a brief message into 46 lines?

Here are some of the techniques Andrew Marvell uses to achieve irony in his poem.

Use of subjunctive mood

Using the subjunctive "Had" in line 1 immediately designates the ideal situation of the prolonged courtship described in the next few lines to the realm of impossible fantasy.

Use of hyperbole

The poet's lengthy list of hyperbolic statements is intended to flatter the listener. Phrases such as "Thou by the Indian Ganges' side / Shouldst rubies find" and "I would love you ten years before the flood" are examples of Marvell's craft of exaggeration.

Use of excessive flattery

In the 17th century, the notion of "long-preserved virginity" would be a flattering idealization of a young female, as would "quaint honor." The poet's elevation of the young woman to a pedestal is an example of a romantic ideal.

Use of flowery figurative language

Marvell uses figurative language, such as metaphor ("at my back I always hear /Time's wingèd chariot hurrying near" and "Deserts of vast eternity"), simile ("like morning dew" and "like amorous birds of prey"), and personification ("Thus, though we cannot make our sun / Stand still, yet we will make him run").

Contrast of realism and bluntness

The contrasting thread of blunt realism that runs though the poem defines the ironic tone by implying the difference between appearance and reality. The poet's reminder to the girl that her beauty will gain her no suitors once she is in the marble vault of her grave amounts to the harsh and deliberate manipulation of a young person's greatest fear: to die before experiencing the excitement and passion of physical love. The poet's wheedling and self-centred purpose is laid bare in the line about his lust turning to ashes.

In summary, although the poem seems to present a romanticized fantasy as an ideal, in reality, the poet is promoting immediate gratification in favour of long-term commitment.

For fun, a modern poet, A.D. Hope, wrote a response to Marvell's "To His Coy Mistress." Hope uses the same language and poetic form as Marvell but speaks from the point of view of the woman to whom Marvell addresses his poem. The speaker of Hope's poem has managed to see through Marvell's persuasive language and eloquently rejects the urgency of the love that Marvell's speaker professes. Observe how Hope's speaker responds to the imagery and arguments from Marvell's poem.

2.2.2d   assess the use of musical devices, figures of speech and sensory details to create effects in a variety of print and nonprint texts

ALLEGORY AS A LITERARY DEVICE

Allegory is a literary form that uses extended metaphors, giving objects, characters, and actions meaning beyond the actual story. The meaning of the story, in other words, is both literal and figurative. Fables are perhaps the simplest allegories in literature because they are stories that convey a moral lesson. Stories that convey social, religious, or political significance can also be allegories. In such stories, a writer may deliberately personify characters to represent abstract ideas such as charity, greed, and envy. Allegories date back many years, but they have found their way into modern stories, films, and even art.

Here are some allegorical books:

• *Aesop's Fables*

• *Gulliver's Travels* by Jonathan Swift

• *Pilgrim's Progress* by John Bunyan

• *Young Goodman Brown* by Nathaniel Hawthorne

• *The Chronicles of Narnia* by C.S. Lewis

• *Animal Farm* by George Orwell

Here are some allegorical films:

- *2001: A Space Odyssey*

- *Star Trek*

- *Star Wars*

- *The Wizard of Oz*

Poetic Language

Poetic language includes many literary devices, including the following ones.

- **Onomatopoeia**: the imitation of sounds through the use of words
  Buzz, splash, and clash sound like the sounds they describe.

- **Alliteration**: the repetition of first letters, often consonants
  "Dim drums throbbing in the hills half heard."

- **Assonance**: the repeated use of a vowel within successive words
  "I had to laugh to see the calf walk down the path."

- **Consonance**: the repeated use of a consonant within successive words
  "The moan of doves in immemorial elms, / And murmuring of innumerable bees."

Word placement and sentence order can also be used to emphasize and suggest ideas or themes.

- **Repetition**: similar to parallelism, although it may be on a smaller scale
  "Break, break, break,
  On thy cold gray stones, O sea!"

Figures of speech are used for effect and sometimes to convey information.

- **Simile**: a comparison that uses the words like or as
  "Her presence at the meeting was like a breath of fresh air."

- **Metaphor**: a comparison that does not use the words like or as and appears to be an actual statement of fact
  "He had the eye of an eagle."

- **Hyperbole**: deliberate exaggeration to make a point, but not to deceive
  "That joke is as old as the hills."

- **Synecdoche**: the naming of one part of something to stand for the whole thing, or of the whole thing to stand for a part.
  "A fine herd of cattle you have there. About a hundred head, I guess?"
  "Thirteen sail appeared on the horizon."

- **Metonymy**: the use of something associated with a second thing to stand for that second thing; the association can be arbitrary, as long as it is widely understood
  "The Crown supports the adoption of this law."
  An apple is often used to represent education.

Metonymy is often visual and is widely used in film as visual shorthand. Rain falling at a funeral is a visual representation of grief because of its physical association with tears.

- **Personification**: the attribution of human qualities or actions to something that is not human; animals, inanimate objects, and ideas can all be personified
  "Life's but a walking shadow a poor player / That struts and frets his hour upon the stage."

- **Symbolism**: the use of something concrete to represent an abstract belief, feeling, idea, or attitude.
  A red rose is often used to symbolize love.

  Certain colours can symbolize abstract ideas. Black, for example, often symbolizes death.

- **Oxymoron**: a two-or three-word phrase that contains opposite words or ideas

  "civil war"
  "military intelligence"

- **Paradox**: an extended oxymoron that appears to have contradictory ideas
  "I must be cruel in order to be kind."

- **Imagery**: words or phrases that appeal to the senses and help the reader imagine sights, sounds, smells, tastes, and touch
  "The children were nestled all snug in their beds."
  "While visions of sugar plums danced in their heads."
  "As dry leaves that before the wild hurricane fly."

- **Idiom**: an expression that means something other than what it actually says and is often associated with colloquialisms and proverbs
  "To make hay while the sun shines."

The following examples demonstrate the appeal of literary devices.

Effects of Literary Devices

When you read poetry, you expect to find figurative language, to help you see, hear, taste, touch—to experience—literature through your senses. Consider the following two poems.

Fog

The fog comes
on little cat feet.

It sits looking over harbor and city
on silent haunches
and then moves on.

—*by* Carl Sandburg

Mother to Son

Well, son, I'll tell you:
Life for me ain't been no crystal stair.
It's had tacks in it,
And splinters,
And boards torn up,
And places with no carpet on the floor—
Bare.
But all the time
I'se been a-climbin' on,
And reachin' landin's,
And turnin' corners,
And sometimes goin' in the dark
Where there ain't been no light.
So boy, don't you turn back.
Don't you set down on the steps
'Cause you finds it's kinder hard.
Don't you fall now—
For I'se still goin', honey,
I'se still climbin',
And life for me ain't been no crystal stair.

—*by* Langston Hughes

When you read the poem "Fog," can you picture a stealthy grey fog creeping over the buildings and out to sea after lingering throughout the early morning over the harbour? Isn't a cat the perfect metaphor to provide readers with a mental image?

In "Mother to Son," "Life," for the mother "ain't been no crystal stair." Can you picture with this metaphor: a smooth and glittering staircase, sparkling under the twinkling lights of a crystal chandelier? What the mother is trying to tell her son is that life is tough and hard, like a neglected wooden staircase with threadbare carpeting, full of splinters and nasty surprises, and she compares her life journey with climbing the staircase while "sometimes goin' in the dark." When the speaker refers to "landin's," and "turnin' corners," she is using symbolism. The "landin's" represent plateaus or small successes that the mother has achieved. The "corners" she turns could be new directions she has taken with her life. The mother ends with words of encouragement: "So, boy, don't you turn back...Don't you fall now—For I'se still goin', honey." Basically, the mother is telling her son to never give up. What is notable is how beautiful and effective simple words of advice become when symbolism and metaphors replace plain language.

2.2.2e   explain the contribution of motif and symbol to controlling idea and theme

SYMBOLISM

COMMON SYMBOLS IN LITERATURE

- Here are some common symbols used in literature.
- Water: fertility, life-giving, rebirth, purification, and redemption
- Stagnant or polluted water: corruption, evil
- Fire: destruction, purification, passion, death
- Earth: baseness, fertility
- Air, wind: spirits, freedom, inspiration
- Sun: wisdom and vision, power, life-giving, regeneration
- Sunrise: birth, rebirth, joy, hope
- Sunset: death
- Mountains: obstacles, achievement, aspirations, awe, glory
- Storms: death, evil, inner turmoil
- Roads, ships, trains, railroads: journeys, changes
- Fork in the road, crossroads: choices, decisions
- Doors, gates, arches: escape, opportunities, utopias, fantasy worlds, freedom
- Bridges: transitions, crossing over
- Walls, fences, hedges: barriers, dividing lines, prisons
- Windows: freedom, longing, imprisonment
- Mirrors: illusion, unreality, passage to other worlds
- Birds, sky: freedom
- Circles: wholeness, unity
- Gardens: Eden, paradise, innocence, fertility
- Deserts: spiritual aridity, death, hopelessness, sterility
- Lambs: innocence, Christ
- Sheep: conformity
- Black: evil, death, despair
- White: innocence, good, redemption
- Red: war, anger, blood, vengeance, love, passion
- Green: growth, renewal, life, nature, envy
- Yellow: sun, happiness, cowardice, betrayal

The following poem contains many examples of effective word use. Diction and figurative language work together to produce a feeling about night: a universally calming experience of peace, beauty, and infinity with which readers can identify. The mood and tone produced by the writer's style also leave the reader with a message or theme, even though the theme is not directly stated. As you read the poem, pay attention to the meaning of the words and figurative language and symbolism used. Think about how they contribute to the mood and tone and how they suggest the theme.

STARS

> Now in the West the slender moon lies low,
> And now Orion glimmers through the trees,
> Clearing the earth with even pace and slow,
> And now the stately-moving Pleiades,
> In that soft infinite darkness overhead
> Hang jewel-wise upon a silver thread.
>
> And all the lonelier stars that have their place,
> Calm lamps within the distant southern sky,
> And planet-dust upon the edge of space,
> Look down upon the fretful world, and I
> Look up to outer vastness unafraid
> And see the stars which sang when earth was made.
>
> —*by* Marjorie Pickthall

UNDERSTANDING THE WORDS

Understanding the meaning of each word is the first step to understanding the whole poem. Here are some words and phrases that you might want to focus on and think about.

Word	Meaning or Explanation
the West	West is a compass direction; when capitalized, it represents a region
slender moon	Crescent moon means the moon is either waxing or waning
glimmer	A faint, intermittent light
stately	Impressive, dignified, and graceful
pace	Speed of walking, running, or other movement
Orion, the Pleiades	Two constellations, or groups of stars, named after characters from Greek mythology; Orion was a hunter, and the Pleiades were seven sisters
-wise	In a certain way, direction, or manner
jewel-wise	In the manner of a jewel (think of the characteristics of a jewel)
planet-dust	Vast dust clouds in space are compressed by gravity to form planets and stars
edge of space	Astronomers have known since ancient times that the universe is vast, but until the 1920s and the discovery of galaxies, no one knew quite how vast it really is. This may refer to knowledge that was considered accurate, but now has changed. It may also be a figure of speech.
fretful	Agitated, disturbed

UNDERSTANDING IMAGERY

The poet's emotional response to the night sky (and to all of life) is carefully developed through a series of motifs and images. She looks up at the night sky and sees the moon and stars.

Image	Meaning or Explanation
slender moon lies low	The crescent moon is setting.
Orion glimmers through the trees	The stars are seen through branches, the leaves must have fallen, and it is fall or winter.
clears the earth	The constellation is rising in the east.
overhead	The Pleiades rise before Orion and are high in the sky. The placement of the moon and stars are correct for a night in November in the early 1900s.
jewel-wise upon a silver thread	The jewels are compared with a necklace. The thread is an allusion to star charts that show the stars connected with lines. The entire image recalls the beauty of diamonds and silver.

In the poem, the night sky is personified. Words and phrases such as "slender," "even pace," "stately-moving," "lonelier," "calm," and "look down" make the celestial bodies appear to be alive and aware. The images are all beautiful and peaceful: "the stately-moving Pleiades, / In that soft infinite darkness overhead / Hang jewel-wise upon a silver thread."

UNDERSTANDING SYMBOLS, REFERENCES, AND ALLUSIONS

Poetry often includes elements that refer to things other than themselves.

A *symbol* is something that stands for something else, especially for something abstract. In this poem, the stars are symbols of peace, order, and purpose.

A *reference* is a direct mention of something that is related to whatever is being discussed.

An *allusion* is an indirect reference. Because they are indirect, allusions can be more difficult to recognize and understand. Writers and poets often expect their readers to have certain knowledge or to be familiar with certain events or writings. References and allusions often refer to historical, mythological, or religious subjects.

The first line of the poem "Stars" contains an allusion to the First World War slang to "go west," which means to die. The term itself is an allusion to the death toll on the Western Front. In the poem, if the moon is waning (becoming less), then "slender moon" would support the interpretation that "the West" is referring to the Western Front. The moon is certainly setting, which does support this interpretation. All this accounts for the capitalization of "west," a word that is not capitalized when used as a direction.

Lines 10 and 11 contain allusions to Blaise Pascal's, (a French mathematician, scientist, and religious philospher), famous words about the vastness of space: "The eternal silence of these infinite spaces terrifies me." However, Marjorie Pickthall feels the opposite: "I look up to outer vastness unafraid."

Line 12 is an allusion to the Book of Job when God speaks to Job about the creation of Earth: "When the morning stars sang together, and all the sons of God shouted for joy." Like "the fretful world," (line 10) Job had suffered greatly, and this line about the creation of the world is part of the response to his suffering.

This poem was published posthumously (after the poet's death) in 1925. This means that the use of the phrase "the West" would have been familiar to the poet and its association to death would have been on her mind during the writing of this poem.

Some words to describe the mood in the poem "Stars" might be reverential, inspired, or full of awe. The mood is conveyed by words and figurative language.

Pickthall seems to be conveying the theme that the night is a living entity or being, with stars moving in jeweled, endless patterns that began long before the dawn of human time. Far above the "fretful" Earth, they rule the heavens with tranquility and bring their calming influence from the vastness of space. There is less figurative language in prose, but the poet's style and diction influences the mood, the tone, and the theme.

2.3.1 a identify and consider personal, moral, ethical and cultural perspectives when studying literature and other texts; and reflect on and monitor how perspectives change as a result of interpretation and discussion

CRITICAL LITERACY

Literature presents the reader with values, perspectives, and world views in a way that invites engaging and thoughtful discussion, interpretation, and comparison. Good literature makes readers think about the ideas it presents and how these ideas might relate to the real world.

VALUES

Values are based on the beliefs and principles that influence your perspective, on the experiences of your life, and on the issues you encounter. Values shape your world view, which influences your decisions and judgements, the way you feel toward and treat others, and the motivations that govern your actions.

In literature, world views are revealed through narration, description, and character motivation. Characters in literature and poetry often become a voice for values, perspectives, and world views. Stories and poems offer perspectives and world views for exploration, interpretation, and comparison. As a reader, you are invited to join the discussion, analyze descriptions and motivations that you see in the text, and agree or disagree with the writer or characters.

Here are some of the ways in which values, perspectives, and world views can be presented.

By the Author

Henry David Thoreau (1817–1862) was an American writer and philosopher. He opposed slavery and was an advocate of independence and simple living. Can you see hints of his values, perspective, or world view in the opening paragraph of one of his most well-known essays, "Waldon; or, Life in the Woods"?

> The mass of men lead lives of quiet desperation. What is called resignation is confirmed desperation. From the desperate city you go into the desperate country, and have to console yourself with the bravery of minks and muskrats. A stereotyped   but unconscious despair is concealed even under what are called the games and amusements of mankind. There is no play in them, for this comes after work. But it is a characteristic of wisdom not to do desperate things.

From a Character

Lester Burnham is the main protagonist in the movie *American Beauty*, written by Alan Ball. As a middle-aged man who values fulfillment in life, Lester finds himself buried in a rut: he hates the mundane predictability of his job and comes home at night to a wife consumed by materialism. One day, Lester meets his daughter's friend, whose youth and beauty jars Lester alive. His quest to recapture a lost youth motivates him to begin working out, to try drugs, to quit his job, and to buy an expensive car. Lester's twisted and adolescent views of self-fulfillment eventually lead him to attempt to seduce his daughter's teenage friend, foreshadowing the tragic denouement of the story. As a cautionary tale, the movie ends with a plastic bag dancing in the wind, reflecting simplicity, which is what makes life beautiful and meaningful.

From a setting

Setting often contributes to a set of assumptions and value systems that can reinforce theme. In William Faulkner's short story "A Rose for Emily," the description of Miss Emily's house reinforces the decline of Miss Emily's influence in the town. Her resistance to change and the changing economic climate are inferred.

> It was a big squarish frame house that had once been white, decorated with cupolas and spires and scrolled balconies in the heavily lightsome style of the seventies, set on what has once been our most select street. But garages and cotton gins had encroached and obliterated even the august names of that neighborhood; only Miss Emily's house was left, lifting its stubborn and coquettish decay above the cotton wagons and the gasoline pumps—an eyesore among eyesores.

From a poem

In Margaret Avison's poem "Swimmer's Moment," the lure of seeking self-fulfillment is compared with a swimmer taking a risk by diving into a whirlpool.

> For everyone
> The swimmer's moment at the whirlpool comes,
> But many at that moment will not say
> "This is the whirlpool, then."
> By their refusal they are saved
> From the black pit, and also from contesting
> The deadly rapids, and emerging in
> The mysterious, and more ample, further waters.

In John Milton's poem "On His Blindness," the poet expresses a less narcissistic, more spiritual world view. The poet, after reflecting on the personal challenges of losing his vision, concludes that while it is a natural outreach of the human condition to question God or fate, dark times do not have to cause the death of dreams and the loss of gifts: "They also serve who only stand and wait."

2.3.2a identify criteria to evaluate the effectiveness of texts, monitor the effectiveness of the criteria, and modify the criteria as needed [for example, use criteria to assess the adequacy, relevance and effectiveness of content and to assess the text creator's voice and style]

STRATEGIES FOR EVALUATING TEXTS

When viewing and reading informational text containing some form of graphics, critical reading skills are still required. However, the addition of graphic text to the written word challenges the reader to employ certain strategies differently, since graphs, charts, diagrams, drawings, or photographs convey meaning in a more subtle or unusually structured way. Be aware that conventional syntax can be dramatically influenced by an accompanying graphic. Word text used in graphic communication has the following unique characteristics:

- fragmented syntax

- irregular word placement

- spatial grouping of text (columns, boxes, bubbles)

- use of different font types and sizes

- application of bold and italicized text

- inferred connections between words and graphic text

- use of white space and framing for effect

- organization by headings, bullets, and lists

Although charts and tables use fragmented syntax and a unique spatial arrangement of text, the reading process remains logical, since information is organized vertically and horizontally and is typically grouped in a recognizable form. However, when a drawing, diagram, or photograph plays a dominant role in graphic communication, the "reading" process becomes far more intuitive, since the language is frequently subordinate to the image. You will find yourself going through fewer steps and applying fewer strategies, but the key steps remain the same.

- establish your purpose for reading

- understand the writer's purpose

- apply any background knowledge

- identify the building blocks: words and images

- construct a whole meaning: interpretation

- apply critical thinking

- reflect and analyze: accept or reject

APPLYING YOUR SKILLS

Compare the following sample reader reactions to a magazine photograph and a political poster. Keep in mind that the reader's point of view as well as the writer's motivations and intent.

ONE THAT ALMOST GOT AWAY

Final Edit

PUERTO RICO

Why We Pulled the Taffeta

Sample Reader Notes for "Why We Pulled the Taffeta"

- The featured picture of little dresses hanging on a clothesline was to accompany a magazine article on Puerto Rico's rural heartland.

- The word rural is the opposite of urban. It suggests country living, farming, or a more rustic life style.

- Taffetta is a kind of stiff silk cloth with a smooth glossy surface used for clothing requiring stiff, decorative features.

- Commercial photographs are chosen to vivify an impression rather than to record reality. This suggests that what is real and what is perceived are often quite different.

- A possible conclusion is that the editor did not wish to confuse her reading audience with an image that conflicted with the intended theme of her article on the Puerto Rican rural heartland.

- Another possible conclusion is that the details selected by all writers are discriminatory in that they are rejected if they do not contribute to the central purpose of the piece.

- All communication is selective.

MANAGE IDEAS AND INFORMATION

3.1.1a   modify selected strategies as needed to refine the depth and breadth of inquiry or research and to identify the purpose, audience and form of presentation

METACOGNITION

The word *metacognition* refers to thinking about how you think, including thinking about how you learn. As you discover and think about strategies that work best with your individual learning style, you will become a more confident and productive learner. It is important to think about your own learning and to ask yourself questions about how it works for you. Do you work better in groups or on your own? Do you memorize things visually? What kind of reading do you like to do best? The more time you spend analyzing how you think, the better able you will be to pinpoint the areas where you excel and the areas where you have trouble.

The following section of the *KEY* gives many examples and guidelines on metacognition. The examples are designed to show how an individual student performs metacognition activities. Keep in mind that the way you think and learn is unique, so different methods may appeal to you more than others. Learning what appeals to you is also a part of metacognition.

SETTING GOALS

One of the keys to improving your English skills is to set personal goals for language growth. You may wish to use the following rubric that identifies some of the major English skills needed to identify your strengths and areas for growth. Reviewing assignments and assessment rubrics from your current or past English courses will help you to assess your strengths and the areas that need improvement.

Skill	Yes	Needs Improvement
Read regularly		
Predict and ask questions while reading; discuss unfamiliar concepts with others		
Take note of words I am not sure of and use context or references to find meanings		
Re-read passages to clarify meaning		
Use visualizing and graphic organizers as aids to analyzing text and planning for communicating ideas		
Connect what I am reading to what I know about and to other texts I have read		
Understand symbols, archetypes, and literary devices and use them to enhance understanding of texts		
Use ideas in texts to better understand and communicate understandings of self and the world around		

Skill	Yes	Needs Improvement
Know how to effectively introduce and conclude topics in writing or oral presentations		
Connect all ideas to a controlling idea		
Fully support ideas with explanations and examples		
Identify when ideas are not communicated clearly		
Use a variety of sentences and precise diction for effect		
Find and correct errors in spelling, usage, and punctuation		
Understand oral instructions		
Listen carefully, build on the ideas of others, and ask questions to help others clarify ideas		
Feel comfortable making formal presentations		
Use voice effectively—volume, rate, tone, and pacing to communicate effectively and convey emotion		
Use eye contact and gestures for emphasis		
Use charts, graphs, and visual aids to contribute to presentations		
Know how to find resources, effectively record information, and correctly reference sources		

3.1.2a *reflect on and describe strategies for developing an inquiry or research plan that will foster understanding, select and monitor appropriate strategies, and modify strategies as needed to plan inquiry or research effectively [for example, use a research journal to keep and record reflections on the research process, clarify thinking, revisit initial perceptions and ask questions that lead to new research].*

3.1.2b *select from a repertoire of effective strategies to develop appropriate inquiry or research plans that will address the topic and satisfy contextual and presentation requirements [for example, questions within questions, inquiry charts, preliminary interview, and consultations with the teacher /librarian].*

APPLYING SKILLS: USING RESEARCH IN PROJECTS

Research is a vital part of writing formal papers. Metacognition can be applied to your research in order to see where you can improve your researching techniques. In the following fictional account, two students were given a news article about a local issue and were asked to use research to clarify and extend their understanding of the article and the issues it presents. As you read about their assignment, try and think about how you might go about researching this issue if it were your own assignment. How might the techniques you would use be different from the ones used by the fictional students in the following example?

The students are given two weeks to work on a project about current events. They are asked to identify an issue raised in a news article that they are given, track the issue for two weeks, consider perspectives and possible outcomes of the issue, and engage their classmates in the issue.

The article is about an airport safety issue arising from a recent crash landing at Pearson International Airport in Toronto that could have resulted in a tragic loss of lives. According to the news item, an Air France jet carrying 309 passengers and crew landed halfway down the runway during a summer rainstorm. Overshooting the 90-metre buffer zone at the end of the runway, the plane careened over a bank and finally came to a stop. Fortunately, before the damaged aircraft burst into flames, everyone on board was safely evacuated and removed from danger. The accident was caused by human error, but the issue arising from this incident involved passenger safety and accident prevention. After reading the information, the students felt that the runway buffer zone should be extended to 300 metres, the required length at most major European airports.

The students decide to use a kind of tracking log to record what they did to clarify or extend their understanding of this story and the issues it raised. This is what they recorded over their two-week assignment:

Class Project: The Pearson Airport

We collected stories on the topic from the newspaper, television, and the Internet for about two weeks. We ended up with a total of 21 news items.

We recorded facts or messages common to all of the stories, including:

- the Pearson runway has a 90-metre buffer zone

- the weather conditions were severe

- the pilot landed halfway down the runway

- incidents such as this happen more frequently than is commonly believed

We looked for public reactions on the newspaper and television websites and on the editorial page of the newspaper, and recorded repeated responses, such as:

- safety is of major concern

- the expense of extending the runway is worth possibly saving lives

- Pearson Airport should have the same standards as the rest of the world

We watched for different opinions on the issue, and found opinion articles from:

- the Airline Pilots' Association

- the Ontario Department of Tourism

- city and provincial governments (about who would bear the cost of a runway upgrade)

Based on all that we found, we predicted this outcome:

- the runway extension will be built over the next two years, funded by the province

- We watched to see if the issue was resolved in two weeks. It was not, but the matter was under review by a transportation committee.

We summarized our findings and prepared our class presentation.

After our presentation, we will allow a brief time for discussion on our issue. We will then ask Miss Fergusen to review business letter format and take us to the computer lab to write letters to the Transportation Safety Board of Canada, to be forwarded to the Honourable Lawrence Cannon, Minister of Transport, Ottawa. The purpose of the letters will be to request mandatory lengthened buffer zones for major Canadian airport runways by 2010.

Our Concluding Comments:

Through reading, research, and discussion, we clarified and extended our understanding of an important and newsworthy safety issue. We came to have a strong personal interest in the outcome of this issue because, like most Canadians, we will use air travel throughout our lives. If a shortsighted decision is made, we could someday be victims.

Research is critical to writing non-fiction text. The more you learn about an issue, the better able you will be to form an opinion that is informed and balanced. It can be difficult to find information that is accurate and that does not have a bias. As you become a better researcher, understanding information and how to find good information will become easier.

Use metacognition the next time you are researching for a project. Think about areas of research you may have missed and about ways of effectively using your research.

EVALUATING YOUR PROCESS

Metacognition consists of two processes occurring at the same time: monitoring your progress as you learn, and changing and adapting your strategies if necessary. In writing, this involves identifying what strategies you found most helpful before, during, and after writing and considering what steps you can take to improve as a writer. After you have finished a writing project, think back to how you developed your ideas for writing, the research you did, and how you sorted and organized it. This will help you to identify the strategies you used. The next time you do similar writing, use the strategies that worked the best for you and reconsider the others.

For example, a Grade 12 student came up with the following examples of strategies he had used during the first half of the year.

My Writing Strategies

Before Writing

- Went online to find information about topics such as the topic "natural disasters" after we read the short story "The Worst Day Ever"

- Jotted down books, TV shows, and music titles related to topic

- Talked with mom about topic choice

- Wrote down purpose and audience

- Made a web plan and outline

During Writing

- Spread out notes and outlines

- Tried to follow outlines

- Checked the assignment criteria

- Tried to write correctly

- Tried to use good transitions

- Tried to include things teacher was emphasizing, like different sentence openers and replacements

After Writing

- Labelled my revisions to make sure I was intentionally including the teacher's suggestions

- Read drafts aloud from computer screen while revising and editing

- Paid attention to my peer partner so we could help each other improve

---

Next, the student explained the strategy he found the most helpful, which was the idea of labelling revisions because it required him to think specifically about what he was changing and why. Since the students were sharing their metacognition activities with the teacher, he submitted the following paragraph:

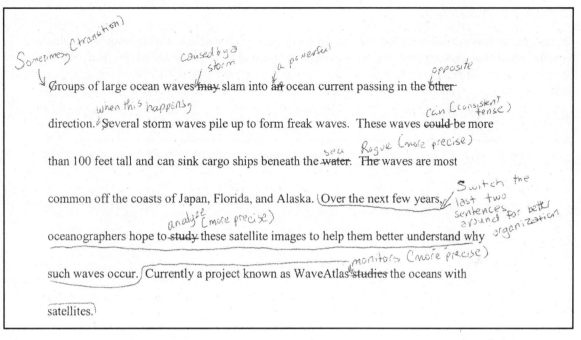

Finally, the student identified several steps he could take to improve as a writer. His list included the following ideas.

- Keep a writing log, with sections for Spelling Errors, Writing Errors, Story Ideas

- Start a list of words I want to use in my writing

- Look online for sites where I can share some of my writing

After collecting the class's reflections, the teacher gave each student two 4 × 6" cards to tape inside his or her writing log. The cards contained reminders to help the students think about each piece of writing.

This Piece

- What is best?

- What could I improve?

- What stage was smoothest?

- What ideas could I use for new writing?

Learning from This Piece

- Have I learned any new techniques?

- Did I try something new?

- Have I eliminated personal errors such as sentence fragments, that I have commonly made in the past?

WRITER'S REFLECTION

Reflecting on your writing is something you probably have to do in class. In the following example, a fictional student has written answers to metacognition questions she has reflected on. You may have to answer questions similar to these about your own writing and language skills. See if you can answer the following questions yourself.

Example

> **Before Grade 12, what did you know or understand to be your strengths as a writer? Has this changed?**
>
> I always thought that my greatest strength was writing humour. It was because I found it easy to remember the punch line of a good joke, and I could always seem to make my friends laugh. Sometimes at the wrong time, like in the middle of your class on sentence fragments! When you asked us to think hard about our strengths in September and to think of ways to branch out from those strengths, I realized that one reason I can describe things in a humorous way is that I am a people watcher. I am always watching what people do, how they react, and what they say in certain situations. I used that strength to branch out when I wrote my one-act play on peer pressure. With realistic sounding dialogue and characters based on what I had really seen around me, I think I was able to get some serious points across using humour. After my group presented my play, you said our dialogue was convincing and real.

> **What did you learn about yourself as a writer as a result of the group writing experience?**
>
> You mean the short story project. The truth is, I wasn't too happy at first. I actually like writing independent stories from my own head, so it was annoying to have to stop and pay attention to the other two guys in my group. One hated writing, period, and the other didn't want to write anything but fantasy, which I have never read. We wasted a bit of time in the beginning, but when you started posting deadlines on the board we had to think of something. We had just learned about parodies, so we decided to write a modernized parody of a well-known fairy tale. The partner who hated writing didn't mind working from a basic plot we all knew—"Little Red Riding Hood." He even started to contribute a few ideas. My other partner added some twists, I added some ideas for humour, and we all liked the result, because it turned out like a bit of a fantasy. What I learned about myself as a writer was that:
>
> • I am more creative than I realized
>
> • sometimes other points of view can improve writing
>
> • I can motivate a peer who thinks writing is an unpleasant chore

> **How do you determine whether the peer feedback you receive is valid?**
>
> I pay the closest attention to revision ideas. I figure that if my ideas are boring or confusing to any reader, especially a peer, I need to fix that. Sometimes it's just the organization that is confusing, so I make my work more chronological or use better transitions. When a peer suggests different spelling or punctuation, I look at it, but not as closely unless the peer is a classmate I know to be a strong speller or one who makes very few errors in his or her own writing. Even when I don't agree with the peer feedback, it does force me to take another look at my writing before publishing the final draft.

How you learn matters. Keeping track of what has affected your language skills is important. How easy was it to answer the three questions above? Could you think of any other questions that might be good to ask about your learning? Metacognition means thinking about your learning while you are learning. The more you ask yourself questions like the ones in the given example, the more aware you will become of your learning.

INTERCONNECTED SKILLS

Learning to be a good writer does not happen in isolation. What you hear, speak, and see influences what you write. Many of the skills you practice every day help you develop as a writer. In fact, everything you do and experience can become part of your writing experience, if you take time to reflect on it. To start thinking about how language skills are connected, consider the following questions.

- What do you know about different media texts that might help when you are writing? Media texts are found in newspapers and magazines as well as in advertising, posters, and leaflets.

- In what way do you think that the reading you do helps you as a writer? Can you give an example?

- What do you listen to that might help you as a writer?

- Have you ever seen a picture or a movie that made you think of a story? Or, have you ever written a story based on something you saw?

To understand more about how different skills interact, read the following fictional experience of Timothy, a Grade 12 student. His experiences describe how interconnected skills played a part in his learning to write more effectively. As you read, think about how your own experiences in English class can be improved by using a variety of skills.

Listening

Timothy is sitting with his friends in a Grade 12 assembly. He does not know what to expect as his English teacher, Mr. Kennedy, introduces the guest speaker:

"Ladies and gentlemen, our guest today was once a teacher like me, and like me, he too wracked his brains on a daily basis, trying to think of ways to encourage his students to write and to get them excited about writing. He came up with the idea of writing a novel for them. The novel, Stand Your Ground, was set in the school where he worked. The setting was his community. Many of the characters had the same names as his students. That novel came out in 1993. It was a big hit, especially with the students who found their names in the book.

Since 1993, our guest has given up his teaching career to become a full-time writer of over 45 novels, with more on the way. He has won more than 30 awards, including the Ontario Library Association Silver Birch Award three times. The selection panel was made up of over 750,000 young people from across the country who voted for Mr. Eric Walters. It is my honour to present him to you today. Eric Walters is a man who loves a great story and who knows how to turn young people into fans of his books."

As the writer approaches the podium, Timothy starts to pay attention, especially when Mr. Walters launches into the dramatic reading of a chapter from his novel Shattered. The chapter is about a 15-year-old boy, Ian, starting to work as a volunteer in a soup kitchen as part of a social studies project. After a near mugging, in which Ian is saved by a homeless man, Ian later spots the man at the soup kitchen. It turns out he is a returned member of the Canadian Armed Forces whose last tour had involved peacekeeping duties in Rwanda.

Mr. Walters also reads a foreword from the book Shake Hands With the Devil by Canadian Forces General Romeo Dallaire, Force Commander for the United Nations Mission to Rwanda at the time of the 1994 Rwandan genocide.

The rest of the presentation is a blur. Mr. Walters calls on a couple of students who have prepared some interview questions. He is both entertaining and serious. He talks about writing and about researching historical events in Canada to get ideas for writing. All Timothy can think about is getting his hands on Shattered. Timothy is not from Rwanda, but his parents did come to Canada from Zaire before it was renamed Congo. He was too young to remember, but he wants to find out about why his parents ended up in a refugee camp for a year before they emigrated.

Reading and Viewing

Timothy signs out the novel *Shattered* from the school library. The librarian suggests that he might also like to watch the movie *Hotel Rwanda*, which is about a courageous hotel manager who saved people from being caught in a tribal massacre during the Rwandan crisis. Timothy rents the movie after he finishes the book.

Writing

Mr. Kennedy has encouraged his students to try writing some form of historical fiction, using suggestions from Eric Walters. Timothy decides to create five journal entries written by a fictional character, Akunda, who lives with his parents in a refugee camp in Congo, from where they are hoping to emigrate to Canada.

Speaking

Timothy tapes his journal entries to play for his writing group. He gets his older brother to be the voice of Akunda, and he reads the part of the narrator. As a writer, Timothy is supposed to use the group's suggestions to help him revise his writing.

Reflection

Mr. Kennedy poses the following two questions to his student writers, which they are to answer and then attach to the final draft of their writing before handing it in. Read Timothy's answers to both questions.

How did listening to the taped reading of your writing help you to revise it?

One of my peer listeners suggested that I write two more entries to show a contrast with the time when Akunda started his new life in Canada. He thought that the journal ended too abruptly. I thought that was a good idea, so I added those to my assignment. They also thought I could make the African entries a bit more realistic if I used actual places, so I looked up a map of the Congo on the Internet and changed a couple of location names.

What did you discover from reading young adult fiction that you could apply to your own story?

After Mr. Walters spoke to us a month ago, I read his novel Shattered. I tried to make my character, Akunda, seem as real as Ian seemed to me when I read the book. I also did some research on the Congo and talked to my parents about their experiences in order to make the journal entries as authentic as I could. I went on Eric Walters' website for more ideas, but what I learned from that one novel was to:

- *use real places and events*
- *make the main character have the same worries and concerns as young people all over the world— with dreams of a better life, a successful future, and solid friendships*

The great thing about all your language skills being connected is that you can tailor your learning to how you learn best. If you learn better by talking to others or by speaking out loud about your ideas, do that. Maybe you need to write out what you think before you prepare a formal essay. Some people learn best by reading, some by listening to others speak, and others by watching visual demonstrations.

It is important to remember that related skills in listening, speaking, reading, viewing, and representing contribute to improving your proficiency as a writer. The more you are able to recognize these connections, the better your writing will become.

3.2.1a reflect on and describe strategies that may be used to select, record and organize information; select and monitor appropriate strategies

ORGANIZING IDEAS

Most forms of writing can be categorized according to how they are organized and developed. When you write about what you think, know, or feel about a subject, try to communicate in a unique and personal way. Even in unique and personalized writing, using organizational patterns will help you to give your message the most impact. The following organizational structures help ensure your ideas are presented in an interesting and original manner.

INDUCTIVE AND DEDUCTIVE REASONING

Inductive reasoning consists of gathering facts and then using those facts to formulate a more general statement. It is important to have enough examples to justify your conclusion, but you also need to be prepared to review or alter your conclusions as new evidence comes to light.

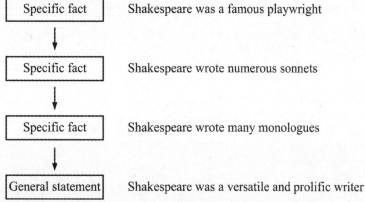

Deductive reasoning involves a different process. It begins with a generalization that you assume is true, and then specific facts are used to confirm that assumption.

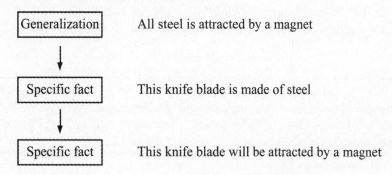

ANALOGY

Analogy is reasoning by using a comparison; i.e., by reasoning that if two things are similar in one respect, they will be similar in other respects. For example, imagine that you were outside one day and got sunburned. If you did not know why you got sunburned, you might think of reasons for it. Perhaps you would guess that it was because you were outside. If you thought this was the reason you got burned, through analogy you would guess that any time you were outside at all, even if it were nighttime, you would get sunburned. This is why analogy often does not make sense.

PROCESS ANALYSIS

Process analysis is used specifically in writing that informs or explains. In process analysis, the writer explains how something works, how it is defined, or how it has been made. In a process analysis, chronological order is the most common structure used because it outlines the steps in which something occurs.

Example

How to program a VCR

1. Turn on VCR

2. Set channel on VCR to match channel on TV from which show to be recorded will be on

3. Set timer on VCR to indicate time that show starts and finishes

4. Press record

CLIMACTIC ORDER

Climatic order is achieved by developing a sequence of events or conflicts that build toward a climax. A climatic order chart would look something like this:

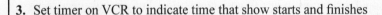

CHRONOLOGICAL ORDER

Chronological order is often used to organize ideas in narrative and descriptive writing. It is a good idea to use transitions, such as first, second, then, finally, next, and later to connect your ideas.

Example

One wintry day in 1926, as Lindbergh was flying his plane delivering mail, he was caught in a snowstorm. When his plane became unmanageable, he parachuted out. As he descended, he saw a barbed-wire fence below him, which he failed to miss—landing directly on top of it. Once he had untangled himself, he walked to the nearest farm to report the accident.

CAUSE AND EFFECT

Cause and effect is frequently used in explanatory writing in order to present information clearly. Writers often present information by explaining why something happened, what specific conditions exist, or what resulted from a certain action or condition. Cause and effect can be used in narrative writing to explain characters' actions, or it may be used in essays or reports to discuss how something progresses or the results of certain actions.

Cause-and-effect writing can be organized three ways:

• Effect to Cause

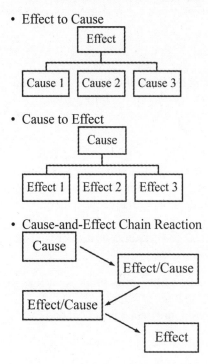

• Cause to Effect

• Cause-and-Effect Chain Reaction

Regardless of the type of writing that you are doing (narrative, essay, critical reviews, or reports), make sure that you organize your writing well so that your ideas and information are logically presented. Logical organization gives your writing clarity. Experiment with different organizational methods to find the one that best suits the type of writing you are doing. An organizational structure gives you a skeleton upon which you can flesh out your ideas.

3.2.2c assess the accuracy, completeness, currency and relevance of information selected from sources; and assess the appropriateness of the information for purpose.

RESEARCH

The Internet allows anyone to make information public, so you must be very careful when performing research using Internet resources. Not everything you read will be true, and if it is, it might not be totally accurate. Although you should be critical of any text you read, it is especially important to use critical reading with Internet resources. Critical reading is especially necessary to check the quality and reliability of the information on the Internet.

HOW TO READ A WEBSITE

Reading any text requires you to think critically and ask questions about the truth of the text. You should ask yourself questions that will help you to determine the validity and reliability of the information presented on a website.

Things to Consider When Conducting Internet Research

1. Take a look at the writer or editor of the website. Is it a professional academic journal or an amateur blog? How professional the writing sounds and polished the site looks are factors that can help you determine how reliable that site is. Does the site post information about the writer of the materials that are found there? Does the writer have training or recognized expertise in the field that the web site represents? Can you find any other sites that mention that writer? Well-known writers or well-regarded experts will usually be referred to on many sites.

2. What is the content like? Is the information consistent with information from other sources, such as books or other websites? Usually, academic publishers are reliable sources of information about a subject. Is the information easy to understand? Does the site present more than one side of an issue?

3. Who is the intended audience? Does the writer seem to have a specific audience in mind? Does the site have advertisements? At whom do you think such ads are targeted? How has the site been funded—through corporate sponsorships or through non-profit organizations?

4. How is the site structured? Is it easy to navigate? Can you exit at any time? Can you go back to a previous page without hitting the "Back" button on the browser? Are there links to other sites that give you additional information?

After you have analyzed the different features of a site, it is time to evaluate the usefulness of the information on the site. Does it fit the topic of your research? Some sites may look great and have reliable information, but it may not necessarily relate to your assignment. Make sure not to fill up a research paper with lots of citations from sites that do not have much to do with what you are writing about. More is not always better. You may only find a few websites that help you, but if they are comprehensive and large sites, you may only need a few Internet sources for your writing. Finally, remember that the Internet should not be the only resource you use. Books, newspapers, interviews, or academic journals are all excellent resources as well.

Create and Enhance

CREATE AND ENHANCE

4.1.1a   reflect on the purposes for text creation [for example, to inform, explain, persuade, entertain or inspire] and on own motives for selecting strategies to engage audience [for example, to communicate information, promote action or build relationships]; and consider potential consequences of choices regarding text creation [for example, follow-up action may be required to clarify information, a position may need to be defended and opposing viewpoints addressed, and tone and style must be appropriate for intended audience]

REFLECTING ON WRITING

A READING METACOGNITION CHECKLIST

The following questions are examples of questions that you can ask to examine your learning.

- What is the best way to approach this learning task?

- At this point, how well do I understand information, concepts, and characters?

- How can I maintain my motivation to complete what I have started?

- Am I using the best tools for this learning task?

The following checklist shows different strategies that you can use to get the most out of your reading. More importantly, the checklist can help you to think about how you approach various reading tasks. You could use this checklist several times during the school year to help you understand or change your approach.

Using the Checklist

- Put check marks in the "Most Effective for Me" column next to the five strategies that work best for you.

- Write a number beside each check mark to show how effective the strategy is for you (1 is most effective, 5 is least effective).

- Think of logical reasons for the order you have chosen.

- Discuss and compare your top five most effective strategies with a peer.

- Collaborate to identify the top five strategies from you and your peer, and describe the best uses for each strategy.

- List five ways that you and your peers can become better readers.

Thinking About My Reading Strategies	Most Effective for Me	Use Most Often	Use Sometimes	Should Try
Before Reading I *preview* (look over exams, texts, stories, articles, and assignments) to determine: • What is involved in this text? • What is my purpose for reading? • How should I approach this? • How should I read (speed, etc.)?				
I think about my *prior knowledge*—what I already know that might be relevant to the topic or task in front of me.				
I *visualize* or try to picture the characters, setting, what I hope to find out, etc.				
While Reading I **check back** to verify a definition, information about a character, etc.				
I use vocabulary strategies, such as context clues, root words, prefixes, and suffixes, to understand unfamiliar words and phrases.				
I make point-form notes or use *graphic organizers* when I need to remember plots, key ideas, etc.				
I pause while reading and *predict* what I think will happen next in the story.				
I *tag text* with sticky notes or mark parts I find confusing, so I can ask about them later.				
I use a *highlighter*—when I am allowed—to mark the text (notes, handouts, etc.) for key phrases and important ideas.				
I write *notes*, *questions*, and *comments* in margins if I am allowed. Sometimes, I use these later on to clarify information.				

Thinking About My Reading Strategies	Most Effective for Me	Use Most Often	Use Sometimes	Should Try
I ask questions to *monitor my understanding* of what I read: • Does this make sense to me? • What exactly is the writer saying? • What is the narrator's point of view? • Do I agree? Why or why not?				
When the text does not state something directly, I make *inferences* and draw *conclusions* from my reading.				
I deliberately use *skimming* and *scanning* skills when appropriate, such as to locate a specific answer or idea in the text.				
I *adjust my reading rate* as needed, slowing down for detailed information, etc.				
I *pay attention* to diagrams, pictures, charts, and graphs—anything that may help me make more sense of the text.				
After Reading I *summarize*, using notes or a graphic organizer.				
I write my thoughts, questions, and reactions in a *personal response journal*.				
I share with a peer in the following ways: • in written form, such as a double-response journal, in which we write back and forth • by discussing informally within a share-pair or small group • by explaining a newly learned concept I try to *support my own opinions* and to *show respect* for the opinions of others.				
I write critical responses to text when invited to do so. I try to include comments on the form, purpose, writer's viewpoint, historical context, mood, imagery, etc. When possible, I make comparisons with other texts or draw from my personal experiences to deepen my response.				

SAMPLE APPLICATIONS OF METACOGNITION

The following section shows you some strategies that involve metacognition. Journals, visual charts, and literature circles and book clubs are all great methods of making yourself more aware of how you read. Some of these may be more useful to you than others. Figuring out which methods work best for you will give you insight into your learning style.

Personal Response Journal

A personal response journal can be a great record of what you read. A journal can also be a good starting point to get ideas for assignments. A journal entry should include the date, title, and name of the work that you describe. The entry should express your connections with the text. How does the work connect to your experiences? How does it relate to your opinions?

Consider the following example of a poem and one student's personal response journal entry regarding that poem. The personal response describes that student's individual experience with the poem. To practice metacognition skills, try writing your own response to this poem.

Dragon Night

Little flame mouths,
Cool your tongues.
Dreamtime starts,
My furnace-lungs.

Rest your wings now,
Little flappers,
Cave mouth calls
To dragon nappers.

Night is coming,
Bank your fire.
Time for dragons
To retire.

Hiss.
Hush.
Sleep.

—*by* Jane Yolen

Personal Response Journal Entry: "Dragon Night" by Jane Yolen

February 27, 2008

Although this poem seems to be written as a lullaby for baby dragons, it means something different and very personal to me. Of all the poems we studied in our September poetry unit, this is my absolute favourite. It brought back lots of memories of the summer, sitting with my family on the deck of our cottage at Muskoka Lake, relaxing and looking at the lake. As I read the poem, I thought of tiny flashes of light down by the lakeshore—fireflies flicking their mini-lanterns on and off. The poem has lots of summer and evening imagery. I felt quiet and relaxed by the end of the poem.

The great thing about journal entries is that you do not have to worry that you are being too casual with your language. Even though the entry may be casual and talk about your own life experience, the information about your opinions can be used to write something more formal later on. Keeping a journal about what you read is a great tool for keeping track of your learning.

4.1.3d   develop supporting ideas, by using developmental aids appropriate to form and purpose [for example, use chars to collect and assemble details in creating character comparisons when developing a comparison and contrast essay, or use a think aloud reading strategy to make notes from informational text when writing a summary]

DEVELOPING WRITING TASKS

By Grade 12, you should be confident using various forms of writing. The form of writing you choose will change according to your purpose for writing and your intended audience. These forms include analytic and argumentative essays, critical reviews, expressive works such as narrative or dramatic scenes, and independent research essays and reports. Because the general emphasis by the end of high school is on critical thinking essays (analytic and argumentative) and expressive works (narratives, dramatic scenes), examples of those forms are demonstrated for you in this ***KEY***.

ANALYTIC ESSAY: CHARACTER

Before reviewing a sample essay analyzing the character of Miss Brill from Katherine Mansfield's short story "Miss Brill," it is helpful to consider some key concepts related to characterization. These concepts are common to any narrative work containing one or more characters—short stories, plays, novellas, novels, narrative poems, films, and other narrative texts.

Recognizable Characters

- Picking *stock characters* that have been read or seen over and over again. The audience knows what to expect and can be immediately drawn into the story. It is then possible to move the character toward reality, or at least individuality.

- Assigning archetypal qualities to characters. One technique used in literature is to select and emphasize certain enduring character traits. These are archetypal qualities. Certain archetypes are instantly recognizable, such as the hero, the sidekick, and the foil (a character whose contrasts with the hero show off the hero's qualities). The reason stock characters work is that they share in the archetypes that most people recognize and accept, and sometimes the distinction can be a matter of taste.

How Character is Revealed

In this context, *character* refers to qualities such as courage, honesty, generosity, and intelligence—and their opposites. *Character* also refers to fundamental ideas and beliefs held by the character, which can be revealed through:

- actions

- dialogue

- thoughts revealed through interior speech or through other thought-revealing techniques such as stream of consciousness narration

- the writer's narration

One limitation of film is the difficulty of revealing thoughts in any way other than action or dialogue. Voice-over narration is one way that filmmakers try to get around this limitation.

Personality

Personality refers to things such as mannerisms, social skills, sense of humour, and all traits that contribute to the words and actions of a person.

Motivation

Motivation is essential to character development and plot.

• Well-developed characters have believable motives—even multiple and conflicting motives.

• Motivation takes time to develop. That is one reason that characters in movies often have simple motivation.

Appearance

Except in a movie, appearance is usually an unimportant part of character, unless the story is actually about appearance.

• Some writers do not describe their characters' appearance at all. A reader is left to imagine what the character looks like.

• When appearance is described, first-person narration and third-person limited narration can present a problem as a result of a narrator's subjectivity.

UNDERSTANDING CHARACTER

Understanding fictional characters requires the same analytical, inferential, and interpretive skills that are used to judge people in real life. Conclusions are made through the reader's observations and through what is revealed by the narrator. It is possible to make supported assumptions and to draw logical conclusions about fictional characters, as will be demonstrated in the essay on Miss Brill.

People share human thoughts, emotions, and motives. Through an active and sympathetic imagination, it is possible to understand other people who are genuinely different from one's own self. Understanding is possible through one's own experiences and seeing something of oneself in a character's experiences. By coming to know others or through observing others in real life, characters in fictional texts can be easier to understand. The better you know yourself and others, the better able you are to know characters in fictional texts.

Skillful fiction and non-fiction storytellers can make a character's feelings and motives so clear that the world and the individual have new meaning. Empathy—the sense of personal identification with the experiences of a character—develops when a reader can identify with or relate to a character's experiences.

CHARACTERIZATION

Everything that a writer does to portray characters is called characterization. Characters can be described directly or indirectly. The following chart contains examples of both types of characterization.

Direct characterization is received:	**Indirect characterization** is inferred:
• from what one character says or thinks about another character	• from what a character says—sometimes from what a character says about another character
• from the writer's statements about a character; for example, "Jane was stubborn and persevering"	• from what a character thinks about self, others, and the world
• from "indirect characterization" that is obvious or contrived	• from what a character does, especially in small things or when under pressure
	• from other characters' reactions to a character

One of the basic methods of characterization is to invent different kinds of characters that serve different purposes. Characters can be classified by type and function.

Types of Characters

flat	have only one quality or character trait; are one-sided; always act the same way
round	have different, even contradictory traits; are more like real people
stock	are like flat characters, except that stock characters have been used over and over and are instantly recognizable
archetypal	are like stock characters, except that archetypes are meant to be typical (even universal) examples of certain character traits
dynamic	change or grow in some way either for good or bad; are altered by events and by their own actions and choices
static	do not change; flat, round, stock, and archetypal characters can all be static
foil	used as a contrast to the main character or protagonist; the difference between the foil and the main character emphasizes the main character's qualities; the foil is used for indirect characterization

Good storytellers use all of these types of characters. The most important character in a story is usually round and dynamic. However, a minor character such as a taxi driver whose only function is to delay the protagonist by taking a wrong turn is usually flat and static. In fact, some characters must be flat because there is no time or space to portray them as real people.

The amount of characterization that a character receives is generally a function of the character's role in the story.

Characters Classified by Function

protagonist	the main character; often the hero, but not always because sometimes the main character is a villain; often a dynamic character
antagonist	the character the protagonist struggles against; often the villain, but not always
major	help move the plot forward in some way; they are often round and dynamic; the protagonist and antagonist are major characters
minor	have minor roles; they affect an event in the plot, but they do not move the whole plot forward; are often flat or stock because they do not appear long enough to be fully developed

4.1.3e develop appropriate, relevant and sufficient content to support a controlling ideas or unifying effect [for example, relate supporting details, examples and illustrations to a controlling idea when creating a critical/analytical response to literature]

THE ANALYTIC ESSAY

"Miss Brill" is an example of a short story in which character and theme are the dominant elements. This makes the story a natural choice for a character analysis. Because the theme is so closely related to Miss Brill's character and limited outlook on life, an analysis of theme and character is necessary.

In the context of a literary essay, supporting detail can refer to an actual detail, like a single incident, scene description, sensory image, or metaphor. At the same time, supporting detail can mean a discussion or explanation of plot, setting, the use of imagery, or the use of figurative language.

USING A MODEL

If you have difficulty in devising your own structure for essay writing, you may want to follow a straightforward structure, such as the one modelled below, that includes:

• an introductory paragraph that introduces your thesis and the text(s) that will be examined to support it

• three body paragraphs, each establishing and developing support for the thesis

• a concluding paragraph that unifies the writing

CREATING A THESIS STATEMENT

Your thesis statement often comes at the end of your introductory paragraph to provide guidance through the rest of your response. Your thesis statement contains the controlling idea for your essay. This idea may be either implicit in your thesis statement or may be stated explicitly. Analysis of character, goal, conflict/obstacle, and realization/resolution should lead naturally to your thesis statement/ controlling idea.

Example

> "Miss Brill," a short story by Katherine Mansfield
>
> Character: Miss Brill, a woman who lives in a fantasy world. She imagines that she lives a glamorous life and that she plays an important part of the lives of others.
>
> Character's Goal: Contentment, escape from isolation of her real life
>
> Conflict/Obstacle: She is mocked by a young couple.
>
> Realization/Resolution: She eventually sees herself as others see her, realizes the loneliness and emptiness of her life, and is ultimately devastated.
>
> Themes: Reality versus illusion, desire for companionship versus the struggle to belong
>
> Thesis Statement (controlling idea is implicit): Miss Brill [character/goal] lives in an imaginary world where she experiences a sense of contentment as she imagines herself an important part of other people's lives. She is eventually forced to face the gloomy reality of the life she lives [conflict], and her feelings of contentment and self-worth are destroyed [realization/resolution].

Stated explicitly, the controlling idea is that allowing imagination to blur one's reality can lead to both positive and negative consequences.

INTRODUCTORY PARAGRAPH

If you have difficulty writing introductions, use some of the following hints to help make the process easier.

- Write a sentence that introduces the topic and text(s) you will be using.

- Write several sentences that explain the topic and present your thesis statement, including the order of the evidence you will be supporting.

- Explore alternative beginnings to find the one that works best for the idea that you are developing. The first sentence is an important sentence because it introduces the mood and tone of your writing.

Example

Introduces the topic of imagination and the text	In the short story "Miss Brill," Katherine Mansfield depicts an elderly woman who lives in a fantasy world created by her imagination. She creates this world to escape from the isolation and loneliness of her real life and, in so doing, her life becomes more interesting and fulfilling. In her fantasy world, she experiences a sense of contentment as she images herself as an important part of other people's lives and as possessing a life better than those around her. Unfortunately, her fragile world is shattered, forcing her to face the gloomy reality of the life she truly lives. Her feelings of contentment and self-worth are destroyed once she realizes the emptiness and loneliness of her real world.
Thesis statement—opinion with the three supports identified as: 1. She experiences a sense of contentment 2. She imagines herself an important part of others' lives	

PARAGRAPHS IN THE BODY

Paragraphs in the body of the essay are used to support your thesis. The first support for the main idea or the thesis is given in Body Paragraph A, the second support for the thesis in Body Paragraph B, and the third support for the thesis in Body Paragraph C. Body paragraphs B and C follow the same pattern as Body Paragraph A. Each paragraph should contain the following elements.

- An effective introductory and topic sentence that focuses on the support for the thesis that you will develop in the paragraph.

- The development of the supporting idea through explanatory sentences. To bring power to your position, you must include concrete evidence from the text(s). Direct quotations are only useful if they precisely support your idea. Direct references to events, character traits, and literary symbols are all considered useful evidence.

- Your interpretation of the evidence, explained in detail. Readers need to see evidence of your thinking. You need to demonstrate your intellect, your thinking, and your ability to interpret literature.

- Specific and overt connections of the information in this paragraph to your thesis.

- A transition sentence must be considered. Transitions are necessary between paragraphs. They can be given at the end of paragraphs or in the introduction to a new paragraph.

Example

Miss Brill is content and happy to live within her fantasy world; a world wonderful within her own mind. This world affords her delightful routines, which, on most occasions, bring her to the Jardins Publiques where she enjoys the surroundings of nature, music, and contented people. On one particular Sunday afternoon, she dresses up for her outing, completing her ensemble with her fox fur piece; a piece she has had for a long time and of which she is very proud. From her position on a park bench, she watches and internally comments on what she sees. Miss Brill is a keen observer of the people around her, and she weaves what she sees and hears into imaginative, glamorous events. She notices an elderly gentleman in a velvet coat and a woman with knitting in her lap. She is disappointed that they are not speaking as she had become quite expert "at listening to people's conversations, as though she wasn't listening." She turns her attention to other people and their activities around her. As she sits, she does not ponder her own solitary life as she is happy to enjoy the splendour of the day.	Topic sentence clearly identifies the first support: she experiences a sense of contentment Specific details from the story to demonstrate her contentment Concluding sentence

Ironically, as Miss Brill observes the other people—especially those occupying benches and chair—she fails to see the parallel between herself and them. She notes that Sunday after Sunday the same people are drawn to the park and something is "funny" about all of them. They were odd, silent, nearly all old, and from the way they stared, they looked as though they'd come from dark little rooms or even cupboards. She perceives these people as being different; as being "less" than what she is. As well, she does not see herself as being rejected like the violets the young woman throws away or like the woman in the ermine toque who is being carelessly cast aside by the man in the suit. Miss Brill, wearing her own outdated piece, cannot see her image mirrored in the woman who does not perceive herself to be as shabby as the ermine toque she wears. Rather, Miss Brill imagines herself as being superior to these people; an intricate part of the stage performance that is re-enacted in the park each week. She fantasizes that her absence would be noticed if she were not present, so integral is her role. She takes delight in this fantasy and envisions telling the old gentleman to whom she reads that she is not a mere English teacher, but an actress. She is enthralled by this fantasy and feels as though she is one with all the members of the company. Her imaginary world is, indeed, fulfilling.

Transition and topic sentence that clearly identify the second support: imagining herself as superior to others and as an important part of their lives

Support, including symbols of her rejection that she ironically does not perceive

Concluding sentence

Despite her excitement with her imaginary world, Miss Brill overhears a conversation that completely shatters her illusions and alters her life. A boy and girl, in love, sit near her, and Miss Brill prepares to listen. The boy wishes to kiss the girl but she insists that she cannot let him because of that stupid old thing at the end there. The girl then begins to giggle at the poor soul wearing the fur that looks like a fried whiting (fish). Miss Brill is shattered when she realizes that the young couple is mocking her. She leaves the park, not bothering to stop for her ritualistic slice of honey cake, and hurries home. Once inside, she realizes how dark her room is, like a cupboard. Her world is no longer bright and splendid, but depressing and stark in reality. This reality is even bleaker when compared with the imaginary world of her fantasies. Her fur piece symbolizes the shabbiness of her life, and as she replaces it in the box, she imagines she hears something crying. Although she tries to deny that she is the one who is crying, she has come to an unhappy epiphany: the loneliness of her life is devastating.

Transition and topic sentence clearly identify the third support: that her fragile world is shattered

Support, including —symbolism of her dark room and fur piece

Concluding sentence

CONCLUDING PARAGRAPH

In your concluding paragraph, you should always

• Generalize your thesis beyond the text—make your idea explicit

• Summarize your major or points

• End with a strong sense of closure

In "Miss Brill," Mansfield emphasizes both the positive and negative effects of the imagination and what results when imagination is allowed to blur one's view of reality. Initially, Miss Brill is content living within the parameters of her fantasy world. Feelings of fulfillment are deepened as she perceives herself as being integral to the performance and the people around her; she views her own life as being more than what it truly is. When her illusion is shattered; however, the harshness of the reality she is compelled to face is devastating.	Topic sentence explicitly states the controlling idea as a generalization beyond the text Summary of support and significance of support Thoughtful observation connected to resolution/effect on character

Be sure to stay focused on your controlling idea or thesis right through to the concluding sentence of your essay.

4.1.3f   develop content consistent with form and appropriate to context [for example, link questions and answers when reporting the results of an interview]

THE ARGUMENTATIVE ESSAY

The argumentative essay is an example of persuasive writing. Supporting a position is different from supporting a character analysis. In an argumentative essay, you adopt a particular point of view on an issue and attempt to persuade an audience to agree with your position. Your arguments should be logical in order to be persuasive. Arguments can be strengthened through supporting details in the form of natural logic, examples, statistics, expert opinions, facts, and anecdotes.

An important component of a formal debate is the ability to give a speech that can convince an audience of the debater's position. Therefore, a speech format naturally lends itself to argumentative writing. You still need to follow essay guidelines for organization, as you will see from the example provided below. Your controlling idea, or thesis, is a clear statement of your position on the issue.

The following speech was written in response to two articles on poverty. The writer has taken the role of the chairperson of the local teen council and prepared a speech to present at a town hall meeting of a group of local politicians in order to convince them to increase funding for social services.

Good Evening Ladies and Gentlemen.

If each of us were to put ourselves into the situation of having no place to live, or hardly being able to make it from month to month, what would we want? We would want a little help. If anyone were to place himself or herself in the shoes of those with special needs or those who are homeless, I think that society would no longer have a problem with the lack of housing. Those who could imagine what it would be like to have that sort of life would realize that it is a way of living they would not wish on even their worst enemy, and they would want to do anything to have the problem fixed. That means putting more money into social services. Toronto needs 5,000 low income homes. We are one of the richest provinces in all of Canada, and the government could certainly afford to build those 5,000 homes within the next ten years.

Twenty-two million dollars is a lot of money. This sum of money can make a very big difference in a lot lives. That is the amount of money that has been cut from Children's Services. If the problems are not going away, why should money be cut from Children's Services? If things are getting worse, should we not be putting more money into such programs? If we take away that money, the cuts within the Children's Services will be mainly in the early intervention and prevention program, both of which I believe are very important. When kids are on a path that will harm them and others, it is best if they are helped onto another path. Some kids see stealing and selling drugs as their best way to make money. If we can prevent kids from doing those things, we can decrease the amount of drugs circulating in Toronto and we could decrease the number of crimes.

If we do not help the people who need it most now, when will we? Will it be too late at that point? I would much rather have my tax dollars spent on these two issues than on anything else. The government wasted 12 million dollars last year on the area surrounding the CN Tower. It was not a necessary change; that money would have been better spent on building homes or on Children's Services. I propose that the government make budget cuts to those things that are not so important. Stop spending money repairing things that are not broken, and start spending some money on the things that do need to be fixed. Thank you.

What aspects of argumentative writing can you identify in this example? What is different about writing intended for a speech and writing intended for a reading audience?

4.2.3c assess syntax for appropriateness and effectiveness, and revise sentence structures as needed to create intended effects

SENTENCE CRAFT AND FLUENCY

A sentence is a group of words that expresses a complete thought, begins with a capital letter, and ends with a period or other end punctuation. Every sentence contains at least one noun (or pronoun) and one verb; a sentence must have a subject and a predicate. Parts of speech, which include nouns, pronouns, and verbs, are the building blocks of sentences.

Example

The *subject* is a noun and everything attached to that noun.	The *predicate* is a verb and everything attached to that verb.
Cattle graze	
A tall *girl ran* to the gate.	
Penelope, the faithful wife of Odysseus, slowly *wove* an intricate tapestry.	

Sometimes, a complete sentence seems to be missing a necessary part. "Stop!" is an example of a sentence that seems incomplete because it does not seem to have a subject. However, the subject, you, is implied and understood. Similarly, some sentences contain parts of speech that are understood and are omitted:

Here is a copy of the assignment I gave you. (that I gave to you)

Write me when you find work. (write to me)

When you are editing your work, look for any incomplete sentences or fragments, and be sure to rewrite them so that they are complete.

SENTENCE VARIETY

Sentence variety is a key element of efficient writing. It is a good idea to keep your ideas flowing smoothly using a mixture of long, short, or complex sentences.

KINDS OF SENTENCES

There are different kinds of sentences:

- declarative sentences, which make statements

- interrogative sentences, which ask questions

- exclamatory sentences, which express strong emotion

- imperative sentences, which give instructions or commands

Remember that exclamation marks should rarely be used except in dialogue. Exclamation marks are not advisable in formal writing. If you want to stress a point, try using words that have intensity. It takes a lot more creativity and thought to emphasize using the best words possible rather than it does to a sentence with an exclamation point when you want to show that you feel strongly about something.

Simple Sentences

Independent clauses that contain one subject and one verb make a simple sentence:

• The boy stood on the garden wall.

Sentence order can be altered for variety or for emphasis. The part to be emphasized usually comes first:

• On the garden wall stood the boy.

Compound Sentences

Two independent clauses that are joined by a coordinating conjunction make a compound sentence. The two sentences "The boy stood on the garden wall" and "No one noticed him" are correct sentences on their own, but they can also be joined in a variety of ways:

• The boy stood on the garden wall, but no one noticed him.

• No one noticed the boy as he stood on the garden wall.

Complex

Two clauses joined by a subordinating conjunction make a complex sentence. One clause must be independent and one clause must be dependent (subordinate):

• Although the boy stood on the garden wall, no one noticed him.

• No one noticed the boy, although he stood on the garden wall.

• While the firefighters were distracted by brush fires, three houses burned to the ground.

• Three houses burned to the ground while the firefighters were distracted by brush fires.

Changing the order of the words in a sentence changes the emphasis. Consider the sentence "An actress who has won three Oscars will be present tonight" compared with the sentence "Present tonight will be an actress who has won three Oscars."

The order of the first sentence puts more stress on the accomplishments of the actress, whereas the second sentence puts more stress on the fact that the actress will be present.

Compound-Complex Sentences

A compound-complex sentence contains at least two independent clauses and one dependent clause:

• While I slept, the sun rose and the birds began to sing.

• Although she didn't win a medal, Janine competed at the Olympics and she has never forgotten the wonderful experience.

When writing or editing your work, pay attention to how you structure your sentences. Consider varying sentence structure, length, and order for variety and for emphasis. A succession of short sentences can be used for strong effect after a series of longer sentences. Use transitional devices (words like although, next, or consequently) to order and link ideas.

Transitions

Transitional words and phrases, which are used at the beginning of sentences or in the middle to join compound or compound-complex sentences, enhance sentence variety. The following chart contains examples of useful transition words and phrases.

Purpose	Transitional Words and Phrases
To show differences	On the other hand In contrast In opposition to Instead Unlike However In comparison
To show similarity	Just as important Not very different from In the same manner Similarly Hence Alike Also
To show preference	In preference to Preferred by more people However Nevertheless
To indicate time	At the same time A few days prior Following the completion of Next Soon In subsequent months
To indicate more	In addition to To add to On top of this Furthermore Moreover It is also true that Another example of

Conjunctive Adverbs

Conjunctive adverbs are used in compound sentences, while the subordinating conjunctions introduce subordinate clauses in complex or compound-complex sentences.

Adverbs can be used with a semicolon to join independent clauses into compound sentences.

Examples

> We have presented our case completely; on the other hand, there is no telling how the judge will respond.
>
> I like your pitch; however, it sounds too similar to other movies.

The following chart contains examples of conjunctive adverbs.

accordingly	incidentally	on the contrary
as a result	indeed	on the other hand
at the same time	instead	otherwise
consequently	likewise	similarly
finally	meanwhile	so far
for example	moreover	still
for instance	namely	thereafter
furthermore	nevertheless	therefore
hence	next	thus
however	nonetheless	undoubtedly
in fact	of course	

Subordinating conjunctions

Subordinating conjunctions introduce a subordinate clause.

Example

> After the party we will need to lock the hall.
>
> Unless you go, the party will be a bore.

The following chart contains common subordinating conjunctions

Example

after	even though	until
although	if	when
as	than	where
as if	that	whether
because	though	while
before	unless	

Sentence Beginnings

The basic subject–verb pattern that forms the primary English sentence pattern can be varied in a number of ways at the beginning of the sentence. The following section contains examples of how sentences can begin in English.

- Basic Pattern
  "The cowboy rode into the sunset."

- Inverted Order
  "Did the cowboy ride into the sunset?"

- Begin with a participle [verbal adjective]
  "Sunburned and dejected, the cowboy rode into the sunset."

- Begin with an adjective
  "Victorious, the cowboy rode into the sunset."

- Begin with an adverb
  "Swiftly, the cowboy rode into the sunset."

- Begin with a participial phrase
  "Having delivered his message, the cowboy rode into the sunset."

- Begin with a prepositional phrase
  "Into the sunset rode the cowboy."

- Begin with a subordinate clause
  "Once he had delivered his message, the cowboy rode into the sunset."

Deliberate Sentence Fragments

Normally, a correct sentence requires a minimum of one main clause containing both a subject and a predicate. Occasionally, writers deliberately use sentence fragments as a part of their writing style.

> The last cowboy rode into the sunset. Alone. A solitary reminder of the relentless passage of time.

Sentence and Word Order

The most important part of a sentence can be emphasized by using it to begin the sentence. NASA might note that "A meteorite hit a man in London," while the *London Star* might report "London Man Hit by Meteorite."

Word order is closely related to sentence order. Word placement and sentence order can be used to emphasize and also to suggest things. For example, compare the quotations "accused mass murderer Goneril Brocadie" with "Goneril Brocadie, who is accused of mass murder." Because the first quotation has "mass murderer" so close to the man's name, it implies guilt more strongly than does the second quotation. The adjectives closest to the noun imply the message "mass-murderer-Brocadie."

Parallelism

Parallelism is the deliberate repetition of sentence elements or of another structural pattern.

Example

> Alone, alone, all, all alone,
> Alone on a wide wide sea!
> And never a saint took pity on
> My soul in agony.
>
> —*by* Samuel Coleridge

4.2.3.a reflect on personal vocabulary and repertoire of stylistic choices and on their effectiveness; and expand vocabulary and repertoire of stylistic choices.

4.2.3.d explain how stylistic techniques and rhetorical devices are used to create intended effects

PORTFOLIOS

A portfolio is a collection of your writing pieces, usually representing a time period of at least one school year. Keeping your writing together allows you to:

- see your growth as a writer

- review topics and writing forms that you have tried

- evaluate your writing skills

- set writing goals for improving or refining your skills

A portfolio may also contain a writer's log or journal, personal spelling list, personal error record, or reflections about your writing. In this section, you will find some examples of ways you could use your portfolio as a resource to help you improve your writing skills.

In the following example, a student compares a first draft with a final draft, both of which she has found in her writing portfolio.

Example

Revised Final Draft of Rogue Waves Paragraph

Sometimes, groups of large ocean waves caused by a storm slam into a powerful ocean current passing in the opposite direction. When this happens, several storm waves pile up to form rogue waves. These waves can be more than 100 feet high and can bury cargo ships beneath the sea. Rogue waves are most common off the coasts of Japan, Florida, and Alaska. Currently, a project known as WaveAtlas allows scientists to monitor the oceans with satellites. Over the next few years, oceanographers hope to analyze these satellite images to help them better understand why freak waves, or "rogue waves" as they are known to scientists, occur so that scientific warnings can prevent unnecessary tragedies at sea.

Improvements Made

- Used better transitions

- Used more precise and consistent vocabulary

- Used consistent verb tenses throughout paragraph

- Created a more logical order in last section of paragraph

- Added a safety reason for scientific studies to round out paragraph

What I Learned from the Redrafting Process

- Read out loud to make sure writing flows smoothly

- When you use consistent verb tenses throughout a piece of writing, the ideas are clearer to the reader

- Your writing can sound better if you take the time to think about changes for improvement

- It is more satisfying to hand in redrafted work because you are sure that it is clear and says what you want it to

Here is an example from a fictional student's writing portfolio. The student was given the following point-form information from a local television news broadcast during a week of bitter cold in the city:

- only 826 of 1 200 available overnight shelter spots being used

- fears homeless people not using shelters

- hot line number to call 416-SHELTER

- citizens urged to cooperate to prevent homeless from freezing

- city spokesperson Ellen McCall

The assignment that accompanied this information required the student to write a poem and a news report based on it. The student was asked to include a reflection with his writing, comparing the processes he used in writing each form, and identifying any challenges he had to overcome.

The following section includes the student's two writing pieces, followed by the reflection that accompanied the pieces in the portfolio.

Deep Freeze Increases Risk to Homeless
Fears Grow for Unsheltered
By E. Meyer
Toronto Sun City Desk

Toronto – While most of us struggle with getting the car to start and risking a fender-bender on the way to work, the homeless of our city struggle with survival in the frigid temperatures that have gripped the region this past week.

Ellen McCall, spokesperson for city shelter coordination, reports that 1200 beds prepared for weather emergencies are being filled nightly.

While no one is being turned away from shelter facilities, it is feared that some people needing shelter may not be receiving it for a variety of reasons, including voluntary choices to spend the night in makeshift temporary shelters outside.

Bus drivers and police have been cautioned to be on the alert for anyone needing assistance or shelter.

Citizens are asked to report possible shelter-related emergencies to the shelter hotline at 416-SHELTER (743-5837). All calls will be treated as urgent.

So far, there have been no reported deaths due to freezing. However, each period of severe cold in the past has generated at least one fatality in the city. It is hoped that 2008 will remain fatality-free.

Ballad of a Cold Man

The winds they chill me to the bone,
A man who calls Toronto home,
My cardboard walls are way too thin
I wish I could go home again.

Chorus

Home again, yes home again,
I wish I could go home again,
To Mother's stew without the pain,
I wish I could go home again.

The streets they mock me with their ice,
The cops assume I act with vice,
My cardboard walls no shelter give,
Must move if I expect to live.

Chorus

How did I reach this point so low?
How did my dreams descend below?
The ice outside, that's not so bad,
It's ice within that makes me sad.

And so if winter's got you down,
And risky drivers make you frown,
Just pause while at that traffic light,
And say a prayer for someone's plight.

I too was once a man like you,
The 401 my trial too,
But life can change and paths can turn,
So don't complain, be still, and learn.

My Challenges for this Writing Assignment

The news story was not too difficult to write because of the notes we had from class on the inverted pyramid format for news reporting. Most of the key facts were provided in the points listed on the board, so I tried to be as factual as possible. To create the byline and dateline correctly, I checked a newspaper at home and tried to make it look similar with my computer, using special fonts and the column feature. I sometimes make spelling mistakes on words like "frigid," so I used spellcheck and also had my older sister proofread my draft for spelling. I remembered that newspaper reports should always be written in correct English, so I used sentence patterns that I could use with confidence and did not try anything fancy.

I was able to be more creative with the poem. I chose the ballad form because of the repetitive rhyme scheme and chorus, which I thought I could imitate, and because I think the misfortunes of the homeless make a sad story that seems to have no end, just like a sad ballad that goes on and on. I struggled with the line in the chorus, "To Mother's stew without the pain," because I didn't really like the effect of that wording, but I could not seem to come up with a better line that would express the emotional pain against something comforting like a mother's cooking. My favourite line was "It's ice within that makes me sad" because of the figurative language in it. Other than that, I think my biggest challenge was expressing the ideas I had according to the form I had chosen.

METACOGNITION AND MAKING REVISIONS

In this third example from a fictional student's writing portfolio, the student was asked to revise a descriptive paragraph by creating a variety of sentence beginnings using different openers, such as adjectives, prepositional phrases, and past participles to replace the overused pattern of "the" with a noun. The original draft and the revised paragraph are reproduced below. A student reflection in which the student comments on the effect of the revision on the writing follows the two paragraphs. Both drafts and the reflection would be kept in the student's portfolio. Take a look at the revisions and make a note of what has changed and see if you prefer the revisions. What might you change about the original paragraph?

First Draft of Descriptive Paragraph

The room in which I feel most relaxed is my bedroom. Mother and I painted it in my favourite colour scheme, pale green and navy blue. The wide south window looks out over our sweeping back lawn with its massive weeping willow, where I once played as a child. I would play house, pretend it was a robbers' hideout, or even read a book under the umbrella of its cool shade on a hot July afternoon. The window is framed in white, with a softly draped sheer navy valance across its top. I like to sit by that window in my white wicker armchair during a thunderstorm, watching lightning stab the sky in jagged tears as angry raindrops pound against the glass. I feel cozy and secure. This is my own special place.

Paragraph with Revisions

Painted in my favourite colour scheme of pale green and navy blue, the room in which I feel most relaxed is my bedroom. (*Began sentence with a past participle*) The wide south window looks out over our sweeping back lawn with its massive weeping willow where I once played as a child. Under the umbrella of its cool shade, I would play house, pretend it was a robbers' hideout, or even read a book on a hot July afternoon. (*Began sentence with two prepositional phrases*) The window is framed in white, with a softly draped, sheer navy valance across its top. In my white wicker armchair, I like to sit by that window during a thunderstorm, watching lightning stab the navy sky with jagged tears as angry raindrops pound against the glass. (*Began with a prepositional phrase*) Cozy and secure, I burrow deeper into my chair. (*Began with two adjectives*) This is my own special place.

Student Reflection on Revisions

I thought my original draft was quite good, probably because I enjoy describing things, and my room is a special place that I was able to share through precise description. When you taught us about sentence beginnings, I could see right away from your examples that this was a good way of adding variety to my writing. It is hard to believe that we fall into the habit of repeating the same sentence pattern, even while using lots of effective descriptive phrases. Here is how I thought the revisions improved my writing with this paragraph.

1. Placing the participle "Painted" at the beginning of the first sentence helps the reader to immediately see the colour scheme, which is probably the most striking feature of the room.

2. The prepositional phrases in this sentence ("Under the umbrella of its cool shade") provide a good transition and link with the "weeping willow" that I introduced in the preceding sentence.

3. This prepositional phrase ("In my white wicker armchair") provides a change from the more predictable beginning of the sentence just before it ("The window is...").

4. These two adjectives ("Cozy and secure") describe the atmosphere of my room and how I feel there during the storm. By moving them to the beginning of the sentence, I was able to give the adjectives a more important status and to stress the mood in the room.

I like the freedom to move words and phrasing around to add variety to my paragraph without eliminating vocabulary that I had carefully chosen for the description. I thought the overall effect was much improved!

The applications of metacognition in this section are only examples. You can apply the language skills you have learned in many different ways. Reading out loud, reading with others, discussion, writing, and reworking texts are useful exercises. As you try different methods, you will begin to see which ones are the most effective for your learning style. The more information you can process and understand, the better able you will be to interact with and interpret the world.

Taking time to focus on metacognition will improve your skills in language arts. There is not one correct method for metacognition. It is best to use a variety of methods in order to determine how you learn best. Reflecting on how you learn should be an ongoing process. Metacognition is something that you can use throughout your life in school and in work. Examining how and why you do certain things gives you insight on how you can change and improve. Reflecting on how you read and write also helps you practise your reading and writing skills.

4.2.3e develop a repertoire of stylistic choices that contribute to personal voice

VOICE

Voice refers to how the narrator or speaker of a text sounds to the reader. Did you notice that the voice and style of the speech "Good Evening Ladies and Gentlemen" are considerably less formal than the voice and style evident in the "Miss Brill" essay? Using a voice and style appropriate to academic and personal writing and format is an important choice that should be evident in your writing. As an analytical essay, the "Miss Brill" essay requires an observational style using standard formal English. The speech, on the other hand, is written in the voice of the chairperson of the local teen council. Even though the young person is addressing a group of local politicians, the language will still genuinely represent the youth of the person speaking. A youthful voice is evident in the more informal tone of the essay. Sentences like "Twenty-two million dollars is a lot of money" and the use of more colloquial words add to a youthful-sounding voice.

EXPRESSIVE WRITING

Creating your own expressive writing in response to texts that you have read in class can help you to understand those texts in greater detail. For example, writing an expressive poem or dramatic scene based on a novel can help you to pinpoint main themes or symbols within the novel. That is one reason that your teacher may require students to adapt an episode in a novel to a different time period or setting, or to create a dramatic scene from a short story. For example, many students have recreated scenes from Shakespearean plays and put them into the language of modern English. Expressive writing is enjoyable and it can teach you how to change the voice of your writing.

The following example shows how using a voice different from the one you would naturally use can be a creative challenge. Learning how to change the voice of your writing can help you to develop your own unique writing style.

Imagine that your class is reading Hamlet and that you have begun Act III, where you have encountered one of the most famous soliloquies in literature, "To Be or Not to Be."

Example

> To be, or not to be: that is the question:
> Whether 'tis nobler in the mind to suffer
> The slings and arrows of outrageous fortune,
> Or to take arms against a sea of troubles,
> And by opposing end them? To die: to sleep;
> No more; and by a sleep to say we end
> The heart-ache and the thousand natural shocks
> That flesh is heir to, 'tis a consummation
> Devoutly to be wish'd. To die, to sleep;
> To sleep: perchance to dream: ay, there's the rub;
> For in that sleep of death what dreams may come
> When we have shuffled off this mortal coil,
> Must give us pause: there's the respect
> That makes calamity of so long life;
> For who would bear the whips and scorns of time,
> The oppressor's wrong, the proud man's contumely,
> The pangs of despised love, the law's delay,

The insolence of office and the spurns
That patient merit of the unworthy takes,
When he himself might his quietus make
With a bare bodkin? who would fardels bear,
To grunt and sweat under a weary life,
But that the dread of something after death,
The undiscover'd country from whose bourn
No traveller returns, puzzles the will
And makes us rather bear those ills we have
Than fly to others that we know not of?
Thus conscience does make cowards of us all;
And thus the native hue of resolution
Is sicklied o'er with the pale cast of thought,
And enterprises of great pith and moment
With this regard their currents turn awry,
And lose the name of action.—Soft you now!
The fair Ophelia! Nymph, in thy orisons
Be all my sins remember'd.

Now imagine that your teacher has invited the class to reproduce the soliloquy in the voice of an antagonist from the play. A soliloquy for Polonius, for example, would reflect different concerns than Hamlet's soliloquy. Observe how the voice has been adapted to match the kind of language used in Hamlet.

Example

Polonius

[*Reflecting on his daughter's love for Hamlet*]
To spy, or not to spy: that is the question:
Whether 'tis nobler in the dark to suffer
The whims and nonsense of that mad fool, Hamlet
Or to speak forth against his dubious intentions
And so protect Ophelia's honour? To fret: to warn
Once more: And by his vow to say we end
Her heartache and the thousand broken dreams
That girl embraces, tis a consummation
Devoutly to be wish'd. To fret, to warn.
Once more: perchance they'll wed: ay, there's the rub.

Changing the voice of your writing involves thinking about a vocabulary that you might not normally use to express yourself.

4.2.4b know and be able to apply capitalization and punctuation conventions correctly, including end punctuation, commas, semicolons, colons, apostrophes, quotation marks, hyphens, dashes, ellipses, parentheses, underlining and italics

PUNCTUATION

Imagine if people never paused when they were speaking. It would be difficult to understand when thoughts started and began or if someone were asking a question. Punctuation translates many conventions of speech, such as pausing, into writing. It has its own set of rules that are necessary for clear writing. Punctuation gives clarity and definition to your writing and can be used for a wide variety of rhetorical and stylistic effects.

PERIODS

The period is used at the end of most sentences and after fragments used as sentences:

> "I walked to the end of the world. And stopped."

Do not use a period after a complete sentence that is contained by brackets or quotation marks within another sentence:

> "The company then sent him a registered letter (he was not answering e-mails or telephone messages) to explain the situation."
>
> "That's my friend Sonja (the Matchmaker)."
>
> "When she said, 'Class dismissed,' chaos erupted."

Notice that the bracketed sentences in the first and second examples do not begin with a capital letter, but the quotation in the third example does. The quotation is also set off with both quotation marks and commas.

PUNCTUATING POSSESSIVES

Most possessives are formed by adding an apostrophe and an s:

- a girl's smile

- one country's history

- a coat's buttons

The possessive of a noun that ends in s is generally formed with an apostrophe and an *s*:

- the boss's car

- the countess's speech

- James's, Charles's, Alex's

Watch for the possessive of plurals. The rule is to add an apostrophe after the *s* of the plural:

- five girls' smiles

- three countries' histories

- the actresses' Oscars

- the girls' car

COMMAS WITH CONJUNCTIONS

Coordinating conjunctions (*for*, *and*, *nor*, *but*, *or*, *yet*, *so*—think FANBOYS) are used with a comma if they join two independent clauses:

> "He will be late, *for* he must complete the game."
>
> "Go to the edge of the cliff, *and* tell me what you see there."
>
> "She will not learn from her failures, *nor* will she learn from her successes."

When a coordinate conjunction joins two short independent clauses, a comma may not be necessary:

> "She's late *and* she's tired."

When subordinating conjunctions (which include after, because, although, before, since, though, and unless) are used in an introductory clause, a comma follows the clause:

> "*Because* you have been elected, you must serve."
>
> "*Before* she leaves, she plans to write a note of farewell."

Do not use a semicolon to follow an introductory clause:

> "Because you have been elected; you must serve." (*incorrect*)

When a subordinate clause follows an independent clause, a comma is usually not used:

> "She plas to write a note of farewell *before* she leaves."
>
> "You must serve *because* you have been elected."

However, a comma should be used when it is necessary to avoid confusion:

> "He has done all his work since his failure last term threatened his final grade." (*unclear*)
>
> "He has done all his work, since his failure last term threatened his final grade." (*clear*)

The original sentence seems to mean that he has done all his work from the time that his failure threatened his final grade. It is only once you reach the end of the sentence that the meaning can be understood. A comma after "work" makes it clear that "since" is a subordinating conjunction and not a preposition.

Wanted: Designers, Creators, Inventors, Thinkers, Dreamers

Work in teams.

Bring ideas to life.

Use creativity to solve problems.

Impact the world around you.

Help people live longer, healthier lives.

Make communities healthier,
happier, safer.

Become an engineer.
Visit www.engineering.ualberta.ca

 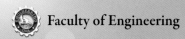

CASTLE ROCK

RESEARCH CORP

Castle Rock Research is a Canadian company dedicated to supporting student learning through the development of proven educational resources. The core strength of Castle Rock Research is the company's ability to create study guides, workbooks, and online assessment tools that are 100% aligned with the Alberta curriculum. Using breakthrough technology for developing, managing, and implementing content, Castle Rock educational resources are blueprinted to accurately reflect the weighting of standards in the Alberta curriculum. Our unique products serve students, teachers, school jurisdictions, education ministries, colleges, and universities.

THE KEY

THE KEY *Study Guide* helps students prepare for course assignments, unit tests, final exams, and provincial assessments. Each **KEY** includes teaching pieces, questions with detailed solutions, and practice tests that correlate 100% to Alberta curriculum expectations.

SNAP (Student Notes and Problems)

The **SNAP** *Workbook* provides lessons for each of the course expectations, detailed explanations of concepts, and practice exercises with detailed solutions to take students from guided learning to independent practice.

brain fuel

People who eat breakfast perform better in school and at work. This is just one of the many ways good nutrition contributes to a healthy lifestyle.

Aim to meet your nutritional needs as recommended in *Eating Well with Canada's Food Guide*.

Teens 14–18 years old need the following number of servings each day from the 4 food groups:

	females	males
vegetables and fruit	7	8
grain products	6	7
milk and alternatives	3–4	3–4
meat and alternatives	2	4

Find a complete food guide on line at: **www.healthcanada.gc.ca/foodguide**

To learn more about healthy eating, visit **www.saveonfoods.com** and send your nutrition questions to our dietitians, register for an in-store Nutrition Tour or find healthy recipes and eating advice.

THE BEAR CHILDREN'S FUND

Think of it as 'Tough Love'

Since 1992, The Bear has been giving back to Edmonton's kids through The Bear Children's Fund. In the years since the Fund's inception, over $1,500,000 has been directed back into the greater Edmonton community and its charities. To make the Fund work requires the dedication of both management and staff, who have volunteered thousands of hours of their time to this worthwhile cause. As a rock station, The Bear may be loud, but it's proud too. Proud to be a part of a community as generous as Edmonton.

Edmonton's Best Rock 100.3 fm

To apply for grants from the Bear Children's Fund please visit **www.thebearrocks.com**

Alberta Committee for Citizens with Disabilities | Alberta Rose Chapter | Alberta Special Olympics | Arbutus Volunteer Foundation Belmont Elementary School | Ben Calf Robe Native Elementary & Junior High Catholic School | Bent Arrow Traditional Healing Society | Boyle Street Co-op Playground | Boys & Girls Club of Edmonton | Canadian Progress Club | Century Services Inc. Stollery Children's Hospital Foundation | Children's Heart Society City Centre Education Project | CNIB | Cross Cancer Institute Early Head Start Program | Edmonton City Police D.A.R.E. Program | Edmonton Food Bank | Edmonton Garrison Base Fund Edmonton Jaycees | Edmonton School Lunch Program | Edmonton Spring Board & Platform Diving Club | Employabilities | EMS Social Club | Firefighter's Burn Unit | Fort Saskatchewan Boys & Girls Club | Friends of Rosecrest | Garden Valley Pony Club | Glenrose Rehabilitation Hospital | Griesbach School Council | Inner City Youth Development Association | Head First Foundation | Hug-A-Bear Express | Kid's Kottage | Kinsmen Club of St. Albert | Mansion Youth Drop-In Centre for Teens | McCauley Community After School Care Association | Morinville Panthers | New York City Police & Fire Widows' & Children's Benefit | Northern Alberta Brain Injury Society | Norwood Community Centre | Nottingham Playground Association | Parents Empowering Parents | P.A.R.T.Y. Program Project Literacy | Queen Mary Park School | Rainbow Society Ronald McDonald House | Royal Alexandra Hospital | Southwest Area Council of Community Leagues | St. Michael's School | St. Patrick's School (Edmonton) Parents Society | Terra Association | Uncles At Large | Various Trust Funds & Confidential Donations | Westview Regional Health Authority Youth Health Centre | Wetaskiwin Head Start Society | Yellowhead Youth Centre | Youth Emergency Shelter Society | Skills Woodcroft Respite Home | Royal Alexandra Hospital NICU Family Room (Bear Den) | Brightview Elementary School

YOUR QUEST STARTS HERE!

Learn full-time, part-time, online…
on your time

NorQuest College is your community college, providing career education through diplomas and certificates in health, human service, business and industry.

Need pre-requisites or language training to go on to further study or a better job… we can help with that too!

DIPLOMAS:
- **Business Administration**
- **Digital Graphics Communications**
- **Mental Health Rehabilitation** (Diploma or Certificate)
- **Pharmacy Technician**
- **Physical Therapy Assistant**
- **Practical Nurse**
- **Social Work** (with a multicultural focus)
- **Therapeutic Recreation** (Diploma or Certificate)

CERTIFICATES:
- **Aboriginal Community Support Worker**
- **Aboriginal Policing & Security**
- **Administrative Professional** (six specializations)
- **Apprenticeship Prep**
- **Building Service Worker**
- **Day Home Provider**
- **Facility Service Management**
- **Health Care Aide**
- **Hospital Unit Clerk**

For more information, call
780-644-6000 in Edmonton,
1-866-534-7218 toll free or visit
www.norquest.ca

COLONS

When used in sentences, a colon can only follow an independent clause to introduce a list, explanation, or appositive:

> "You should bring the following items: a sleeping bag, a change of clothes, and matches."
>
> "There is only one honest thing to do: admit you made a mistake and apologize."
>
> "Everything about him was summed up in his nickname: Old Ornery."

When a list is set up in point form, the same rule applies:

> The introductory course will cover three topics:
> 1. algebra
> 2. geometry
> 3. trigonometry

If a list does not follow an independent clause, no colon is used:

> "You must bring a sleeping bag, a change of clothes, and matches."

Similarly, the following list does not require a colon:

> The introductory course will cover
> 1. algebra
> 2. geometry
> 3. trigonometry

A simple way of checking colon use is to cover up all the words after the colon. Can the first part of the sentence now stand alone as a sentence? If it does, use a colon. If not, then do not use the colon.

QUOTATION MARKS

Use quotation marks at the beginning and end of all words in a direct quotation. Watch for the use of quotation marks before and after speech tags:

> Alfred said, "We are ready."
>
> "I'm finished the job," said Alfred. "We can go now."
>
> "When we are ready," said Alfred, "we will go."

Notice that the closing quotation mark is placed after a comma or a period and that a comma is used after a speech tag ("Alfred said,").

Closing quotation marks are also used with exclamation marks and question marks. When these punctuation marks belong to the sentence, they are placed outside the closing quotation marks:

> Didn't you hear him say, "I'm in trouble"?

If the punctuation marks belong to the quotation, they are placed inside the quotation marks:

> He said sadly, "Why is it always me?"

The same rules apply to closing quotation marks used for other purposes. Periods and commas always belong inside the quotation marks:

> You could say that her acting was "over the top."

Exclamation marks and question marks belong either outside or inside the quotation marks, depending on whether they belong to the sentence as a whole or to the words inside the quotation marks:

> She asked, "Are these seats taken?"
>
> I can't believe you call that dilapidated wreck a "car"!

Indirect quotations never require quotation marks:

> Alfred asked if we were ready.
>
> Alfred said that he had finished the job and that we could go.
>
> Alfred said that when we were ready, we could go.

Quotation marks are also used for the titles of short stories and poems and to indicate that a word is being used in an unusual sense:

> "Housekeeping" on the space station is challenging.

Quotation marks can also indicate sarcasm or irony:

> The "suicide" of Jan Masaryk marked the end of democracy in Czechoslovakia.
>
> It seems that their "help" has put this project three weeks behind.

PUNCTUATION FOR EFFECT

Consider the following examples, remembering that punctuation is your tool, not your taskmaster.

- John closes the door and asks Alice what is wrong.

- John closes the door and asks Alice, "What is wrong?"

- John closes the door and asks, "Alice, what is wrong?"

- We mustn't believe everything we hear is the truth.

- We mustn't! Believe! Everything we hear is the truth!

- Consider yourself one of the family.

- Consider yourself one of the family!

- Consider yourself one of the family? Never!

- Why? Because we can. Because we must. Because we care.

Sentence fragments can be used deliberately with sentence punctuation to create a rhetorical effect.

ITALICS AND UNDERLINING

Certain titles are printed in italic script. Italicize or underline the titles of all major works, such as books, long poems, newspapers, magazines, movies, and television series.

Example

A Tale of Two Cities
Time Magazine
The Times
The Wizard of Oz
Star Trek

Italics are also used to indicate words and sometimes letters that are considered as objects rather than as structural parts of a sentence:

"The word *since* can be a subordinate conjunction or a preposition."
"Add *s* or *es* to form the plural of a noun."

Italics should be used sparingly for emphasis. It is more acceptable to use italics for emphasis in creative writing than it in formal writing. Formal writing should use words and arguments so compelling that no extra emphasis is needed. In creative writing, it can be useful to use italics for showing emphasis in, for example, the dialogue of characters.

Use quotation marks to set off shorter works or parts of works, such as chapters, short stories, short poems, songs, articles, and episodes in a television series.

4.2.4c   know and be able to apply spelling conventions consistently and independently

SPELLING

Correct spelling is necessary for clear and effective writing. By Grade 12, your writing should demonstrate a practical understanding of spelling patterns, rules, and strategies. It is a good idea to maintain a growing list of words that are difficult to spell and a list of words that you frequently misspell. Make a conscious effort to spell correctly.

Use print resources to check your spelling. Print resources include a dictionary as well as textbooks and class handouts to check academic spelling. Often, a definition in a textbook will be better tailored to explaining the meaning of the word in context. Use electronic resources like your computer's spellcheck only as an initial tool to weed out obvious errors. Your computer's spellcheck is not enough for proofreading. The computer usually cannot correct homonyms (their, there, they're) or misused but correctly spelled words, such as accept and except. It is a good idea to occasionally refresh your memory of basic spelling rules as well as exceptions to those rules.

SPELLING RULES

You may have heard the complaint that there are always exceptions to spelling and grammar rules. However, spelling rules are still a good place to start. The rules take care of most cases and leave you free to pay attention to exceptions. The "I before E" rhyme is a good example:

> I before E except after C, unless it sounds "A", as in neighbour and weigh.

The rule that this rhyme explains covers the majority of cases. It is possible to sort the common exceptions into groups:

- Words of foreign origin: German (Geiger, stein, poltergeist) or Greek (protein, kaleidoscope, seismograph)

- Words that have some connection: A group of words loosely connected with government, law, or property can be matched with reign, which does follow the rule. Then think of reign, sovereign, foreign, heir, heiress, seize, counterfeit, and forfeit as being a group.

- Words whose pattern matches a subset of words that follow the rule: height and sleight match neighbour, weigh, weight, and freight.

- A few more or less common words are left over. Simply pay attention to their spelling: either, neither, leisure, weird, heifer, feisty.

- Words like reinforce can be ignored, since the pronunciation of the prefix makes it just about impossible to spell the ei incorrectly.

Use a writing guide or the Internet to look up a list of spelling rules for review.

HOMONYMS AND OTHER EASILY CONFUSED WORDS

Words can be confused because they sound exactly the same (its, it's) or almost the same (insure, ensure).

Certain contractions (when two words are combined with an apostrophe) and pronouns are also easily confused:

> "Your list is complete."
> "You're almost ready."
>
> "Their supper is ready."
> "They're about to sit down."
> "There is the book."
>
> "Its collar came off."
> "It's a great pity."

Remember that no possessive pronoun is ever written with an apostrophe. Because possessives written with apostrophes sound the same as plural forms when spoken, they are often confused when written.

> "The quarter's shape is distinctive."
>
> "I have four quarters in my pocket."

The list of homonyms, near-homonyms, and easily confused words is long. The following list shows some examples of commonly confused homonyms.

• allowed, aloud	• seen, scene
• bow, bough	• sight, site, cite
• not, knot	• sign, sine
• pore, pour, poor	• slight, sleight
• principal, principle	• sweet, suite
• prophet, profit	• there, their, they're
• red, read	• to, too, two
• waste, waist	

The following chart displays more examples of easily confused words that a computer spellcheck might not find.

all right, alright	In standard written English, only *all right* is recognized. Alright is strictly informal.
practice, practise	*Practice* is a noun (two hours of practice). *Practise* is a verb (He has been practising for two hours).
licence, license	*Licence* is a noun (driver's licence) and *license* is a verb (The state licenses us to drive).
stationary, stationery	*Stationary* means staying in one place; *stationery* is the writing materials sold by a *stationer*, originally a merchant who set up a station, or booth, to sell pens and paper.
a lot, allot	There is only one way to spell these two words when they are used together: *a lot*. The word *allot* means to allocate or give out.
it's, its	All the possessive pronouns are formed the same way: yours, his, hers, *its*, theirs, whose. Pronouns spelled with apostrophes are contractions: you're (you are), he's (he is), she's (she is), it's (it is), they're, (they are), who's (who is).

FREQUENTLY MISSPELLED WORDS

Certain words in the English language are frequently misspelled, even by people who consider themselves to be good spellers. Some of these words are listed below. Try to master them now. The tricky parts of these words have been underlined for you.

across	conscience	experience	immediate	really	schedule
argument	definitely	foreign	lightning	relevant	separate
calendar	discipline	government	neighbour	restaurant	until
column	embarrass	grateful	occasionally	rhyme	weird
committed	equipment	height	possession	rhythm	

Here are some examples of frequently confused words.

- accept/except: Everyone was pleased to *accept* their reward, *except* Melody.

- a lot: Two words, as in "*a lot* of homework." This word gets confused with *allot*, which means to distribute a portion: Each child was *allotted* some personal space in the new classroom.

- believe/receive: These two words follow the i before e rule: "i before e, except after c."

- its/it's: "Its" without the apostrophe is a possessive pronoun, as in "The cat injured *its* tail." The word itself shows possession, just like the pronoun "yours." With the apostrophe, "*it's*" is a contraction of the phrase "it is." The apostrophe is used to replace the missing letter.

- principal/principle: A *principal* is the administrator of a school, as in "the *principal's* office." *Principal* also means main, as in "The *principal* reason I am moving is…" The word "*principle*," however, refers to a moral belief, as in "The school's anti-bullying policy is based on the *principle* that all children deserve to feel safe at school."

- their/there/they're: "*Their* new house," "They live over *there*," and "He said *they're* coming."

- to/too/two: "*To* the track meet" is a preposition, "*Too* much" means also, and "*Two* lists" represents a number.

- weather/whether: "*Whether* we attend the game depends on the *weather*."

SPELLING AND PROOFREADING

When proofreading for spelling, not every mistake will jump out at you. Look for mistakes like *vallies* (for valleys), *recieve* (for receive), or *resent* (for recent). Mistakes like these can be hard to catch. A good method for finding easy-to-miss mistakes is to read sentences backward. This allows each word to be seen as an individual item and not as part of a sentence. With the pattern of meaning removed, it is easier to find errors. The same method may help you to proofread your own work in the written-response questions on exams.

4.2.4d understand the importance of grammatical agreement; and assess and revise texts in progress to ensure correctness of grammatical agreement, including correct pronoun reference and pronoun antecedent agreement, and correct use of modifiers and other parts of speech

GRAMMAR

Grammar gives structure to language so that communication can be as clear as possible. Understanding grammar—the names of the parts of speech, kinds of sentences, rules for the agreement of sentence parts—gives you a common vocabulary so that you can speak about language. If your teacher gives you a comment on a paper such as "use the objective case of that pronoun," then it would be helpful for you to understand the objective case.

Pronouns take the place of nouns: *I*, *she*, *it*, *we*, *that*, *all*, *whatever*, *some*. In your writing, ensure that there are no misunderstandings regarding the nouns to which your pronouns refer.

Example

Both girls agreed that their projects had been prepared thoroughly. They were ready for the science fair. (*What or who was ready? The girls? The projects?*)
When I got to the tax office, they told me they were closing for the day. (*This sentence if fine for informal speech, but in written English, they can only refer to the tax office, and a tax office cannot be they.*)

Ensure that your pronouns and their antecedents are clear.

The most basic group of pronouns is the personal pronouns. These pronouns replace persons or things and are used to identify point of view, particularly in narrative texts, such as short stories, novels, and plays.

First Person: I/Me, We/Us

Second Person: You

Third Person: He/Him, She/Her, They/Them, It

USING THE CORRECT CASE

For the most part, English is not inflected. That means that most words do not change their endings to show how they are used in sentences. Pronouns are one exception: they are inflected.

Pronouns have three cases, as shown in the following chart.

Whenever you use these pronouns, check the pronoun case and check for the correct spelling.

Subjective case is used for the subject of a sentence or clause and for the complement of a linking verb	Objective case is used for the object of a verb or preposition, gerund, participle, or infinitive	Possessive case is used to show ownership	
		Used as an adjective	Used as a subject or as the complement of a linking verb
I	Me	My	Mine
You	You	Your	Yours
He/she/it	Him/her/it	His/her/its	His/hers/its
We	Us	Our	Ours
You	You	Your	Yours
They	Them	Their	Theirs
Who	Whom	Whose	Whose

The possessive pronoun its follows the same pattern as his, hers, yours, and theirs. Remember that the possessive of pronouns is never formed with an apostrophe.

When the pronoun is the subject, use the subjective case:

- *You* have been elected.

- Despite the weather, *we* are certainly going.

- *He* and *she* ran the marathon.

- Even after a late start, *they* still won the marathon.

If the pronoun is the subject and a possessive, use the second form of the possessive case:

- *Mine* is nearly ready.

- *Yours* is already finished, but theirs is not ready.

When the pronoun is the object (either direct or indirect), use the objective case:

- Give it to *her*.

- The government mailed *me* a letter.

- The fall smashed *it* to pieces.

- When the paper is ready, give *it* to *her* and *me*.

A pronoun following a linking verb is a noun complement (or predicate nominative or subject completion) and it is in the subjective case:

- It is *he*.

- Yes, I've seen Miss Jones. It was *she* who walked past just now.

- I am *he*.

- It is *I*.

When writing comparisons using than or as, use the objective case:

- He likes me more than *him*.

- Evan can type as accurately as *her*.

These examples suggest the problem of different levels of language in different situations. Consider the sentence "It is I." The sentence is correct, but it might appear to be stuffy, even pretentious. However, in a formal or solemn context, such sentences are not only correct, they are suitable. On the other hand, in everyday life, few would complain about, "It's me." Sometimes, the pronoun agreements cause trouble. Here is a useful rule of thumb.

> Most of those who might say *Him and me did it*, would never say *Me did it* or *Him did it*. Whenever you have more than one pronoun, try the sentence with one of the pronouns at a time. *He* did it + *I* did it = *He* and *I* did it.

When the pronoun that follows a linking verb is a possessive, use the form of the possessive case that would be used for the subject of a sentence:

• The red one is *mine*. Did you hear me? *Mine* is the red one.

• This car is *hers*—or is it *theirs*? No, *theirs* is the car on the right.

Note the difference when a pronoun is used as an adjective and when it is used as a predicate complement:

• *Their* win was amazing.

• The win was *theirs*.

You would not want to memorize all the pronouns, but it is a good idea to be aware of them and of their uses.

Kinds of Pronouns	Examples
Demonstrative I want to enter *this* in the exhibition.	This, that, these, those
Interrogative *Who* said that?	Who, whom, which, what, whoever, whomever, whichever, whatever
Relative Choose *whichever* you like.	Who, whom, that, which, whoever, whomever, whichever
Indefinite *Many* have asked that question.	All, another, any, anybody, anyone, anything, each, everybody, everyone, everything, few, many, nobody, none, one, several, some, somebody, someone
Reflexive She did the job *herself*.	Myself, yourself, herself, himself, itself, ourselves, yourselves, themselves
Intensive The professor *himself* was not sure of the answer.	Myself, yourself, herself, himself, itself, ourselves, yourselves, themselves

Notice the reflexive and intensive pronouns, which are often used incorrectly: "Give it to myself." The examples given in the chart show the only correct uses of the reflexive pronoun. Notice that when the reflexive is used immediately after the noun, it is an intensifier.

What about the pronouns *who* and *whom*? Although the distinction between these two pronouns may be disappearing in spoken English, you should be able to use each of them correctly in formal writing. *Who* is an interrogative subjective pronoun. Use it whenever the pronoun is the subject of a sentence or a clause:

• *Who* are you?

• *Who* is going?

• The candidate *who* should be elected is Julia.

Whom is an interrogative objective pronoun. Use it whenever the pronoun is the object of a predicate or a preposition:

- The prize will be given to *whom*?

- *Whom* did you tell?

- To *whom* did they refer?

A simple mnemonic for remembering the difference is "he/who" and "him/whom." If the sentence could use he, then use who; if the sentence could use him, then use whom:

- *He* will win. *Who* will win?

- Give it to *him*. Give it to *whom*?

- The crowd followed after *him*. The crowd followed after *whom*?

- The robbers left *him* for dead. The robbers left *whom* for dead?

- For *him*, we would do anything. For *whom* would we do anything?

Of course, there is an extra mental step if the pronoun is not masculine:

- Give it to *her*. Give it to *whom*?

- For *her*, we would do anything. For *whom* would we do anything?

- Yes, it is *she* that won. *Who* was it that won?

Verbs: Voice and Mood

The mood and voice you choose for the verbs you use in your writing makes a difference. The following section describes different voices and the subjunctive mood in writing.

Active and Passive Voice

The active voice is transitive, which means that it requires an object. Active voice is stronger and more direct than the passive voice, and it usually makes your writing more effective. A sentence is written in the active voice when the subject clearly does the action; a sentence is written in the passive voice when the subject of the sentence receives the action. The following examples will help you to understand how much stronger and direct the active voice is than the passive voice.

- "John completed his exam."

The active voice emphasizes the "doer" of the actions. This makes a stronger statement and helps the writer to avoid dangling or misplaced modifiers:

- "Her dog was walked in a bright orange skirt." (incorrect)

- "In a bright orange skirt, she walked her dog." (correct)

The placement of the modifier makes it seem that the dog is wearing the skirt.

The passive voice is intransitive, which means that there is no object. The action is implied:

- "The exam was completed early."

The passive voice emphasizes the receiver of the action and minimizes the importance of the doer. Here are more examples of active and passive voice.

Active Voice	My dad packed the car for the trip.
Passive Voice	The car was packed for the trip by my dad.
Active Voice	Sue ate her birthday cake.
Passive Voice	The birthday cake was eaten by Sue.

Passive Voice in Writing

The passive voice can come across as unnecessarily wordy. The passive voice is a form of the verb where who or what is doing the verb is implied but never actually stated. The active voice is preferred over the passive voice for clear, engaging writing. The active voice indicates the agent who performs the action.

Politicians often use the passive voice because they do not want to identify a specific individual responsible for some problem in government. They may say, "There has recently been a decline in economic activity." The passive voice does not state who or what is responsible for this economic decline. Critics of government, on the other hand, use the active voice because they do want to identify who is responsible for some government problem. They may say, "The finance minister's recent budget has caused a decline in economic activity." The active voice, "The new budget has caused…," offers an agent that the critics feel is to blame for the economic decline.

In the active voice, the subject of each sentence is placed before the object. Active language conveys the same ideas in fewer words.

Subjunctive Mood

The subjunctive mood expresses a wish or condition that is not actually true. Verbs such as *could*, *would*, and *should* are commonly used in the subjunctive mood.

Example

> If I *were* prime minister, I *should* allow everyone to work a four-day week.
>
> If Colin *could* take his dream vacation, he *would* spend it in Antarctica.

4.2.4 g assess and revise texts in progress to ensure the correct use of clauses and phrases, including verbal phrases (participle, gerund and infinitive), and to ensure the correct use of structural features [such as appositives and parallel structure]

PROOFREADING

Proofreading to edit your writing is a crucial stage of the writing process. Do not underestimate the power of using correct English. While the content of your ideas may be substantial, it is the clarity achieved through correct expression that often persuades or impresses your reader. Careless usage, spelling, and punctuation, on the other hand, tend to produce the opposite effect. You do not want your ideas being dismissed or actually missed altogether because you did not edit or proofread carefully.

The following information provides you with some specific areas to be aware of when you are proofreading your writing.

GRAMMAR

- Verb Tense

- Subject/Verb Agreement

- Complete Sentences

- Comparative and Superlative Forms of Adjectives and Adverbs

- Subordinate Clauses and Coordinating Conjunctions

- Modifier Placement

- Correct Word Usage

VERB TENSE

The tense of a verb tells the reader when the action happens. The most common verb tenses you will use in your writing are the past tense (before), the present tense (now), and the future tense (later).

Here is an example of the three tenses of the verb to work.

Past tense	Present tense	Future tense
He worked.	He works.	He will work.

When planning a story, think about when your story will take place: the past, the present, the future, or some combination of these time frames. You may decide to begin your story in the present but include flashback sequences. Make sure that when you are writing in the present, your verbs reflect the present tense. When you use a flashback sequence, make sure that the verbs are written in the past tense. Whatever you decide, make sure that you use consistent verb tenses in your narrative writing.

Example

Consistent: Her uncle often *came* to visit her. One day he *asked* her…

Inconsistent: Her uncle often *comes* to visit her. One day he *asked* her…

SUBJECT-VERB AGREEMENT

Most of the difficulties in subject–verb agreement are caused by the inability to recognize singular and plural subjects.

When subjects are joined by or or nor, the verb agrees with the nearest subject:

> "Either Miller *or* Smith *is* guilty."
>
> "Neither Miller *nor* Smith *wants* to confess."
>
> "Neither the *speaker* nor the *listeners are* aware of the irony."

When one part of the verb is singular and the other plural, write the sentence so that the plural part is nearest the verb:

> "Neither *band members* nor the *conductor* is satisfied." (*weak*)
>
> "Neither the *conductor* nor the *band members are* satisfied." (*better*)

Nothing that comes between a singular subject and its verb can make that subject plural. Students should not make the verb agree with the nearest noun:

> "Our school basketball team, the Gerbils, is victorious again."
>
> "The prime minister, accompanied by several cabinet ministers, arrives at the airport shortly."
>
> "Either Miller or Jones—both are suspects—is guilty."
>
> "The contestant with the most votes is now on stage."
>
> "One of the girls sings better."
>
> "The ringleader who was at the head of the rebellious miners is sorry."

Indefinite pronouns, such as each, each one, either, neither, everyone, everybody, anybody, anyone, nobody, somebody, someone, and no one, are singular:

> "Each of the contestants wins a prize."
>
> "Everybody near the river is in danger."
>
> "No one who wants to be successful in the exams is likely to be late."

Collective nouns are singular unless there is a reason to consider them as plurals:

> "The group works well."
>
> "The company is bankrupt."
>
> "The jury is deliberating its verdict."
>
> "The jury are arguing among themselves."

Using the correct pronoun is often a problem because the form of a pronoun varies depending on how the pronoun is used. Use I, you, he/she/it, we, you, they, and who as the subject of a sentence or clause and for the complement of a linking verb:

"You have been chosen."

"We will be the last of the contestants."

"Who is going to be next?"

"It is she who will be chosen."

Use me, you, him/her/it, us, you, them, and whom as direct or indirect objects of verbs or as the object of a preposition:

"Give it to me."

"Hit the ball to them."

"Ask them the time."

"The child next to him laughed suddenly."

Use my, your, his/her/its, our, their, and whose as adjectives:

"my car"

"your umbrella"

"its fur"

Use mine, yours, his/hers/its, ours, theirs, and whose as subjects of sentences or as the complement of a linking verb:

"Yours is the one on the left."

"This is mine."

"Theirs is next."

The possessive pronouns my, your, his, hers, its, our, yours, theirs, and whose never use an apostrophe to show possession.

Complete Sentences

As a general rule, all sentences should be complete sentences:

"He went ahead with his plan. Even though it was faulty." (*incorrect*)

"He went ahead with his plan, even though it was faulty." (*correct*)

Occasionally, an incomplete sentence is used deliberately for effect. Fragments that are used deliberately are sometimes called minor sentences:

> "Is anyone in favour of dictatorship? No? Well, of course not." (*correct*)

Dialogue and reported speech are exceptions to the rule about fragments:

> "Ready yet?"
>
> "Not yet."
>
> "Well then—!"

The opposite error exists in run-on sentences (in which punctuation between sentences has been omitted) and with sentences containing a comma splice (in which a comma has been used to join two sentences).

> "We went to Toronto we decided to visit the zoo." (*run-on sentence*)
>
> "We went to Toronto, we decided to visit the zoo." (*comma splice*)

These errors can be fixed by correcting the punctuation or by rewriting:

> "We went to Toronto. We decided to visit the zoo."
>
> "We went to Toronto. Then, we decided to visit the zoo."
>
> "After we went to Toronto, we decided to visit the zoo."
>
> "We went to Toronto, and then we decided to visit the zoo."

Comparative and Superlative Forms of Adjectives and Adverbs

Comparatives and superlatives are special forms of adjectives and adverbs. They are used to compare things. When comparing two things, use the comparative form:

> "A car is much *more expensive* than a lollipop."
>
> "Five plus five is *greater* than four plus four."

When comparing more than two things, use the superlative form:

> "That was the *best* movie I have ever seen."
>
> "I wanted to buy the *largest* dog in the window."

The following chart provides some examples that compare the base form of an adjective or adverb with the comparative and superlative forms of the same word.

Base	Comparative	Superlative
fast	faster	fastest
good	better	best
wide	wider	widest
bad	worse	worst
quickly	more quickly	most quickly
harmful	more harmful	most harmful

Subordinate Clauses and Coordinating Conjunctions

A clause is a group of words containing a subject and a predicate. A subordinate clause is a group of words that cannot stand alone as a sentence. Using subordinate clauses allows you to create interesting sentences by combining ideas:

> "My sister, *who is a doctor*, has four children."
>
> "*While I clean my room*, I like to listen to music."

The clauses who is a doctor and while I clean my room cannot stand alone as sentences and are therefore called subordinate clauses. Subordinate clauses add information to a sentence but are not complete ideas on their own.

Coordinating conjunctions are words used to join two clauses together. Some examples of coordinating conjunctions are for, and, not, but, or, yet, and so. These simple words can be used to join ideas and create complex sentences:

> "Wendy loved to read books *but* did not enjoy magazines."
>
> "John heard the weather report *and* hurried home."
>
> "The sun was shining brightly, *yet* the air was still cold."

Modifier Placement

As a general rule, a modifier, which is usually an adjective or an adverb, should be placed as close as possible to the word being modified.

Example

> *Vague*: Entering the room, the door was shut by mother.
> *Clear*: Entering the room, mother shut the door.
>
> *Vague*: At six years of age, my parents started me in piano.
> *Clear*: At six years of age, I started taking piano lessons.

Correct Word Usage

The following words are easily confused:

Lie, which means "to recline" Lay, which means "to place"	• Father would lie down for a ten-minute nap after lunch. • We were asked to lay our uniforms neatly on the shelf.
Accept, which means "to receive" Except, which means "with the exception of"	• Jeremy will accept the reward on behalf of his brother. Everyone in the family except Nolan came down with the flu.
Borrow, which means "to have borrowed from" Lend, which means "to lend to"	• May I borrow your baseball glove? • Could you lend me your textbook?
Their, which is a possessive adjective, means "it belongs to them" There, which is an adverb that denotes a place, position, or existence They're, which is a contraction of "they are"	• The students will take their final exam on Friday morning. • We decided there were enough people present to take a vote. • The Smith family lived there for eight years. If they're arriving Tuesday, someone should meet them at the airport.
Its, which is a possessive pronoun It's, which is a contraction of "it is"	• The cat injured its front paw. • It's been snowing for three days.
Lose, which is a verb that means to be deprived of something Loose, which is an adjective that refers to something that is not tightly in place	• Try not to lose your backpack. • Our mechanic discovered that a loose bolt caused the problem.
Can, which means "are able to" May, which means "are allowed to"	• Most children can print their own name. • You may watch a movie on Saturday.
In, which is a preposition that expresses a situation Into, which is a preposition that expresses movement or action	• The key is in the mailbox. • Sara needs the key to get into her house.
Whose, which means "belonging to whom" Who's, which is a contraction of "who is"	• I don't know whose wallet is missing. • Who's willing to help pick up this litter?
Good, which is an adjective Well, which is an adverb that means "in a satisfactory way"	• It seemed like a good idea. • Terri didn't feel well after her game.

| Could have, should have, and would have are correct usages.

Using of with these verbs (could of, should of, would of) is always incorrect. | • I could have spelled that word correctly.

• I should have spelled that word correctly.

I would have spelled that word correctly had I been paying attention. |
| Different from is correct usage.

Using different than is always incorrect. | • Cabbage is different from lettuce. |

Capitalization

Although there are many special rules for capitalization, the following rules are the most important to practice for now.

• Capitalize the first words of sentence, including sentences used in quotations.

• Capitalize proper nouns, including any specific person or place (John Doe, Calgary, December).

• Always capitalize the word "I."

• Capitalize some abbreviations. For example, R.S.V.P. (please respond), WWF (World Wildlife Federation), Ave. (Avenue), Dr. (Doctor).

• Capitalize the main words in a title, such as The Cat in the Hat or My Summer in Mexico.

The following proofreading checklist may help you make sure that your revised draft is ready for publishing or handing in. Always save your working draft on the computer in case you have to make changes after proofreading. Proofread both silently and out loud, if possible.

• Check for smooth flow of ideas, with all of your revision made to the draft

• Sentences: varied lengths, beginnings, types, and no run-ons or fragments

• Punctuation: all end marks, commas, and quotation marks

• Capitalization

• Spelling: use your computer's spellcheck and a dictionary

• Subject–verb agreement

• Pronoun–antecedent agreement

• Check with your "personal alert" list from your writing binder:

  – your most frequent usage errors; for example, run-ons or verb agreement problems

  – your most frequent punctuation and capitalization errors

  – words you have misspelled this year

• Print or write your final edited copy

Peer Conferences

Peer conferences can be helpful both at the revision and the proofreading stages of your writing. At a peer conference, always read your work out loud. Peer conferences work very well in a partner situation.

Tips for Readers	Tips for Listeners
1. Show your punctuation through pauses. 2. Do not rush your reading. 3. Be open to suggestions. 4. Jot notes for changes on your draft. 5. Clarify your partner's comments with questions as needed. 6. Thank your partner. 7. Appreciate that your peer is trying to help you improve your writing.	1. Listen carefully and pay attention to your reader's ideas. 2. Make sure to tell the reader what they have done well. 3. Be specific in criticism: "That sentence is confusing," "you need a stronger verb there" 4. Try to be constructive: "What if you switched those two ideas to make the argument flow better?" 5. Remember that you are only trying to help. The writer may choose not to follow some of your suggestions.

Appropriate Modifiers

Adjectives modify nouns by telling what kind of person, place, or thing they are.

Example

> *Wild* geese, *high-flying* geese, *honking* geese, *southbound* geese, *excited* geese; *those* geese, *that* goose, *my* geese, *six* geese, *some* geese, *your* goose

Adverbs modify verbs or other modifiers by telling when, where, how, or how much.

Example

> The wild geese flew *south yesterday*.
>
> The wild geese flew *noisily* and *swiftly in a 'V' shape*.

Modifiers can also be phrases that do the work of a single adverb.

Example

> The geese flew *toward the south*.
>
> *With loud honking and flapping of wings*, the geese flew south.

This section is intended to help you develop vocabulary and grammar skills. Remember that both careful reading and writing will help you to better understand how proper grammar works and help you to expand your vocabulary. The rules and guidelines that you have learned in this section of your *KEY* offer tools that are meant to be used when you are reading and writing. After you have finished reading something, take another look at the text, carefully considering the grammatical structures and vocabulary that you have used. Note how sentences are made, which words are being used, and how they are used. Remember that your vocabulary and grammar will improve not only through knowing and following rules and guidelines: reading and being curious and observant in your reading will also help improve your vocabulary and grammar.

4.2.3b assess the appropriateness of diction and revise word choice as needed to create intended effects

REVISING YOUR WRITING

When you are reviewing the first draft of your writing, focus on the following areas.

1. The appropriateness and clarity of your controlling idea

2. The evidence provided to support your arguments

3. The clarity of the sentences, the effectiveness of your sentences, and your use of vocabulary

To better understand your own revision process, it is helpful to see how others revise and edit their work. The following writing is a student's first draft with revisions. Review the revisions the student has made and answer the questions that follow the passage.

Example Revisions

HATS ON[1] FOR TEENAGERS

Paragraph 1   "Colin, bathroom's yours," declares my mother. It's seven a.m. Monday

bellows

morning; school starts in an hour. "Colin, are you up?" my mother ~~asks~~

groggily

now. "Yes, yes, yes," I ~~slowly~~ reply. I am awake but in no mood to be torn away

from the warm comforts of my bed. I rise anyway. I run to the bathroom, turn on

5   the shower (hopefully she left me some hot water) and instinctively moved

under the warm stream. The shower is the highlight of my morning as it is

about as close to a warm bed as I'll get, and, without it, I would be half

asleep the rest of the day.

proceed

After my shower I dress, eat breakfast, and by about seven-thirty ~~go~~ upstairs

10   to brush my teeth and attempt to conquer my hair. Since grade eight my hair

has become gradually curlier. Armed with a blob of gel, I push my hands

presentable

up, down, across, and around my hair, attempting to give it a ~~good~~ look.

Unfortunately, six to seven days a week my hair does not cooperate; but I always

have a backup plan—my hat.

15   Wearing a hat may seem lazy or inconsiderate to some, but for me it is a

Paragraph 2

saviour. My hat saves me a lot of grief, embarassment, and time. Without it,

I feel as though everyone is looking at my hair and so I am constantly

touching it, feeling for any giant sproings of uncooperative curls. I know

that I shouldn't care what others think, but I am still concerned about my

20   appearance and image. My hat is my safety net; with it on I can walk down

the halls comfortably and in style. Relaxed, I show up for class on time—

ready to give my full attention to the teacher and feeling neat and in style.

Paragraph 3   There is a fairly large importance placed on the stylish hat in and out of

school. Not just any old hat is acceptable. There are five major kinds: the

25   baseball hat (a favourite); the NFL hat; the NBA hat; the college hat; and the

name brand hat. At the moment I have three hats: a Blue Jays hat (baseball), an Argonauts (football) hat, and a UCLA (college) hat. Some

NHL hockey team hats are acceptable. The kind of hat a person wears helps

them to make a personality statement. ~~The hat a person wears reveals~~

30 ~~his identity~~. The colour is important too; no fluorescent colours please!

Cost is somewhere from ten to forty dollars.

Paragraph 4 You're probably wondering—why not get a haircut for that price? I find

a hat a better investment. I can never count on getting a good haircut unless

I'm willing to pay thirty or forty dollars to a good stylist, whereas a hat is

35 always dependable. I have to get my hair cut once a month or I start to

resemble Kramer from *Seinfeld*. A hat can last for as long as I can put my

hands on it. Whenever someone finds out that I have naturally curly hair,

they always gawk and say, "Geez, I wish I had curly hair; you're so lucky."

It's not as great as it is made out to be. It's like trying to control a cat—no

40 matter what I say or do, it's going to do what it wants to. My hair

never looks the same at school as it did when I sculpted it at home in front of

the mirror. Sometimes I'm afraid to look in the mirror at school to see how

it turned out! In my case, a hat is a sensible alternative to poor and/or

expensive haircuts.

45
Paragraph 5

Another reason to wear a hat is for safety. During the summer wearing a

hat is not only comfortable but wise. With global warming and dangers of

skin cancer increasing, wearing a hat is a crucial part of protecting myself,

especially if I'm outside on the golf course in the middle of the day. I know

you're thinking that a hat is fine outside but not inside. Have you ever

50
seen what wearing a hat for a few hours can do to a hairstyle? Especially a

thick, curly head of hair? I do understand that at some point in my life I may

have an occupation that will force me to get a stylish haircut and go

hatless (unless I golf for a living). I also understand that there are certain

places where a hat is never acceptable, no matter what my hair looks like.

55
My grandparents constantly remind me of that. I do remove my hat when

necessary or when asked, but until the job comes or I can easily afford to pay

someone who can give me a good haircut, the hat will be the solution of

choice.

Paragraph 6
I do not consider myself lazy or rude for wearing a hat. I have more

60
important things to take care of than constantly doing my hair, such as

getting to school on time, earning honours and scholarships, wondering

where I'm going to go to university, spending time with my family and friends, working at my job and on top of that, finding time to relax. When

65   the hatless head becomes a more essential part of my life, I will somehow

change my hair or pay for more expensive haircuts, but until then, I won't

leave home without it—my hat, that is.

¹ Hats On – a word play on the phrase "hats off," which refers to the custom of gentlemen removing their hats as a gesture of respect or honour

EXAMPLE REVISIONS QUESTIONS

1. Paragraph 1 is developed **mainly** through the use of
    A. a definition
    B. an anecdote
    C. cause and effect
    D. comparison and contrast

2. The sentence "I run to the bathroom, turn on the shower (hopefully she left me some hot water) and instinctively moved under the warm stream" contains an error in
    A. tense
    B. context
    C. emphasis
    D. punctuation

3. The writer's revisions to Paragraph 1 result in vocabulary choices that are more
    A. concise
    B. familiar
    C. colloquial
    D. descriptive

4. The **main** function of Paragraph 2 is to
    A. create mood
    B. provide contrast
    C. amuse the reader
    D. expand the thesis

5. In Paragraph 3, the punctuation that should be used after the phrase "There are five major kinds" is a

   A. colon

   B. period

   C. comma

   D. semicolon

6. The sentence "The kind of hat a person wears helps them to make a personality statement" contains an error in

   A. tense

   B. spelling

   C. agreement

   D. punctuation

7. The writer's decision to delete a sentence in Paragraph 3 is appropriate because the sentence's

   A. tone is too informal

   B. content is redundant

   C. wording is awkward

   D. word count is too low

8. The writer has used a comma between the words "increasing" and "wearing" in the second line of Paragraph 5 in order to

   A. set off an appositive

   B. indicate coordination

   C. indicate items in a series

   D. set off an introductory phrase

9. The first sentence of Paragraph 5 has been included to provide

   A. humour

   B. contrast

   C. emphasis

   D. transition

10. Which of the following words did the writer fail to correct in the passage?

    A. Highlight

    B. Necessary

    C. Dependable

    D. Embarassment

11. The writer's purpose in writing this story is **most** likely to

    A. criticize a fad

    B. narrate an event

    C. persuade the reader

    D. describe a situation

SOLUTIONS TO REVISIONS QUESTIONS

1. B

The story about the narrator's morning routine is an anecdote to develop the introductory paragraph.

2. A

If a change in tense is not necessary, sentences should be written consistently using one tense. In this sentence, the narrator runs to the bathroom, in the present time, thus justifying the use of this tense for the verbs "to run" and "to turn on." Even though stepping into the shower happens last in the sequence of events, this action still requires the present tense of the verb because the other verbs are in the present tense as well, so "moved" should read move.

3. A

Each of the changes was made to either verbs (the action words) or adverbs (words that modify action words) to describe the writer's story with greater description. The word "bellows" is a more descriptive word to show how the narrator's mother was asking, "groggily" more precisely describes his sleepiness, "proceed" more accurately describes how he "goes," and "presentable" more precisely defines the way in which his hair should be "good."

4. D

When the writer concludes the introduction with "I always have a backup plan—my hat," he is stating his purpose, which, in this case, is to explain why his hat helps him on "bad hair days."

5. A

A colon is used to introduce lists. In this case, the list is of different kinds of hats. A period closes sentences, a comma separates clauses, and a semicolon separates longer phrases in a list.

6. C

The pronoun "them" is plural, but the noun it replaces, "person," is singular, so the two disagree in number. There is an error in agreement. The tenses are consistent in this sentence, and the sentence contains no spelling or punctuation errors.

7. **B**

Since this sentence is very similar in meaning to the one that precedes it: "The kind of hat a person wears helps them to make a personality statement," the content is redundant, or repetitive.

8. **D**

An appositive is a part of a sentence that parallels another with similar information and grammatical structure. Similarly, coordination and a series are not features of this sentence. Because the first clause of the sentence introduces the idea of the increasing dangers of cancer, the remaining parts of the sentence are separated with a comma.

9. **D**

Since the sentence begins with the phrase "Another reason to wear a hat," a transition is created from the reason cited in the previous paragraph and the one that is discussed in this paragraph.

10. **D**

The only mistake the writer has made is that of not including enough r's in the word "embarrassment."

11. **C**

The speaker tries to persuade the reader that wearing a hat is an appropriate way to handle his situation.

KEY Strategies for Success on Tests

KEY STRATEGIES FOR SUCCESS ON TESTS

AN OVERVIEW OF THE TEST

This section is all about the skills and strategies you need to be successful on the Alberta Provincial Diploma Examination. It is designed for you to use together with your classroom learning and assignments.

Finding Out About the Examination

Here are some questions you may wish to discuss with your teacher to help you prepare for the Alberta Provincial Diploma Examination:

1.	What is the purpose of the exam?	The purpose is to see how well you construct meaning, reflect on reading, and understand what you read. The test will focus on comprehension, variety of texts, and vocabulary.
2.	What do I need to know to do well on the assessment?	By the end of Grade 12 you are expected to actively make meaning by understanding explicitly stated information and ideas; understand implicitly stated information (make inferences) and respond to reading by making connections between text information and personal knowledge.
3.	What must I bring for the test?	You may bring a dictionary, a thesaurus, and a writing hand book for Part A. You must bring a pencil and an eraser for Part B.
4.	Will there be graphics?	Yes, diagrams, pictures, and illustrations.
5.	What kinds of questions are on the test?	There will be two parts. Part A will consist of a writing assignment and Part B will have 70 multiple-choice questions.
6.	How important is this edam to my final grade?	This examination is worth 50% of your final Grade 12 mark.

Having a good understanding of effective test taking skills can help your performance on the exam. Being familiar with the question format may help you in preparing for quizzes, unit tests or year-end assessments.

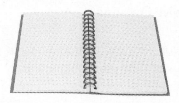

TEST PREPARATION AND TEST-TAKING SKILLS

Things to Consider When Taking a Test

- It is normal to feel anxious before you write a test. You can manage this anxiety by
    - thinking positive thoughts. Visual imagery is a helpful technique to try.
    - making a conscious effort to relax by taking several slow, controlled, deep breaths. Concentrate on the air going in and out of the body.
- Before you begin the test, ask questions if you are unsure of anything.
- Jot down key words or phrases from any oral directions.
- Look over the entire test to assess the number and kinds of questions on the test.
- Read each question closely and reread if necessary.
- Pay close attention to key vocabulary words. Sometimes, these are bolded or italicized, and they are usually important words in the question.
- Mark your answers on your answer sheet carefully. If you wish to change an answer, erase the mark and then ensure that your final answer is darker than the one that you have erased.
- On the test booklet, use highlighting to note directions, key words and vocabulary that you find confusing or that are important to answering the question.
- Double-**check** to make sure you have answered everything before handing in your test.

When taking tests, some words are often overlooked. Failure to pay close attention to these words can result in an incorrect answer. One way to avoid this is to be aware of these words and to <u>underline,</u> circle or **highlight** these words while you are taking the test.

Even though these words are easy, they can change the meaning of the entire question and/or answer.

all	always	most likely	probably	best	not
difference	usually	except	most	unlikely	likely

Example

1. During the race, Susan is **most likely** feeling

   A. sad

   B. weak

   C. scared

   D. determined

Helpful Strategies for Answering Multiple-Choice Questions

A multiple-choice question provides some information for you to consider and then asks you to select a response from four choices. There will be one correct answer. The other answers are distractors, which are incorrect.

Here are some strategies to help you when answering multiple-choice questions.

- Quickly skim through the entire test. Find out how many questions there are and plan your time accordingly.

- Read and reread questions carefully. Underline key words and try to think of an answer before looking at the choices.

- If there is a graphic, look at the graphic, read the question, and go back to the graphic. Then, you may want to circle the important information from the question.

- Carefully read the choices. Read the question first and then each answer with it.

- When choosing an answer, try to eliminate those choices that are clearly wrong or do not make sense.

- Some questions may ask you to select the "best" answer. These questions will always include words like best, most strongly, and most clearly. All of the answers will be correct to some degree, but one of the choices will be "best" in some way. Carefully read all four choices (A, B, C, D) before choosing the answer you think is the best.

- If you do not know the answer or if the question does not make sense to you, it is better to guess than to leave it blank.

- Do not spend too much time on any one question. Make a mark (*) beside a difficult question and come back to it. If you are leaving a question to come back to later, make sure that you also leave the space on the answer sheet.

- Remember to go back to the difficult questions at the end of the test; sometimes clues are given throughout the test that will provide you with answers.

- Note any negative (e.g., no, not) and be sure your choice fits the question.

- Before changing an answer, be sure you have a very good reason to do so.

- Do not look for patterns on your answer sheet.

Helpful Strategies for Answering Open-Response Questions

A written response requires you to respond to a question or directive such as **explain, predict, list, describe, use information from the text and your own ideas; provide the main idea and supporting details.** In preparing for open-response tasks you may wish to:

- Read and re-read the question carefully.

- Recognize and pay close attention to directing words such as explain, predict, and describe.

- Underline key words and phrases that indicate what is required in your answer such as explain, summarize, mainly about, what is the meaning of, best shows…

- Write down rough, point-form notes regarding the information you want to include in your answer.

- Think about what you want to say and organize information and ideas in a coherent and concise manner within the time limit you have for the question.

- Be sure to answer every part of the question that is asked.

- Stick to the question, be brief and only answer what is asked.

- Answer in full and correctly written sentences keeping your answer within the space provided.

- Re-read your response to ensure you have answered the question.

- Think! Does your answer make sense

- Listen! Does it sound right?

- Use the appropriate subject vocabulary and terminology in your response.

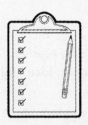

TEST PREPARATION COUNTDOWN

There is little doubt that if you develop a plan for studying and test preparation, you **will** perform well on tests.

Here is a general plan to follow seven days before you write a test.

Countdown: 7 Days before the Test

1. Use "Finding Out About the Test" to help you make your own personal test preparation plan.

2. Review the following information:
     - areas to be included on the test
     - types of test items
     - general and specific test tips

3. Start preparing for the test at least 7 days before the test. Develop your test preparation plan and set time aside to prepare and study.

Countdown: 6, 5, 4, 3, 2 Days before the Test

1. Review old homework assignments, quizzes, and tests.

2. Rework problems on quizzes and tests to make sure you still know how to solve them.

3. Correct any errors made on quizzes and tests.

4. Review key concepts, processes, formulas, and vocabulary.

5. Create practice test questions for yourself and then answer them. Work out many sample problems.

Countdown: The Night before the Test

1. The night before the test is for final preparation, which includes reviewing and gathering material needed for the test before going to bed.

2. Most important is getting a good night's rest and knowing you have done everything possible to do well on the test.

Test Day

1. Eat a healthy and nutritious breakfast.

2. Ensure you have all the necessary materials.

3. Think positive thoughts: "I can do this." "I am ready." "I know I can do well."

4. Arrive at your school early so you are not rushing, which can cause you anxiety and stress.

SUMMARY OF HOW TO BE SUCCESSFUL DURING THE TEST

The following are some strategies that you may find useful in writing your test.

- Take 2 or 3 deep breaths to help you relax.

- Read the directions carefully and underline, circle, or highlight any KEY words.

- Survey the entire test to get a flavour of what you will need to do.

- Budget your time.

- Begin with an easy question or a question that you know that you can answer correctly rather than following the numerical question order of the test.

- If you "draw a blank" on the test, try repeating the deep breathing and physical relaxation activities first. Then, move to visualization and positive self-talk to get you going.

- Write down anything that you remember about the subject on the reverse side of your test paper. This activity sometimes helps you to remind yourself that you do know something and you are capable of writing the test.

- Look over your test when you have finished and double-check your answers to be sure you did not forget anything.

NOTES

A GUIDE TO WRITING THE DIPLOMA EXAMINATION

The Diploma Examination section contains all of the questions from the June 1998 and January 2004 diploma examinations.   It is recommended that students work carefully through these exams as they are reflective of the format and difficulty level of the final exam that students are likely to encounter.

THE KEY contains detailed answers that illustrate the problem-solving process for every question in this section.

When writing practice exams, students are encouraged to simulate actual Diploma Exam conditions. This will help students become:
- *aware of the mental and physical stamina required to sit through an entire exam*
- *familiar with the exam format and how the course content is tested*
- *aware of any units or concepts that are troublesome or require additional study*
- *more successful in managing their review effectively*

To simulate the exam conditions, students should:
- *use an alarm clock or other timer to monitor the time allowed for the exam*
- *select a quiet writing spot away from all distractions*
- *place their picture ID on the desk or table where the exam is being written*
- *assemble the appropriate materials that are allowed for writing the exam such as pens, HB pencils, calculator, dictionary*
- *use "test wiseness" skills*
- *complete as much of the exam as possible within the allowable time*

In writing the practice exam, students should:
- *read instructions, directions, and questions carefully*
- *organize writing time according to the exam emphasis on each section*
- *highlight key words*
- *think about what is being asked*
- *plan their writing; once complete, proof for errors in content, spelling, grammar*
- *watch for bolded words such as most, least, best*
- *in multiple-choice questions, cross out any choices students know are incorrect*
- *if possible, review all responses upon completion of the exam*

Diploma Examinations

DIPLOMA EXAMINATIONS

TABLE OF CORRELATIONS

Specific Expectation	June 1998	January 2004
2.1.1a explain the text creator's purpose, including implicit purpose when applicable; describe whether or not the purpose was achieved	18	31, 33
2.1.1b analyze elements or causes present in the communication situation surrounding a text that contribute to the creation of the text	13, 17, 54, 60	5, 8, 34, 47, 49, 70
2.1.1c explain how understanding the interplay between text and context can influence on audience to appreciate a text from multiple perspectives	26, 48	
2.1.1d identify the impact that personal context -experience, prior knowledge – has on constructing meaning from a text	14, 43	
2.1.2a use a variety of strategies to comprehend literature and other texts, and develop strategies for close reading of literature in order to understand contextual elements	3, 6.8, 32, 33, 43, 47, 48, 54, 55, 57	12, 17, 18, 20, 33, 41, 47, 56, 61,
2.1.2b analyze the relationships among controlling ideas, supporting ideas and supporting details in a variety of texts	1, 5, 26, 28, 30, 34, 38, 52, 70	65
2.1.2c assess the contributions of setting, plot, character, and atmosphere to the development of theme when studying a narrative	45, 61, 62, 63, 65	9, 19, 25, 26, 31, 32, 34, 44, 45, 54, 61,
2.1.2d analyze the personality traits, roles, relationships, motivations, attitudes and values of characters developed/persons represented in literature and other texts; and explain how the use of archetypes can contribute to the development of other textual elements, such as theme	2, 7, 9, 11, 15, 16, 20, 21, 25, 37, 42, 49	70
2.1.2e relate a text creator's tone and register to the moral and ethical stance explicitly or implicitly communicated by a text	12, 50	22, 28, 42, 53, 64
2.1.2f assess the contributions of figurative language, symbol, imagery and allusion to the meaning and significance of texts; and appreciate the text creator's craft	4, 39, 50, 51, 53, 66	16, 27, 28, 37, 38, 39, 40, 43, 56, 69
2.1.2g assess the contributions that visual and aural elements make to the meaning of texts	56	23, 46, 48, 49, 50
2.1.3a reflect on and describe strategies used to engage prior knowledge as a means of assisting comprehension of new texts; and select, monitor and modify strategies as needed	55, 58	6, 14, 21, 23, 30, 35
2.2.1a analyze a variety of text forms, explain the relationship of form to purpose and content, and assess the effects of these relationships on audience	27, 31	3, 15, 54
2.2.1c apply knowledge of organizational patterns and structural features to understand purpose and content, and assess the effectiveness of a text's organizational structure		17, 29, 63
2.2.2a assess the contributions of rhetorical devices and stylistic techniques to the clarity and coherence of print and non-print texts, and assess the various means by which devices and techniques are used to emphasize aspects or portions of a text	4, 18, 19, 27, 31, 66	1, 58
2.2.2b assess the contributions of textual elements and stylistic techniques to the creation of atmosphere, tone and voice	31, 53, 61, 65, 67	4, 7, 13, 50, 66
2.2.2c analyze the use of irony and satire to create effects in print and non-print texts	10	18, 60, 67

2.2.2d	analyze the use of irony analyze the use f irony assess the use of musical devices, figures of speech and sensory details to create effects in a variety of print and nonprint texts	39	
2.2.2e	explain the contribution of motif and symbol to controlling idea and theme	50, 51, 59, 68	3, 6, 10, 14, 15, 21, 24, 52
2.3.1a	identify and consider personal, moral, ethical and cultural perspectives when studying literature and other texts; and reflect on and monitor how perspectives change as a result of interpretation and discussion	29, 34, 35, 44	11, 46
2.3.1c	assess the choices and motives of characters and people portrayed in texts in light of the choices and motives of self and others	7, 36, 37	4, 55, 57
2.3.1d	respond personally and critically to the ways in which cultural and societal influences are reflected in a variety of Canadian and international texts	41, 43	
2.3.2b	assess the appropriateness of own and others' understandings and interpretations of works of literature and other texts, by referring to the works and texts for supporting or contradictory evidence		19
2.3.2d	analyze and assess character and characterization in terms of consistency of behaviour, motivation and plausibility, and in terms of contribution to theme	2, 12, 14, 16, 20, 22, 24, 36, 40, 46, 49, 62, 69	16, 25, 37, 38, 59, 60, 68
2.3.2e	analyze and assess images in print and nonprint texts in terms of created reality and appropriateness to purpose and audience		46, 52
2.3.2f	assess the significance of a text's theme or controlling idea, and the adequacy, relevance and effectiveness of its supporting details, examples or illustrations, and content in general	6, 13, 28, 29, 34, 44, 52, 67, 70	11, 20, 32, 44, 51, 52
2.3.3a	use terminology appropriate to the forms studied for discussing and appreciating the effectiveness and artistry of a variety of text forms		58
2.3.3b	appreciate the craft of the text creator and the shape and substance of literature and other texts	11, 19	54

JUNE 1998 DIPLOMA EXAMINATION

I. Questions 1 to 8 are based on this poem.

FOR THE LOST ADOLESCENT

Even before he left for good I heard things in the fire,

heard fundamental moaning,

wind like a shoulder splintering a door.

I'd say, *Come here*, but he was lost to me.

5   I'd say, *Beloved, bring more wood up from the yard.*

But he was lost to me,

locked inside his name, the name itself

too big a house, or simply wilderness I only glimpsed sometimes

And true, those days, looking out of my own eyes

10   I felt some former host behind me,

some bedrock stare, antediluvian, unchanging.

And he was horrified to see me watching

something like birds in the fire,

not their song but a scratching among rubble.

15   Something like rain then surely rain

if I shut my eyes.

Another year, another child,

this might have been the subject—

always penultimate,[1] some claim for the beautiful,

20   the conditions of the lie gone up with goodness, all the same,

log after log, fire after fire, praise beyond pretense

for so primitive a thing, that first warmth

ransomed, a captive

of our need amid the ruin of a modern city!

25   And if I never recognized his voice inside me,

who could know?

A mother learns a code of sounds not yet a voice

and feels her way inside that heat

and then there's the holding while the world heals

30 or does not heal.

Life's long with and without him

where children passing on their way to school

no longer walk into his body.

As for their laughter, it's like the laughter in a dream

35 to which the sleeper barely smiles.

Deborah Digges – American poet/educator

¹ penultimate—second from the last

1. Lines 1 to 3 convey the mother's feeling that her son's leaving was
   A. provoked
   B. accidental
   C. unexpected
   D. foreseeable

2. In context, the phrase "locked inside his name" (line 7) suggests **mainly** that the son is
   A. resistant to change
   B. restrained by expectations
   C. inclined to dominate others
   D. cherished by an overeager family

3. In the context of lines 6 to 11, "antediluvian" means
   A. watery
   B. age-old
   C. mercurial
   D. suspicious

4. That an image of rain (lines 15 to 16) briefly replaces the imagery of fire points to a sense of
   A. reprieve
   B. rebellion
   C. celebration
   D. indifference

5. Lines 17 to 24 suggest **most clearly** that "so primitive a thing" is our

   A. anger

   B. natural environment

   C. struggle to create a life of ease

   D. instinctive desire to have children

6. In the context of lines 17 to 24, the image in "a captive/of our need amid the ruin of a modern city!" reinforces the idea that

   A. urban life is doomed to extinction

   B. disadvantaged adolescents thrive on adversity

   C. children become victims of their parents' longings

   D. parents seek to provide shelter for their children

7. In the context of lines 25 to 30, the line "and then there's the holding while the world heals or does not heal" serve to convey

   A. the inclination of mothers to create conflict

   B. a mother's passive role of patience and hope

   C. a mother's happiness in hearing her offspring learn to talk

   D. the uncertainty that causes mothers to reject their surroundings

8. The central focus of lines 25 to 35 is the speaker's

   A. refusal to accept the desires of the young

   B. acceptance of a mother's role in raising a child

   C. knowledge that a conflict is forthcoming

   D. need to accept blame for her son's leaving

II. Questions 9 to 16 are based on this excerpt from a novel.

from A RIVER RUNS THROUGH IT

In our family, there was no clear line between religion and fly fishing. We lived at the junction of great trout rivers in western Montana, and our father was a Presbyterian minister and a fly fisherman who tied his own flies and taught others. He told us about Christ's disciples being fishermen, and we were left to assume, as my brother and I did, that all first-class fishermen on the Sea of Galilee were fly fishermen and that John, the
5   favorite, was a dry-fly fisherman.

It is true that one day a week was given over wholly to religion. On Sunday mornings my brother, Paul, and I went to Sunday school and then to "morning services" to hear our father preach and in the evenings to Christian Endeavor and afterwards to "evening services" to hear our father preach again. In between on Sunday afternoons we had to
10 study *The Westminster Shorter Catechism*[1] for an hour and then recite before we could walk the hills with him while he unwound between services. But he never asked us more than the first question in the catechism, "What is the chief end of man?" And we answered together so one of us could carry on if the other forgot, "Man's chief end is to glorify God, and to enjoy Him forever." This always seemed to satisfy him, as indeed such a beautiful
15 answer should have, and besides he was anxious to be on the hills where he could restore his soul and be filled again to overflowing for the evening sermon. His chief way of recharging himself was to recite to us from the sermon that was coming, enriched here and there with selections from the most successful passages of his morning sermon.

Even so, in a typical week of our childhood Paul and I probably received as many hours of instruction in fly fishing as we did in all other spiritual matters.

20 After my brother and I became good fishermen, we realized that our father was not a great fly caster, but he was accurate and stylish and wore a glove on his casting hand. As he buttoned his glove in preparation to give us a lesson, he would say, "It is an art that is performed on a four-count rhythm between ten and two o'clock."

As a Scot and a Presbyterian, my father believed that man by nature was a mess and had
25 fallen from an original state of grace.[2] Somehow, I early developed the notion that he had done this by falling from a tree. As for my father, I never knew whether he believed God was a mathematician but he certainly believed God could count and that only by picking up God's rhythms were we able to regain power and beauty. Unlike many Presbyterians, he often used the word "beautiful."

30 After he buttoned his glove, he would hold his rod straight out in front of him, where it trembled with the beating of his heart. Although it was eight and a half feet long, it weighed only four and a half ounces. It was made of split bamboo cane from the far-off Bay of Tonkin. It was wrapped with red and blue silk thread, and the wrappings were carefully spaced to make the delicate rod powerful but not so stiff it could not tremble.

35 Always it was to be called a rod. If someone called it a pole, my father looked at him as a sergeant in the United States Marines would look at a recruit who had just called a rifle a gun.

My brother and I would have preferred to start learning how to fish by going out and
catching a few, omitting entirely anything difficult or technical in the way of preparation
40 that would take away from the fun. But it wasn't by way of fun that we were introduced
to our father's art. If our father had had his say, nobody who did not know how to fish
would be allowed to disgrace a fish by catching him. So you too will have to approach the
art Marine- and Presbyterian-style, and, if you have never picked up a fly rod before, you
will soon find it factually and theologically true that man by nature is a damn mess. The
45 four-and-a-half-ounce thing in silk wrappings that trembles with the underskin motions of
the flesh becomes a stick without brains, refusing anything simple that is wanted of it. All
that a rod has to do is lift the line, the leader, and the fly off the water, give them a good
toss over the head, and then shoot them forward so they will land in the water without a
splash in the following order: fly, transparent leader, and then the line—otherwise the fish
50 will see the fly is a fake and be gone. Of course, there are special casts[3] that anyone could
predict would be difficult, and they require artistry—casts where the line can't go over
the fisherman's head because cliffs or trees are immediately behind, sideways casts to get
the fly under overhanging willows, and so on. But what's remarkable about just a straight
cast—just picking up a rod with line on it and tossing the line across the river?

Well, until man is redeemed[4] he will always take a fly rod too far back, just as natural man
55 always overswings with an ax or golf club and loses all his power somewhere in the air;
only with a rod it's worse, because the fly often comes so far back it gets caught behind
in a bush or rock. When my father said it was an art that ended at two o'clock, he often
added, "closer to twelve than to two," meaning that the rod should be taken back only
slightly farther than overhead (straight overhead being twelve o'clock).

Then, since it is natural for man to try to attain power without recovering grace, he whips
60 the line back and forth making it whistle each way, and sometimes even snapping off the
fly from the leader, but the power that was going to transport the little fly across the river
somehow gets diverted into building a bird's nest of line, leader, and fly that falls out of the
air into the water about ten feet in front of the fisherman. If, though, he pictures the round
trip of the line, transparent leader, and fly from the time they leave the water until their
65 return, they are easier to cast. They naturally come off the water heavy line first and in
front, and light transparent leader and fly trailing behind. But, as they pass overhead, they
have to have a little beat of time so the light, transparent leader and fly can catch up to the
heavy line now starting forward and again fall behind it; otherwise, the line starting on its
return trip will collide with the leader and fly still on their way up, and the mess will be
70 the bird's nest that splashes into the water ten feet in front of the fisherman.

Almost the moment, however, that the forward order of line, leader, and fly is
reestablished, it has to be reversed, because the fly and transparent leader must be ahead
of the heavy line when they settle on the water. If what the fish sees is highly visible line,
what the fisherman will see are departing black darts, and he might as well start for the
75 next hole. High overhead, then, on the forward cast (at about ten o'clock) the fisherman
checks again.

The four-count rhythm, of course, is functional. The one count takes the line, leader, and
fly off the water; the two count tosses them seemingly straight into the sky; the three count

80 was my father's way of saying that at the top the leader and fly have to be given a little beat of time to get behind the line as it is starting forward; the four count means put on the power and throw the line into the rod until you reach ten o'clock—then check-cast, let the fly and leader get ahead of the line, and coast to a soft and perfect landing. Power comes not from power everywhere, but from knowing where to put it on. "Remember," as my father kept saying, "it is an art that is performed on a four-count rhythm between ten and two o'clock."

85 My father was very sure about certain matters pertaining to the universe. To him, all good things—trout as well as eternal salvation—come by grace and grace comes by art and art does not come easy.

So my brother and I learned to cast Presbyterian-style, on a metronome.[5] It was mother's metronome, which father had taken from the top of the piano in town. She would

90 occasionally peer down to the dock from the front porch of the cabin, wondering nervously whether her metronome could float if it had to. When she became so overwrought that she thumped down the dock to reclaim it, my father would clap out the four-count rhythm with his cupped hands.

Norman Maclean – American writer

[1] Catechism—a book of religious instruction in the form of question and answer

[2] state of grace—a state of favour with God; free from sin

[3] casts—the throwing out of a fly or artificial bait at the end of a fishing line

[4] redeemed—rescued, saved, liberated by virtue of performance; often used in the sense of spiritual salvation

[5] metronome—a clockwork device with a pendulum that beats time; used especially for practising piano

9. Lines 6 to 17 suggest **most clearly** that father and sons approached Sunday afternoons with attitudes of

A. apathy and resignation

B. solemnity and resolution

C. dutifulness and anticipation

D. dismay and apprehension

10. The tone of the narrator's comment "This always seemed to satisfy him, as indeed such a beautiful answer should have, and besides he was anxious to be on the hills" (lines 13 to 14) can be described as

A. respectful

B. derogatory

C. gently ironic

D. slightly pompous

11. The narrator's point of view as a child is emphasized by repetition in the phrases

   A. "the sermon that was coming" (line 16) and "the most successful passages of his morning sermon." (line 17)

   B. "had fallen from an original state of grace" (lines 24 to 25) and "by falling from a tree" (lines 25 to 26)

   C. "man by nature was a mess" (line 24) and "man by nature is a damn mess" (lines 41 to 42)

   D. "it trembled with the beating of his heart" (lines 29 to 30) and "not so stiff it could not tremble" (line 33)

12. The narrator's observation "Unlike many Presbyterians, he often used the word 'beautiful'" (line 28) suggests that, in the narrator's view, Presbyterians are characteristically

   A. austere

   B. optimistic

   C. appreciative

   D. hypocritical

13. The seriousness with which the father regards mastery of the art of fly fishing is most emphatically conveyed by the statement

   A. "He told us about Christ's disciples being fishermen" (line 3)

   B. "If someone called it a pole, my father looked at him as a sergeant in the United States Marines would look at a recruit who had just called a rifle a gun" (lines 34 to 35)

   C. "If our father had had his say, nobody who did not know how to fish would be allowed to disgrace a fish by catching him" (lines 38 to 40)

   D. " 'it is an art that is performed on a four-count rhythm between ten and two o'clock' " (lines 80 to 81)

14. The contrast between the attitude of the father toward fly fishing and the attitudes of his young sons toward fly fishing is best revealed in the statement

   A. "we were left to assume, as my brother and I did, that all first-class fishermen on the Sea of Galilee were fly fishermen and that John, the favorite, was a dry-fly fisherman" (lines 4 to 5)

   B. "After my brother and I became good fishermen, we realized that our father was not a great fly caster, but he was accurate and stylish and wore a glove on his casting hand" (lines 20 to 21)

   C. "My brother and I would have preferred to start learning how to fish by going out and catching a few, omitting entirely anything difficult or technical in the way of preparation that would take away from the fun" (lines 36 to 38)

   D. "So my brother and I learned to cast Presbyterian-style, on a metronome" (line 85)

15. The father's dedication to the principle of " 'a four-count rhythm between ten and two o'clock' " (lines 80 to 81) suggests mainly his

A. Christian leadership

B. methodical approach

C. knowledge of sportsmanship

D. inclination to be competitive

16. In this retrospective account of his father's combined roles of father, minister, and fly fisherman, the narrator conveys an attitude of

A. affectionate regard

B. anxious self-doubt

C. criticism

D. cynicism

III. Questions 17 to 26 are based on this excerpt from a play.

from THE MATCHMAKER

CHARACTERS:

MR. VANDERGELDER—wealthy merchant of Yonkers, New York

ERMENGARDE—his niece

AMBROSE KEMPER—an artist

MRS. DOLLY LEVI—friend of Ermengarde's mother

Scene: **VANDERGELDER** house in Yonkers, New York

Time: early 1880s

ERMENGARDE *has consented to marry* **AMBROSE KEMPER***, but* **MR. VANDERGELDER***, because of what he sees as* **AMBROSE***'s deplorable lack of prospects, has furiously forbidden the marriage.* **MR. VANDERGELDER** *is sending* **ERMENGARDE** *away to "get the romance out of her head."*

As this scene opens, **VANDERGELDER** *addresses the audience.*

> **VANDERGELDER**: Ninety-nine per cent of the people in the world are fools and the rest of us are in great danger of contagion. But I wasn't always free of foolishness as I am now. I was once young, which was foolish; I fell in love, which was foolish; and I got married, which was foolish; and for a while I was poor, which was more foolish than all the other
> 5 things put together. Then my wife died, which was foolish of her; I grew older, which was sensible of me; then I became a rich man, which is as sensible as it is rare. Since you see I'm a man of sense, I guess you were surprised to hear that I'm planning to get married again. Well, I've two reasons for it. In the first place, I like my house run with order, comfort, and economy. That's a woman's work; but even a woman can't do it well if she's
> 10 merely being paid for it. In order to run a house well, a woman must have the feeling that

she owns it. Marriage is a bribe to make a housekeeper think she's a householder. Did you ever watch an ant carry a burden twice its size? What excitement! What patience! What will! Well, that's what I think of when I see a woman running a house. What giant passions in those little bodies—what quarrels with the butcher for the best cut—what fury

15 at discovering a moth in a cupboard! Believe me!—if women could harness their natures to something bigger than a house and a baby carriage—tck! tck!—they'd change the world. And the second reason, ladies and gentlemen? Well, I see by your faces you've guessed it already. There's nothing like mixing with women to bring out all the foolishness in a man of sense. And that's a risk I'm willing to take. I've just turned sixty, and I've just

20 laid side by side the last dollar of my first half million. So if I should lose my head a little, I still have enough money to buy it back. After many years' caution and hard work, I have earned a right to a little risk and adventure, and I'm thinking of getting married. Yes, like all you other fools, I'm willing to risk a little security for a certain amount of adventure. Think it over. (*Exit back center. AMBROSE enters from the street, crosses left, and*

25 *whistles softly. ERMENGARDE enters from left.*)

ERMENGARDE: Ambrose! If my uncle saw you!

AMBROSE: Sh! Get your hat.

ERMENGARDE: My hat!

AMBROSE: Quick! Your trunk's at the station. Now quick! We're running away.

30 **ERMENGARDE**: Running away!

AMBROSE: Sh!

ERMENGARDE: Where?

AMBROSE: To New York. To get married.

ERMENGARDE: Oh, Ambrose, I can't do that. Ambrose dear—it wouldn't be proper!

35 **AMBROSE**: Listen. I'm taking you to my friend's house. His wife will take care of you.

ERMENGARDE: But, Ambrose, a girl can't go on a train with a man. I can see you don't know anything about girls.

AMBROSE: But I'm telling you we're going to get married!

ERMENGARDE: Married? But what would Uncle say?

40 **AMBROSE**: We don't care what Uncle'd say—we're eloping.

ERMENGARDE: Ambrose Kemper! How can you use such an awful word!

AMBROSE: Ermengarde, you have the soul of a field mouse.

ERMENGARDE (*Crying*): Ambrose, why do you say such cruel things to me? (*Enter MRS. LEVI, from the street, right. She stands listening.*)

45 **AMBROSE**: For the last time I beg you—get your hat and coat. The train leaves in a few minutes. Ermengarde, we'll get married tomorrow …

ERMENGARDE: Oh, Ambrose! I see you don't understand anything about weddings. Ambrose, don't you respect me? …

50 **MRS. LEVI** (*Uncertain age; mass of sandy hair; impoverished elegance; large, shrewd but generous nature, an assumption of worldly cynicism conceals a tireless amused enjoyment of life. She carries a handbag and a small brown paper bag*): Good morning, darling girl—how are you? (*They kiss.*)

ERMENGARDE: Oh, good morning, Mrs. Levi.

MRS. LEVI: And who is this gentleman who is so devoted to you?

55 **ERMENGARDE**: This is Mr. Kemper, Mrs. Levi. Ambrose, this is … Mrs. Levi … she's an old friend…

MRS. LEVI: Mrs. Levi, born Gallagher. Very happy to meet you, Mr. Kemper.

AMBROSE: Good morning, Mrs. Levi.

MRS. LEVI: Mr. Kemper, the artist! Delighted! Mr. Kemper, may I say something very
60 frankly?

AMBROSE: Yes, Mrs. Levi.

MRS. LEVI: This thing you were planning to do is a very great mistake.

ERMENGARDE: Oh, Mrs. Levi, please explain to Ambrose—of course! I want to marry him, but to elope! … How …

65 **MRS. LEVI**: Now, my dear girl, you go in and keep one eye on your uncle. I wish to talk to Mr. Kemper for a moment. You give us a warning when you hear your Uncle Horace coming. …

ERMENGARDE: Ye-es, Mrs. Levi. (*Exit ERMENGARDE back center.*)

MRS. LEVI: Mr. Kemper, I was this dear girl's mother's oldest friend. Believe me, I am
70 on your side. I hope you two will be married very soon, and I think I can be of real service to you. Mr. Kemper, I always go right to the point.

AMBROSE: What is the point, Mrs. Levi?

MRS. LEVI: Mr. Vandergelder is a very rich man, Mr. Kemper, and Ermengarde is his only relative.

75 **AMBROSE**: But I am not interested in Mr. Vandergelder's money. I have enough to support a wife and family.

MRS. LEVI: Enough? How much is enough when one is thinking about children, and the future? The future is the most expensive luxury in the world, Mr. Kemper.

AMBROSE: Mrs. Levi, what is the point?

80 **MRS. LEVI**: Believe me, Mr. Vandergelder wishes to get rid of Ermengarde, and if you follow my suggestions he will even permit her to marry you. You see, Mr. Vandergelder is planning to get married himself.

AMBROSE: What? That monster!

MRS. LEVI: Mr. Kemper!

85   **AMBROSE**: Married! To you, Mrs. Levi?

MRS. LEVI (*Taken aback*): Oh, no, no … No! I am merely arranging it. I am helping him find a suitable bride.

AMBROSE: For Mr. Vandergelder there are no suitable brides.

90   **MRS. LEVI**: I think we can safely say that Mr. Vandergelder will be married to someone by the end of next week.

AMBROSE: What are you suggesting, Mrs. Levi?

MRS. LEVI: I am taking Ermengarde to New York on the next train. I shall not take her to Miss Van Huysen's, as is planned; I shall take her to my house. I wish you to call for her at my house at five-thirty. Here is my card.

95   **AMBROSE**: "Mrs. Dolly Gallagher Levi. Varicose veins reduced."

MRS. LEVI (*Trying to take back card*): I beg your pardon… .

AMBROSE (*Holding card*): I beg your pardon. "Consultations free."

MRS. LEVI: I meant to give you my other card. Here.

100   **AMBROSE**: "Mrs. Dolly Gallagher Levi. Aurora Hosiery. Instruction in the guitar and mandolin." You do all these things, Mrs. Levi?

MRS. LEVI: Two and two make four, Mr. Kemper—always did. So you will come to my house at five-thirty. At about six I shall take you both with me to the Harmonia Gardens Restaurant on the Battery; Mr. Vandergelder will be there and everything will be arranged.

AMBROSE: How?

105   **MRS. LEVI**: Oh, I don't know. One thing will lead to another.

AMBROSE: How do I know that I can trust you, Mrs. Levi? You could easily make our situation worse.

MRS. LEVI: Mr. Kemper, your situation could not possibly be worse.

AMBROSE: I wish I knew what you get out of this, Mrs. Levi.

110   **MRS. LEVI**: That is a very proper question. I get two things: profit and pleasure.

AMBROSE: How?

MRS. LEVI: Mr. Kemper, I am a woman who arranges things. At present I am arranging Mr. Vandergelder's domestic affairs. Out of it I get—shall we call it: little pickings? I need little pickings, Mr. Kemper, and especially just now, when I haven't got my train fare 115 back to New York. You see: I am frank with you.

AMBROSE: That's your profit, Mrs. Levi; but where do you get your pleasure?

| 120 | **MRS. LEVI**: My pleasure? Mr. Kemper, when you artists paint a hillside or a river you change everything a little, you make thousands of little changes, don't you? Nature is never completely satisfactory and must be corrected. Well, I'm like you artists. Life as it is is never quite interesting enough for me—I'm bored, Mr. Kemper, with life as it is—and so I do things. I put my hand in here, and I put my hand in there, and I watch and I listen— and often I'm very much amused. |

Thornton Wilder – 20th century American playwright

17. In lines 1 to 2, Vandergelder declares the infectious nature of

    A. fear

    B. folly

    C. prestige

    D. perfection

18. The **main** effect of Vandergelder's address to the audience (lines 1 to 21) is to

    A. ridicule marriage

    B. elicit respect for wealth

    C. humorously introduce the theme

    D. establish his intellectual superiority

19. The repeated use of "what" to begin the exclamatory statements in line 11 serves **mainly** to

    A. convey Vandergelder's respect for women

    B. reinforce Vandergelder's condescending admiration

    C. develop Vandergelder's argument that "Marriage is a bribe" (line 9)

    D. emphasize Vandergelder's fascination with ants (line 10)

20. Ermengarde's objections to the idea of elopement are based on her

    A. practical common sense

    B. regard for her uncle's plans

    C. hopes for an elaborate wedding

    D. conventional sense of propriety

21. Ambrose's comment "Ermengarde, you have the soul of a field mouse" (line 40) is an expression of his

    A. fearful sympathy

    B. disguised contempt

    C. shocked indignation

    D. affectionate exasperation

22. Mrs. Levi's observation "The future is the most expensive luxury in the world, Mr. Kemper" (line 74) reflects her

    A. practical nature

    B. pessimistic nature

    C. pretentious behaviour

    D. predictable behaviour

23. The dramatic purpose of Mrs. Levi's cards (lines 90 to 96) is to

    A. justify Ambrose's fear of her

    B. emphasize her resourcefulness

    C. confirm the credibility of her expertise

    D. clarify her association with the Vandergelders

24. Mrs. Levi's comparison of herself to artists (lines 115 to 116) serves to convey that she

    A. is a lover of nature

    B. is undervalued by society

    C. considers herself a professional

    D. tries to improve on things as she sees them

25. The humour of the contrast drawn between Ambrose and Mrs. Levi arises from the contrast between

    A. his doubt and her assurance

    B. his realism and her idealism

    C. his integrity and her cynicism

    D. his worldliness and her naiveté

26. Mrs. Levi's role in this scene is best described in

    A. "I can be of real service to you" (line 66)

    B. "I am a woman who arranges things" (line 108)

    C. "I need little pickings" (lines 109 to 110)

    D. "I'm very much amused" (line 117)

IV. *Questions 27 to 35 are based on this excerpt from an article published in 1989.*

from THE HARD LIFE

Why is life in Japan so hard? I don't mean hard for me, with my battered dollars, but hard for the Japanese, who have supposedly won the world's economic wars. Japan, as everyone knows, now has the highest per capita income of any country, apart from, perhaps, a couple of oil baronies. Yet few Europeans or North Americans would willingly
5   trade places in daily life with the average Japanese, whose living conditions are cramped, working hours are long, and material rewards and chances for recreation are slight compared with those in the rest of the industrialized world. One friend from New York, on his first visit to Japan, walked through our neighborhood in Yokohama on a sunny day and saw laundry flapping from every window and porch. "You mean no one has dryers?"
10   he asked. "This is how I expected Seoul to look." Japan now has enough money to do anything it wants. Why do rich people keep living this way?

The answer to this question is crucial, because it essentially determines whether the world's trade battles with Japan will ever end. If most Japanese people agree with the outside view—that Japanese life is needlessly hard—then trade imbalances will start
15   working themselves out. The Japanese government may try to keep markets closed, but the people themselves will eventually rebel. They will find ways to buy cheaper imports, they will take more time off, they will get tired of tightening their belts in order to increase world market share. They will complain about, and finally change, the regulations and government-sanctioned cartels that thwart the consumer's interest in Japan. But if, for
20   whatever reason, the Japanese public feels that its material desires have been satisfied, then trade problems might never solve themselves. Japanese workers and consumers will have little incentive to behave the way market theory says they should, by using their ever increasing wealth to live in ever more comfortable style.

My impression is that, unfortunately, the second hypothesis is the correct one: the Japanese
25   public is already quite content, or, more precisely, is not unhappy enough to demand a substantial change. Contentment is a plus for any country, but in this case it practically guarantees continued trade friction.…

How, then, can anyone call Japanese life mean or hard? Many Japanese have replied with semi-offended astonishment when I've raised my "low living standards" questions with
30   them; they've taken the very premise of the question as a sneer at what they have achieved. In attempting to explain why it's not a sneer, I've come up with three ways in which this ever more affluent country still seems pointlessly austere.

The first is crowded housing, and daily crowding in general. The typical Japanese dwelling is much smaller, much more expensive, and somewhat worse made than its counterpart
35   in Europe or, especially, the United States. The typical Japanese also spends more of his day fighting for survival space in unending crowds. The second is purchasing power. Japanese factories make many products very efficiently, and Japanese exports are famous for giving overseas consumers more for their money. When they spend their yen at home, however, Japanese consumers are shortchanged no matter what they buy. The third is
40   leisure. Certain categories of Japanese—namely, white-collar salarymen and public-school students—have essentially no free time.

The most interesting thing about such "hardships" is the sharply differing conclusions that

Japanese and foreign observers draw from them. To me they look like totally unnecessary burdens, and to most outside economists they are all symptoms of an economy biased
45   toward "underconsumption." To many Japanese, however, they're part of the broadly accepted social contract that has allowed the nation to succeed.

The high cost and poor quality of housing are the best-known Japanese problems, and the ones that Japanese themselves are most likely to grumble about. But the grumbling does not appear to be the kind that would lead to a change in behavior. Most Japanese seem to
50   view the tight quarters and high prices as part of their fate, since they live (in the boiler-plate phrase that I have heard times without number) in a "small island nation lacking natural resources...."

In actuality, a variety of commercial and political forces leave [the Japanese] with very little choice but to live in expensive, inelegant houses on small plots. Japan's
55   determination to subsidize its high-cost rice farmers means that tiny, inefficient paddies occupy about a quarter of the nation's nonmountainous land. Tax laws discourage the sale and development of land, and further inflate the price of any land that reaches the market. The cost of land makes the dwelling itself seem a trivial, consumable item. In greater Tokyo the value of a house is typically only a tenth of the value of the land it's
60   built on. This means that many houses are built to be torn down in a decade or two, which discourages heavy investment in sturdiness or finishing touches. One neighborhood near our house exemplifies the modern "Japanese dream": brand-new single-family homes, tastefully landscaped on a small scale, many even with carports to hold the meticulously shined Toyotas and BMWs. It would be obvious to any Japanese that these houses
65   represent a tremendous concentration of wealth; a typical house in the neighborhood, with its land, costs several million dollars. Yet most foreigners, passing by, would think the houses attractive but unexceptional. To me, the neighborhood looks like a new development in Silicon Valley[1] with much smaller lots....

Besides the housing shortage, there is the general atmosphere of crowding that throws
70   outsiders like me into a panic and must wear down even people who have been used to it all their lives. Nanjing Road, the main street of Shanghai, is celebrated by the Chinese as an extremely crowded thoroughfare, but to me it can't compare in claustrophobic density to any of Tokyo's big train stations or major shopping streets. Each morning between 7:15 and 8:45 the platforms at my neighborhood train station are patrolled by "packers," ready to cram extra riders into each passing commuter train. Every train that pulls in is already
75   full, but commuters who need to make a certain train take their places in specific areas on the platform. As the doors open, the first dozen or so people in each line push their way in under their own power, often entering backward and digging with their heels for extra traction. Then the packers take over and wedge in anyone else in line. Two or three times a week I make the half-hour trip to Tokyo on one of these trains. As I stand with my arms
80   immobilized against my chest, someone's hip jammed into my groin and odd appendages pressed against my other surfaces, I alternately boil with anger and rejoice that I don't have to undergo this indignity every day. When I get off the train, after giving thanks for my survival and trying to smooth out my jacket and tie, I wonder why no one except foreigners seems to think that a rich country should find a less degrading way for its

85   citizens to get to work.

My intention is not to examine the roots of Tokyo's housing and crowding problems but simply to say that they're not likely to change. All the remedies would involve making frontal assaults on the strongest interests in Japanese politics: changing the tax laws to encourage residential development, driving out the rice farmers, moving the central
90   government away from Tokyo. (Prime Minister Noboru Takeshita often talks about moving government offices to the hinterland, but this seems more like a dream than an actual plan.) If ordinary Japanese had more room to live and play in, they might behave more like consumers in the rest of the world. "I can honestly say there's nothing I want that I don't have," a Japanese journalist friend of mine said one night when we were
85   discussing the Japanese contentment with low living standards. "Oh, come on," said another friend, a professor. "You mean there's nothing you want that will fit in your house." They agreed on one thing: neither will ever have a bigger house.

James Fallows – American journalist

¹ Silicon Valley—region in western California that is a centre for electronics, computing, and database systems

27. The writer's list of the inconveniences experienced by average Japanese (lines 5 to 6) serves **mainly** to

   A. organize the essay

   B. summarize the essay

   C. provide a personal point of view

   D. provide support for the thesis

28. The writer contends that trade imbalances would start working themselves out (lines 12 to 13) if the Japanese were to

   A. consume more astutely

   B. learn to sacrifice even more

   C. consume more like Westerners

   D. overthrow their rigid government

29. The writer bases his belief that friction between Japan and its trading partners will continue on the observation that

   A. "Japanese life is needlessly hard" (line 13)

   B. "the [Japanese] themselves will eventually rebel" (lines 14 to 15)

   C. "[The Japanese] will find ways to buy cheaper imports" (line 15)

   D. "the Japanese public is already quite content" (lines 22 to 23)

30. Lines 19 to 21 indicate that "market theory" is based on the assumption that

    A. increasing wealth produces increasing consumption

    B. decreasing spending produces increasing wealth

    C. decreasing incentive produces decreasing wealth

    D. increasing wealth produces increasing satisfaction

31. The phrases enclosed by dashes in lines 12 to 13 and lines 37 to 38 serve primarily to

    A. create a conversational tone

    B. expand upon the preceding point

    C. interrupt the flow of the argument

    D. provide transition between two thoughts

32. The writer believes that the "broadly accepted social contract" (line 42) of the Japanese is the

    A. preservation of Japanese cultural traditions

    B. legal agreements made to maintain the uniqueness of the culture

    C. sacrifices made by the citizens in order to foster national prosperity

    D. social mores that prevent the country from maintaining a world presence

33. The writer's description of a subway ride in lines 67 to 78 depends for effect on the use of

    A. contrast

    B. suspense

    C. vivid details

    D. figures of speech

34. In noting that his friends agreed that neither of them "will ever have a bigger house" (lines 88 to 89), the writer concludes that the Japanese

    A. are facing political instability

    B. will not break the social contract

    C. have all the material comforts they need

    D. will uphold small-scale housing as a cultural tradition

35. At the time this article was written, the writer believed the prevailing attitude of the Japanese to be one of

    A. acceptance of the status quo and little expectation of real change

    B. ambitions to improve the material status of the average citizen

    C. frustration at the austerity of life and embarrassment at foreign criticism

    D. pride in the simple beauty found in a non-material lifestyle

V. Questions 36 to 44 are based on this excerpt from a novel.

from TENDER MERCIES

Dan, the young man in this excerpt, has grown up and lived his life in a town called Hyland in the state of New Hampshire.

… he smiled at Laura and gratefully made himself quiet.

He began, in fact, to discover the virtues of quietness, the bottomless depths you could suggest for yourself without quite lying. He surprised himself: what was lying and what wasn't? The question opened wide for him, like arms he didn't exactly deserve to rest
5   in. He devoted himself to mastering the signs of her uniqueness: less rather than more, gentleness rather than power; keeping quiet, just reaching out for her, but not demanding. Her hand, barely touching…. The distance between their bare arms so infinitesimal it drew the small hairs up like electricity. Admiring without touching—it was an exquisite challenge….

10 He had not come, after all, from a family of gentle men and it took a painful chastening of his impulses to learn subtlety where braggadocio came naturally. (Braggadocio was his high school English teacher's favorite word; she had beat him over the head with it. He loved it, that anything so flamboyant and mysterious and foreign-sounding could be called his natural style; it sounded like a compliment.)….

15 She was wearing blue jean shorts; the half-invisible hairs on her thighs, like lights on the water, were silver…. She had a slightly flushed, substantial look he thought; not heavy at all but something weighted nearer the bone; maybe she was one of those people who couldn't float. Her thick reddish hair rode all around her neck like a mane, unruly. She kept it in a rubber band but it fanned out anyway. He guessed she'd never been to a beauty
20 shop and what she had for it was lush and inviting, not like his old girls with those thinned-out greased-up gold-streaked piled-on wedding cakes they wore for special occasions and then, when you wanted to most, wouldn't let you mess. There was delicacy and force in her, and that serious listening quality, so that she was very quiet while he talked, she asked him questions and answered his meticulously, just as she sat in her own straightforward
25 way, without coyness. She didn't seem to know or care how the Hyland girls pumped to keep a conversation going, filling in all the blank spaces, playing their desperate background music endlessly like human jukeboxes. Those were the girls his friends had begun to marry and to run from; after a few months they came and stood around with him and the other survivors and holdouts, staring at the floor, trying to be alone in their old
30 familiar company.

By her listening Laura taught him to talk with the expectation that he would be heard….

He tried to step backwards to see himself whole, but that wasn't a direction he was used to; there was nothing to do but bungle straight ahead and hope. He didn't ask himself what he was hoping for. Laura had had two years at a college called Wellesley[1] that sounded like a
35 country club with a library instead of a bar: it was hard to imagine the campus she walked on, deep ridges overwhelmed with lush trees in purple flower; the galleries of paintings, the linen-covered tables with gold samovars,[2] behind them, bowing, silent servants in tuxedos….

He was, in fact, a young man of ordinary tastes and it seemed hopeless to try to dissimulate
40 with her; she would have found him out. Her philosophy [instructor] liked Heidegger,[3] she told him, and he nodded bleakly, wondering if that was a place or a beer or a sport.

What did he like? Tearing up trees on the bush hog. Swimming in heartstopping water.

45 Bobsledding. He liked dogs, all his life he'd put a lot of love into them because they wouldn't laugh or push him away. He liked well-shined shoes; football that's more brains than shoulders; hot pepper sauce; cheeses that don't smell like someone's been sick in the room; all four-wheel-drive vehicles. He had never eaten an artichoke, nor heard a dulcimer.[4] He fell asleep on uplifting music, though he liked to sing, and thought cars should be fast, not solid. The flag of the state of New Hampshire made his stomach sink

50 with a churning excitement, almost a kind of pain, which must have to do with something he'd done as a child: carried the flag? damaged it accidentally and been punished for it? seen it in the V.A.[5] Hospital where his father was dying? He wasn't patriotic, the word would never have occurred to him; why did he feel so unsettled when he saw the high-masted sailing ship against the sun? Once he blew his nose into a silk handkerchief and then and there decided that he would become rich, or wished he could decide: the feeling

55 of luxury where you least expected it, of a private sweetness, meant more than the drape of any suit or even the chrome on a car. He hid this petty preference from his friends who would have thought him a pansy for it. And getting rich was never the point; getting halfway decent might be, if he ever got good and ready for it. He had always thought of himself as someone who got what he wanted: he thought Laura needed to know this, his

60 honor demanded that he warn her so that she might defend herself if she wanted to. As a young boy, the youngest, he could charm his mother, whose experience of grown men had been nothing but mutilating.[6] She would have given him permission to take the world but all she had of it was what he could find in her worn brown change purse.... She worked nights at the paper mill all his life, all hers; she slept most of the day.

65 At school he kept a balance of terror, benign but effective: the annual lecture to the Society of Future Felons of N.H. was directed at his truculent head by Mrs. Hurley, principal.... He was smarter than his friends, played the odds, used his smooth face and eager goodboy looks, the persistent near-smile, the reassuring firm jaw, something clean about him that had to do with a soul that was subsisting on hope faintly warmed by his mother's love,

70 and not with fastidiousness—something of this combination got him behind closed doors, dispersed his enemies, helped him to escape continuous punishment. There had been plenty of need for absolution and escape: he wasn't mean but he'd always been sloppy, had had a childhood, in close quarters, of breaking things, vases and bicycles, and once the top drawer of the only decent piece of furniture they owned.... and breaking hearts,

75 that too. But there was some glamor in him, some obscure enviable energy that made his arrogance only appropriate; didn't he deserve, by taking them, the things he got?

At the worst his friends and he were vandals, irritating as the black flies that came in their season. What trouble and confusion they made was never intolerable. Hyland bored them; they had known each other, known the two main streets that met at a T and the leafy roads

80 and old wooden stores forever: in another life. To keep their hands busy, their adrenalin in working order, they broke into summer homes and hunting camps. Once inside, the conversation was always the same: "Hey look at this!" to signify the discovery of anything worth ten dollars, and "Boy, you got to figure they've got another whole set of this stuff back home, right?" Dan's resentment was real; he never stopped being angry at the

85 summer people and their endless duplications: his mother had patched together a set of china with one representative of every species of flower around the border. Even if

the chipped plates in these strangers' kitchens came from the Ladies Auxiliary Thrift Shop
he was angry; it was excessive. He and his friends would leave by the windows, would
take the highways at unconscionable speed, occasionally in someone else's car. ("Danny's
90 gonna jump-start this hearse," somebody once said.) They were all known to the cops,
as the cops, and the cops' imperfect pasts, were known to them. But they were amateurs,
every one of them; in spite of their noise and their showy toughness, small-town punks
who didn't need, weren't desperate. This was all braggadocio, that ticklish word: blood
made the difference. But they had no blood guilt. They were puppies growing into their
95 feet.

Rosellen Brown – American writer

38. The "survivors and holdouts" (line 27) are those friends of Dan who

   A. are seeking love affairs

   B. are developing material values

   C. have not succumbed to marrying the Hyland girls

   D. have formed a sense of camaraderie in their good fortune

39. The phrase "alone in their old familiar company" (line 27) is an example of

   A. paradox

   B. allusion

   C. analogy

   D. pun

40. The significance of dogs in Dan's life (lines 38 to 39) suggests his

   A. confidence

   B. masculinity

   C. vulnerability

   D. sentimentality

41. In context, artichokes and dulcimers (lines 41 to 42) represent Dan's ideas of

   A. sophistication

   B. pretentiousness

   C. petty preferences

   D. self-improvement

42. Dan's ability to "escape continuous punishment" (lines 64 to 65) appears to be a result of his

   A. hard work at school

   B. prepossessing charm

   C. fear of consequences at home

   D. friends being willing to take the blame

43. The statement "But there was some glamor in him" (line 68) reflects the implications of

   A. "flamboyant and mysterious and foreign-sounding " (line 12)

   B. "a young man of ordinary tastes" (line 35)

   C. "a place or a beer or a sport" (line 37)

   D. "well-shined shoes; football … hot pepper sauce" (line 40)

44. Dan's awareness of his mother's struggles causes him to adopt an attitude to the relative wealth of others (lines 54 to 86) that is based on his resentment of their

   A. gentility

   B. sloppiness

   C. selfishness

   D. extravagance

VI. Questions 45 to 53 are based on this excerpt from a play.

from THE HISTORY OF TROILUS AND CRESSIDA, ACT III, SCENE III

CHARACTERS:

ACHILLES—Greek commander

ULYSSES—Greek commander

Scene: The Greek camp near the city of Troy, during the Trojan war.

ACHILLES, *Greek champion, has recently chosen to indulge his personal whims and not participate in the ongoing battle.* **ACHILLES** *has just been snubbed by his fellow chieftains, causing him to reflect on the possibility of his falling out of their favour. Believing that he can speak freely to* **ULYSSES**, **ACHILLES** *proceeds thus:*

   ACHILLES: Here is Ulysses;

   I'll interrupt his reading.

   How now, Ulysses.

   ULYSSES: Now, great Thetis'[1] son.

   5 **ACHILLES**: What are you reading?

ULYSSES: A strange fellow here

Writes me that man, how dearly ever parted,

How much in having, or without or in,

Cannot make boast to have that which he hath,

10   Nor feels not what he owes[2] but by reflection;

As when his virtues shining upon others

Heat them, and they retort that heat again

To the first giver.

ACHILLES: This is not strange, Ulysses.

15   The beauty that is borne here in the face

The bearer knows not, but commends itself

To others' eyes; nor doth the eye itself,

That most pure spirit of sense, behold itself,

Not going from itself; but eye to eye opposed

20   Salutes each other with each other's form;

For speculation turns not to itself

Till it hath travelled and is mirror'd there

Where it may see itself. This is not strange at all.

ULYSSES: I do not strain at the position,

25   It is familiar, but at the author's drift;

Who in his circumstance expressly proves

That no man is the lord of anything—

Though in and of him there be much consisting—

Till he communicate his parts to others;

30   Nor doth he of himself know them for aught

Till he behold them form'd in the applause

Where they're extended; who, like an arch, reverb'rate

The voice again, or, like a gate of steel

Fronting the sun, receives and renders back

35   His figure and his heat. I was much rapt in this,

And apprehended here immediately

Th' unknown Ajax.[3]

Heavens, what a man is there! A very horse,

That has he knows not what. Nature, what things there are

40	Most abject in regard and dear in use!
	What things again most dear in the esteem
	And poor in worth! Now shall we see to-morrow,
	An act that very chance doth throw upon him,
	Ajax renowned. O heavens, what some men do,
45	While some men leave to do!
	How some men creep into skittish Fortune's hall,
	Whiles others play the idiots in her eyes!
	How one man eats into another's pride,
	While pride is fasting in his wantonness!
50	To see these Grecian lords—why, even already
	They clap the lubber[4] Ajax on the shoulder,
	As if his foot were on brave Hector's[5] breast,
	And great Troy shrinking.

ACHILLES: I do believe it; for they passed by me

| 55 | As misers do by beggars, neither gave to me |
| | Good word nor look. What, are my deeds forgot? |

ULYSSES: Time hath, my lord, a wallet at his back,

	Wherein he puts alms for oblivion,
	A great-sized monster of ingratitudes.
60	Those scraps are good deeds past, which are devoured
	As fast as they are made, forgot as soon
	As done. Perseverance, dear my lord,
	Keeps honor bright; to have done, is to hang
	Quite out of fashion, like a rusty mail
65	In monumental mock'ry. Take the instant way;
	For honor travels in a strait so narrow
	Where one but goes abreast. Keep, then, the path;
	For emulation hath a thousand sons
	That one by one pursue. If you give way,
70	Or hedge aside from the direct forthright,
	Like to an ent'red tide they all rush by
	And leave you hindmost;
	[Or, like a gallant horse fall'n in first rank,
	Lie there for pavement to the abject rear,

75 O'errun and trampled on.] Then what they do in present,

  Though less than yours in past, must o'ertop yours;

  For time is like a fashionable host,

  That slightly shakes his parting guest by the hand,

  And with his arms outstretched, as he would fly,

80 Grasps in the comer. The welcome ever smiles,

  And farewell goes out sighing. Let not virtue seek

  Remuneration for the thing it was. For beauty, wit,

  High birth, vigor of bone, desert in service,

  Love, friendship, charity, are subjects all

85 To envious and calumniating time.

  One touch of nature[6] makes the whole world kin,

  That all with one consent praise new-born gawds,

  Though they are made and moulded of things past,

  And give to dust that is a little gilt

90 More laud than gilt o'er-dusted.

  The present eye praises the present object.

  Then marvel not, thou great and complete man,

  That all the Greeks begin to worship Ajax;

  Since things in motion sooner catch the eye

95 Than what not stirs. The cry went once on thee,

  And still it might, and yet it may again,

  If thou wouldst not entomb thyself alive

  And case thy reputation in thy tent;

  Whose glorious deeds, but in these fields of late,

100 Made emulous missions 'mongst the gods themselves

  And drave great Mars to faction.[7]

ACHILLES: Of this my privacy

  I have strong reasons.

ULYSSES: But 'gainst your privacy

105 The reasons are more potent and heroical

  'Tis known, Achilles, that you are in love

  With one of Priam's daughters.[8]

ACHILLES: Ha! Known?

ULYSSES: Is that a wonder?

110   The providence[9] that's in a watchful state

Knows almost every grain of Pluto's gold,[10]

Finds bottom in th' uncomprehensive deeps,

Keeps place with thought, and almost, like the gods,

Does thoughts unveil in their dumb cradles.

115   There is a mystery—with whom relation[11]

Durst never meddle—in the soul of state,

Which hath an operation more divine

Than breath or pen can give expressure to.

All the commerce that you have had with Troy

120   As perfectly is ours as yours, my lord;

And better would it fit Achilles much

To throw down Hector than Polyxena

But it must grieve young Pyrrhus[12] now at home,

When fame shall in our islands sound her trump,

125   And all the Greekish girls shall tripping sing,

"Great Hector's sister did Achilles win,

But our great Ajax bravely beat down him."

Farewell, my lord; I as your lover speak;

The fool slides o'er the ice that you should break.

William Shakespeare

[1] Thetis—the sea nymph in Greek mythology who was the mother of Achilles; his father was a Thessalian king

[2] owes—owns

[3] Ajax—one of the Greek commanders

[4] lubber—awkward

[5] Hector—the Trojan champion, son of Priam, who is the king of Troy

[6] one touch of nature —one common weakness

[7] drave great Mars to faction—inspired the support of Mars, god of war

[8] one of Priam's daughters—Polyxena

[9] providence—here, timely care rather than foresight

[10] Pluto's gold—the author has confused Pluto, god of the underworld, with Plutus, god of wealth

[11] relation—open statement

[12] Pyrrhus—son of Achilles

45. In calling Achilles "great Thetis' son" (line 4), Ulysses implies that Achilles

    A. is incapable of error

    B. has a reputation to uphold

    C. is unaware of his parentage

    D. has made a mockery of his parentage

46. Achilles' repetition of the words "This is not strange" (line 14 and line 23) emphasizes **most strongly** that his attitude toward Ulysses' commentary is

    A. sarcastic

    B. dismissive

    C. conciliatory

    D. disrespectful

47. Describing Fortune as "skittish" (line 46) means that she is

    A. fancy

    B. erratic

    C. fond of favours

    D. dangerous to pursue

48. Lines 50 to 53 imply **most strongly** that

    A. the Greeks are in need of a hero

    B. Ajax and Hector harbour a personal hostility

    C. the Trojans will surrender once Hector is slain

    D. Hector is the only Trojan left for Ajax to overcome

49. Achilles' words in lines 54 to 56 indicate that he is

    A. ready to do battle

    B. chastizing himself

    C. wise and understanding

    D. feeling sorry for himself

50. The "great-sized monster of ingratitudes" (line 59) is

    A. war

    B. wealth

    C. charity

    D. forgetfulness

51. A phrase that exemplifies the use of personification is

   A. "emulation hath a thousand sons" (line 68)

   B. "thou great and complete man" (line 92)

   C. "case thy reputation in thy tent" (line 98)

   D. "drave great Mars to faction" (line 101)

52. The central point of Ulysses' advice to Achilles is that

   A. the gods will protect Achilles

   B. the Greeks will fail without Achilles

   C. Achilles' reputation has been tarnished and besmirched

   D. Achilles' past honour will fade if he does not earn it anew

53. Ulysses' **main** method of persuasion is through the use of

   A. praise

   B. criticism

   C. anecdote

   D. analogy

VII. Questions 54 to 61 are based on this excerpt from an essay.

from DANCE AT SANTO DOMINGO

The moment the engine was switched off we could hear the drum. I was delighted, for we had come out to Santo Domingo with no more than a good hope of finding a dance in progress; the possibility of it had been whispered in my ear at the New Mexico Museum of Anthropology, but, it was insisted, the news was both secret and uncertain. Now,

5 however, there was no doubt; even in the distant corner of the village where we were parking our car the drum-beat dominated the bright sunny air relentlessly.

I was delighted, yet as we walked between the low houses towards the plaza, I also felt ashamed; yes, just a little ashamed. The Indians do not care for whites to attend some of their more purposeful dances and I am in complete sympathy with them: the moment

10 a ceremony becomes a spectacle for gapers some of the good goes out of it. Yet when I heard of this one by the anthropologists' bush telegraph, I could not resist the lure, being too greedy of the experience. It was understandable. I had given a fair part of my life to prehistory, and here was my first chance to see a primitive people, miraculously saved for us out of the prehistoric past, performing such rites as I had often tried to imaginewhen

15 confronted by their poor, lifeless remains. I had taken seriously the secrecy of my information; I had left behind my camera; I would try to enter imaginatively into the ceremony and not merely to observe it. These were the sops[1] I threw to my conscience as we approached the plaza, our steps affected by the loudening drum …

20 I began to distinguish the larger pattern of the dance. The lines of men and women
seemed to repeat the same series of joining and partings four times, and at the end of
each movement the men raised and lowered their rattles with a fierce vibration that made
a dying fall, a weird yet heart-affecting sound which is said to symbolize the fall of
raindrops. After each movement the leaders, the dancers, the drummer and chanters all
advanced several yards down the plaza before renewing the fourfold pattern of the dance.
25 It was indeed a pattern of four times four; when the movements had been repeated for
this number of times the drumming and chanting were worked up to an intense though
never wild crescendo, and the final dying fall of the rattles was louder, more rending than
before. Then the four lines of men and women fell into a single column which wound out
of the plaza through one of the gaps between the houses and turned into the doorway of
30 a two-storey house on the alleyway beyond. As the whole company tripped, still softly
dancing, into so small a space, it seemed a miracle that the walls did not fall outwards;
yet after the last chanter had entered, the sound of the drum and a glimpse through the
doorway of moving head-dresses showed that the dance was being continued within.
Soon the sense of confined activity, energy and heat, was like that of a wasp's nest
35 humming below ground.

After a spell inside the house the compact mass reshaped itself into a column, and
returned along the same route back to the plaza where the pattern of four times four was
to be repeated; probably, though I am not certain, the whole dance would be complete
when this largest pattern had itself been re-enacted four times. Some western people
40 find this monotonous repetition unbearable; if they do, perhaps it is because they cannot
rid themselves of the idea that a dance must be either a spectacle or an entertainment.
Instead, these Pueblo dances are enactments, celebrations, no more to be censured for
monotony than the perpetual celebration of the Catholic Mass.

One small but most happy change I did notice when the lines re-formed: a small girl
45 and boy had now taken their place at the lower end. Both wore clothes identical in every
detail with those of their elders and performed the steps and movements with equal
perfection; indeed, the little boy in his eagerness and pride seemed even to outdo them in
exactness and force. From afar the two miniature figures, their heads reaching only up
to the waists of their companions, had the appearance of animated dolls drawn into the
50 human dance. It was a glad as well as an enchanting sight, for it meant that an intricate
ritual which had passed from generation to generation through the centuries was to reach
yet another. In twenty years' time, it was possible to hope, these dolls might be leading
the same dance in the plaza of Santo Domingo, maintaining at least one of those unique
forms, peculiar to their own place, which are now fading so fast and leaving us so much
55 the poorer.

The presence of these children, moreover, added a time factor to the all-inness, the
pervading unity, which was what stirred me most in the performance of this November
ritual. The participation of the new generation recalled the old, suggesting the aged men
and women who had led these lines (perhaps even now in the mind of the grandfather
60 on the kiva² roof) and all their forebears stretching back into the prehistoric past. The
dance itself had not greatly moved me, except to admiration; only the strange outcry of
the rattles had taken possession of my feelings. But I was much affected by the sense
of wholeness which dominated the arena where these men and women danced and sang
before the intent eyes of their fellows. They danced for themselves and for the well-being
65 of the village, they danced for the animals whose pelts they carried, they danced

for the cloud expressed by the soft feathers, for the rain repeated by the rattles and by the swinging fringes of their sashes; they danced for the treasure of the earth shown forth in turquoise and silver, and, containing all, they danced for the enduring life of which the spruce twigs were the symbol. The words of the chant, the rhythm of the drum, every
70 step the dancers trod and every pattern, colour and form of their accoutrement, spun out a maze of threads linking the actors with sun, cloud and earth, with village and fields and orchards, with one another and their ancestors and descendants. And all the threads wove together to make a picture of their desire for well-being and continuance. No one will ever be able to express this universal participation in words, for it is essentially a
75 wordless thing. Yet even the outsider, the visitor, can share in it a little as he stands in this earthen place, enclosed by houses and a ring of eyes, watching it expressed in the being of the dancers and their dance.

Does reason say these rites are useless, the enactments of delusions? No dance has ever caused seeds to germinate, rain fall, corn swell and ripen or the sun to turn back.
80 They are embodiments of the images of the psyche and cannot affect the physical world without. Yet undoubtedly as they spring from the psyche so they also satisfy it, embodying the promptings of the unconscious mind and the imagination. So celebration of such rites invigorates, brings confidence and wards off mental ills; it suffuses with meaning a crowd of daily acts related to its purposes. It satisfies that terrible longing to
85 do something to bring the desired to pass, when nothing can be done with hands.

These are reasons, justifications for a ritual which perhaps needs no justification beyond the fullness of its own existence. Yet in a sense it is already ahead of reason, having never left a position to which reason itself now returns. The dances express in the language of poetry the truth of man's unity with nature, the truth that science repeats to
90 us, curing our delusions of grandeur. Yet because of their poetry they offer us visions for which science has no eyes....

As we returned to our car the drum was beating again just as it had been when we arrived. Probably it would go on for hours yet, and afterwards there would be feasting. I felt curiously limp and emptied out as though following the dance had taxed me more than I
95 knew. But the next morning when I woke my memories had revived their colours, and as I examined them it seemed to me they offered some understanding of the ancient tribal life of my kind. Of life, as some would have it, before the Fall.[3]

J.B. Priestley and J. Hawkes – American writers

---

[1] sops—appeasements

[2] kiva—in a Pueblo Indian dwelling, a large room used for religious ceremonies and councils

[3] the Fall—humanity's loss of innocence through its quest for knowledge or the power that knowledge provides

54. The statement that describes the mindset that the narrator adopts as he prepares himself to experience the dance is

   A. "I was delighted, for we had come out to Santo Domingo with no more than a good hope of finding a dance in progress" (lines 1 to 2)

   B. "I was delighted, yet as we walked between the low houses towards the plaza, I also felt ashamed" (line 7)

   C. "I could not resist the lure, being too greedy of the experience" (line 11)

   D. "I would try to enter imaginatively into the ceremony and not merely to observe it" (lines 15 to 16)

55. A synonym for the term "bush telegraph" (line 11), as it is used in this excerpt, would be

   A. grapevine

   B. field telephone

   C. extrasensory perception

   D. primitive telecommunication system

56. The narrator connotatively reinforces the "heart-affecting" sound of the rattles (line 20) with the use of the word

   A. chanters (line 22)

   B. fourfold (line 23)

   C. rending (line 25)

   D. tripped (line 28)

57. The participation of the small girl and boy in the dance (lines 40 to 41) affects the narrator **mainly** through the

   A. sense of gaiety that the children provide

   B. impressive mastery of the children's skills

   C. charm of the children's unconscious mimicry

   D. promise of continuity that the children represent

58. The word "accoutrement" (line 62) is **best** defined as

   A. paint

   B. regalia

   C. discipline

   D. happiness

59. In context, the narrator suggests his inability to cross the boundary of his stance as critical observer when he uses the words

A. "energy and heat" (line 31) and "wasp's nest" (line 32)

B. "Catholic Mass" (line 39) and "kiva" (line 53)

C. "arena" (line 56) and "actors" (line 63)

D. "embodiments" (line 70) and "imagination" (line 73)

60. The narrator's statement "when I woke my memories had revived their colours" (line 84) **most strongly** supports his former observation

A. "the moment a ceremony becomes a spectacle for gapers some of the good goes out of it" (lines 9 to 10)

B. "all the threads wove together to make a picture of their desire for well-being and continuance" (lines 64 to 65)

C. "No dance has ever caused seeds to germinate, rain fall, corn swell and ripen or the sun to turn back" (lines 69 to 70)

D. "because of their poetry they offer us visions for which science has no eyes" (lines 79 to 80)

61. The juxtaposition of references to the narrator's car and to the drums in lines 1 and 5 and line 81 serves to

A. create an impression of cultural alienation

B. contrast material wealth and spiritual poverty

C. indicate a change in mood from uncertainty to fulfillment

D. punctuate the boundary between two worlds or realms of experience

VIII. Questions 62 to 70 are based on this poem.

THE STONES

Tell the other side of it, how longing

galloped beside terror in your chest

when trees stopped and fog reached between the mountains

and hid the painted stripes that marked the path.

5　It started to get dark and cold and nothing

you could see would burn to warm a night,

and inside, next to fear, over the borders

you'd drawn for safety, leaped a wild wish—

stay where there was no sign of the human,

10　forget your bootprints in a gash of snow,

leave the red trail blazes and the cairns[1]

pointing to the cramped shelter below

for forms you couldn't make resemble faces:

endless streambeds paved with shifting scree,[2]

15　clouds of insects, gentians[3] pushed through fissures,

butterflies, rills[4] broken over stones,

the stones themselves. How could they be persuaded

to accept you as an integer, like them:

taught the measurement of time in eras,

20　infinite, no longer lost or small?

Language was as useless as your eyes

until the fog blew higher and withdrew,

and the ancient pools left by the glaciers

looked like postcards again as you climbed down.

Suzanne Gardinier – British poet

[1] cairns—stones piled as a landmark

[2] scree—loose shale; rocky debris

[3] gentians—bright blue-flowered plants

[4] rills—small streams

62. The speaker's experience of isolation is a direct result of the

A. fog

B. snow

C. glaciers

D. mountains

63. In the first three stanzas, the speaker's description of being stranded on the mountain emphasizes feelings of

A. confidence

B. indifference

C. ambivalence

D. disappointment

64. The word "borders" in line 7 refers to

A. imaginary fears

B. human isolation

C. physical barriers

D. emotional control

65. The speaker's "wild wish" (line 8) is the desire to

A. return to the crowded shelter

B. master the mountain singlehandedly

C. shed the predictability of humanness

D. escape the threat of mountainous hazards

66. The choice of the verbs "galloped" (line 2) and "leaped" (line 8) serves to emphasize a sense of

A. despair

B. timidity

C. excitement

D. determination

67. The speaker's sense of the futility of the wish or longing is **best** conveyed in

A. "there was no sign of the human" (line 9)

B. "forms you couldn't make resemble faces" (line 13)

C. "How could they be persuaded / to accept you" (lines 17 to 18)

D. "the fog blew higher and withdrew" (line 22)

68. In the context of the whole poem, the "painted stripes" (line 4), "borders" (line 7), and "postcards" (line 24) represent

   A. familiar security

   B. spiritual challenge

   C. physical limitations

   D. unnatural boundaries

69. As a telling of "the other side of it" (line 1), this poem describes the speaker's response to

   A. human sacrifice

   B. heroic endeavours

   C. nature's indifferent inscrutability

   D. difficulties that are insurmountable

70. The central idea of the poem relates to the

   A. fear of being lost

   B. rewards of challenge

   C. joy of mountaineering

   D. limitations of being human

ANSWERS AND SOLUTIONS—JUNE 1998
DIPLOMA EXAMINATION

1. D	13. C	25. A	37. A	49. D	61. D
2. B	14. C	26. B	38. C	50. D	62. A
3. B	15. B	27. D	39. A	51. A	63. C
4. A	16. A	28. C	40. C	52. D	64. D
5. D	17. B	29. D	41. A	53. D	65. C
6. C	18. C	30. A	42. B	54. D	66. C
7. B	19. B	31. B	43. A	55. A	67. C
8. B	20. D	32. C	44. D	56. C	68. A
9. C	21. D	33. C	45. B	57. D	69. C
10. C	22. A	34. B	46. B	58. B	70. D
11. B	23. B	35. A	47. B	59. C	
12. A	24. D	36. B	48. A	60. D	

"For the Lost Adolescent" – Synopsis

To discover the fundamental meaning of Deborah Digges' "For the Lost Adolescent," start by identifying both the speaker of the poem and the person of whom she is speaking. The speaker is a mother and she is talking to herself about her son's leaving home. We find this relation in line 27, where the speaker talks of the pre-lingual relation a mother has with her child: "A mother learns a code of sounds not yet a voice." If we read the poem closely, we find that it is organized in sections. In the first section (lines 1 to 16), the mother talks of how she comes to know that "he was lost to me" (line 6). In the second (lines 17 to 30), she speaks of parental needs that bring children into the world, "a captive/of our need amid the ruin of a modern city!" (lines 23 to 24). The final section (lines 31 to 35) returns to the idea of her son's being "lost to [her]" (line 6). This section emphasizes his lack of connection with the "children" (line 32) around him.

1.   D

In line 1 of the poem, the mother states: "Even before he left for good." Although it may not seem logical for the mother to hear about her son's departure from "the fire" (line 1) and "wind" (line 3), the fact that she gains knowledge about him from these sources speaks of the strength of the intuitive bond between the mother and her son. Alternatives **B** and **C** are incorrect because both are contradicted by the mother's statement. Alternative **A**, "provoked," refers more to an event that spurs an individual to action of some kind, usually retaliatory. Since the mother only speaks of how she gains knowledge about her son's departure and not about something he has actually done to her, alternative **D**, "foreseeable" is correct.

2.   B

Alternative **B** is the best response because it indicates the son's feeling of frustration at being restricted by the expectations he has inherited along with "his name" (line 7). Alternative **A** suggests the opposite: that the son would rather not break out of restrictions that have been placed on him. Neither alternatives **C** nor **D** are supported by evidence from the text, such as a specific word or phrase that would suggest a different interpretation.

3. B

Although you may never have seen a word like "antediluvian," you can come close to its meaning by looking at the words that are around it. The words "bedrock stare" and "unchanging" (line 11), which appear just before and after "antediluvian," help explain this meaning. Alternatives **A** and **C**, which are almost opposite in meaning to "bedrock" can be ruled out. Alternative **D** is a possible answer since the son may look suspiciously at his mother, but in the context of these other words, "antediluvian" is likely used to emphasize another aspect of his bearing toward her.

Another way to determine the meaning of difficult words is to break them into their parts, to see if you know any of their meanings. For "antediluvian," then, you could tell that it means "before" (ante) and "the flood" (diluvian). This would confirm your selection of alternative **B** as the best answer among those listed here.

4. A

In the poem, the mother is "hearing" things in the fire about her son's leaving (line 1), which has made her terribly sad. The image of rain (line 15) offers a sense of "reprieve," since we can loosely define "reprieve" as "giving someone a break." Neither alternatives **C** nor **D** work very well to explain the mother's temporary relief from the heartache of her son leaving. For these same reasons, we could also rule out alternative **B**, "rebellion," since the poem is spoken in the mother's voice and the "rebellion" expressed in the poem is expressed in the son's getting ready to leave.

5. D

It is important to keep in mind the mother's perspective through which these thoughts are spoken. The mother's reference to "his voice inside me" (line 25) suggests that her mind is occupied with the basic instinct that led her into motherhood in the first place. Both **A** "anger" and **B** "natural environment," although primitive in their own ways, can be excluded because of the context. Although the "struggle to create a life of ease" (**C**) for one's children may be natural, there is nothing in the poem to link it to the primitive need referred to in the poem.

6. C

In this "run-on sentence," the poet piles one clause onto another as if we were in the mother's mind, listening to her think. This technique means that we need to be careful to keep track of the subject clause—in this case, "another child" (line 17). At the end of this sentence, therefore, "a captive/ of our need" (lines 23 to 24) describes children as "victims of their parents' longings" to have families. Each of the other responses may be true to some extent in another context, but since we are not offered any evidence to support these statements in this poem, we have no choice but to discard them.

7. B

If we start by looking at lines 25 to 26: "And if I never recognized his voice inside me,/who could know?" we find a clue to the phrase that is identified in the question. The "holding" (line 29) does not make very much sense outside of this context. This mother "recognized [him]"; that is, while she was pregnant with him—"holding" her child within her. During her pregnancy, she had to passively wait for his birth, developing patience, and, of course, she was full of hope for her unborn child. Now that her son is growing estranged from her, she must again assume a passive role, this time patiently holding him in her heart, hoping that the "world heals" her both her son and this estrangement.

Alternative **C** is true, on a broader level, since mothers do experience happiness in hearing their child talk. Within this poem, though, this response is weaker than **B**. In naming "talk" as the source of the mother's happiness, it too specifically identifies the pre-verbal communication between baby and mother: "A mother learns a code of sounds not yet a voice/and feels her way inside that heat" (lines 27 to 28). Neither alternatives **A** nor **D** find support in the poetic text, and so they can be disregarded.

8. B

The fact that the mother says she "learns" (line 27) to understand the baby's pre-verbal communication of its needs and wants, makes this response the strongest of the ones offered here, immediately ruling out alternative **A** as a possibility. Since the statement in the question asks the reader to identify the "focus" of this passage, the other statements are ruled out as well. Alternative **C**, "knowledge that a conflict is forthcoming," could be drawn from lines 29 and 30, but is not the central idea. Alternative **D**, "need to accept blame for her son's leaving," could seem like a smart, interpretive response, since perhaps the mother feels she did not "learn the code" of her son well enough while he was growing up. But since the focus of these lines is on her accepting the role of motherhood, and trying her best, alternative B is the best answer.

A River Runs Through It – Synopsis

In Norman Maclean's novel "A River Runs Through It," the narrator talks about how he learned fly-fishing from his father, a Presbyterian minister. His religious background colours the imagery that he uses to describe the correct technique required for successful fly-fishing, which he says must be approached "Presbyterian-style" (line 40). We can tell from the detail that the narrator uses to describe correct fly-fishing technique that he has learned his father's values: "To him, all good things— trout as well as eternal salvation—come by grace and grace comes by art and art does not come easy" (lines 82 to 84).

9. C

According to the narrator, his father never needed to "ask more than the first question" (line 11) of the Catechism before they would answer together. The brothers anticipated this and dutifully responded. Therefore, alternative **C** is the most satisfactory answer. Although the brothers may have been resigned (**A**) to the routine of the day, there is nothing to suggest that they were apathetic (**A**) or apprehensive (**D**). Likewise, alternative **B** can be eliminated because even if there was solemnity to the day, no evidence points to an attitude of resolution.

10. C

The irony is in the phrase "as indeed such a beautiful answer should have," since one would not expect a boy to recognize the beauty of language in a catechism. Alternative **A**, "respectful," comes close, but does it not reflect the nuance in the boy's language. Alternative **B** does not have any support in the text and can be disregarded. Alternative **D** can be eliminated by the context of the whole selection; there is no tone of pretentiousness or boastfulness elsewhere, so it is unlikely that the writer meant this statement to be pompous either.

11. B

The narrator links the idea of following from a state of grace with his own experiences of falling out of trees as a child, so this is the best answer. In alternative **C**, the word "mess" is used to describe the father's theological position and is not specifically related to the narrator's own experiences. Alternative **D** indicates that the narrator was very observant (noticing how the trembling of the fishing rod matched his father's heartbeat), but being observant is not limited to the point of view of a child that we are looking for. The narrator's acknowledgement that certain passages of his father's sermon were more "successful" than others (**A**), suggests maturity in the narrator, rather than a child's point of view.

12. A

The word "austere" refers to a severe or stern attitude; an austere person generally avoids things that may soften life's experiences or make life more pleasant. Since his father is distinct from other Presbyterians in his appreciation for beauty, alternative **A** is the most satisfactory answer. None of the other words offered can be defined as an opposite to the appreciation of beauty and so cannot be correct.

13. C

Alternative **C** "most emphatically" conveys the seriousness with which the father regards mastery of the art of fly fishing because it most clearly states the father's feelings about who should be allowed to actually catch fish. Although alternative **A** conveys an idea that might be important to a Presbyterian minister, it does not relate directly to the father's attitude to the "art of fly fishing." Alternative **B** comes closer to being correct because it shows how displeased his father would become if someone called a fishing rod by a wrong name. However, naming a rod is still not as important as actually being able to use it. Alternative **D** refers to correct fly fishing technique but does not express any of his father's displeasure that he would have felt had the art been practised incorrectly.

14. C

This quotation best shows the difference between the young sons' wanting to experience the fun of fly fishing and their father's wanting them to learn technique. Alternative **B** also compares the sons with their father, but since the quotation begins with "after," we can assume they are no longer as young as when they were first learning the art of fly fishing. Alternatives **A** and **D** do not work because they do not offer comparisons between the attitudes of the father and his sons.

15. B

The father's dedication to the four-count rhythm indicates his methodical approach to fly-fishing, an approach that in this story does not have anything to do with being "competitive," having good "sportsmanship," or "Christian leadership."

16. A

You need to find evidence in the text to support claims about that text. In this case, support for alternative A as the correct answer can be found in the description of his father that begins on line 20: "we realized that our father was not a great fly caster, but he was accurate and stylish and wore a glove on his casting hand."

In other words, even though he realizes that his father was not "a great fly caster," he still notes, with affection, the things that distinguished his father as a fly caster. "Cynicism" means an attitude of not caring about what is good or bad, and obviously does not describe the son's attitude. Likewise, there is no evidence to suggest that the narrator has an attitude of "anxious self-doubt" or "criticism."

"The Matchmaker" – Synopsis

As the introduction tells us, Vandergelder is against Ermengarde's marriage to Ambrose. Since both Vandergelder and Ambrose, however, are using the same matchmaker, Ambrose will successfully marry Ermengarde despite Vandergelder's stern pronouncements to the contrary.

17. B

The comment in line 1 that "Ninety-nine percent of the people in the world are fools" suggests that being a fool is a disease that has infected almost the entire population. Alternative **C** "prestige" and alternative **D** "perfection" are therefore wrong because they are not qualities attributed to fools. Alternative A may seem correct because of the reference to the "danger of contagion" but because the question asks what is causing this "contagion," "fear" itself could not be the correct answer. Since fools are people who practice "folly," the correct choice is **B**.

18. C

This question asks you to identify the "main effect" of Vandergelder's speech. While he does "ridicule marriage" (**A**) near the beginning of his speech, it turns out that he is remarrying for reasons of his own. He does show some "respect for wealth" (**B**), but since he only refers to his becoming rich once (lines 5 to 6), this is not likely the "main effect" of his speech. In this speech, Vandergelder estabablishes himself as a "man of sense" (line 17), but not as an intellectual (**D**).

19. B

Although Vandergelder "admires" the work of women because of the "giant passions" that energize their labour, he does so in a way that is condense ding to them, which means that he treats them in a patronizingly superior manner. Thus, he is not really displaying "respect" (A) for women. In this speech, Vandergelder is focusing on marriage rather than "ants" (D), of course. Vandergelder does think of "marriage as a bribe" (C), but the phrases beginning with "what" refer specifically to the amount and efficiency of the work that is completed around the house by the women of whom he is thinking.

20. D

The word "propriety" (D) refers to conformity to predominant customs and attitudes. When Ermengarde says that running away to get married "wouldn't be proper," she is objecting to the impropriety of this act. Thus, "practical common sense" (A), "regard for her uncle's plans" (B), and "hopes for an elaborate wedding" (C) are all incorrect.

21. D

Alternative D is the correct answer since "affectionate exasperation" describes his feelings of both frustration and love. Each of the other phrases describe responses that are more extreme ("contempt," "indignation") or simply inaccurate ("fearful sympathy").

22. A

Being a practical woman who loves to arrange the details of other people's lives, Mrs. Levi's observation reflects her "practical nature." As well, now living in straitened circumstance, Mrs. Levi has learned that one never knows what the future will bring. A person with a "pessimistic nature" (B) would feel that everything were pointless, which does not apply to Mrs. Levi. Similarly, "pretentious nature" and "predictable nature" are incorrect because they describe the opposite of the characteristics that are represented in the excerpt by Mrs. Levi.

23. B

Since the cards identify the different ways that Mrs. Levi has of making money, they certainly serve to "emphasize her resourcefulness." If you thought they "justify Ambrose's fear of her" (A), you might have overlooked Mrs. Levi's statement (with which Ambrose does not argue): "your situation could not possibly be worse." Answers C and D are contradicted by evidence in the text that suggests otherwise. Her credibility, if anything, might be undermined by having this many endeavours. Further, her association with the Vandergelders is not clarified by the cards.

24. D

Mrs. Levi states: "Nature is never completely satisfactory and must be corrected. Well, I'm like you artists" (line 115). This statement makes alternative D the correct selection. Since Mrs. Levi does not explicitly state her feelings about nature or about the way society undervalues her, you would have to rule out alternatives A and B. According to what she herself states, she considers herself to be anything but a professional, only "putting her hand" in different people's affairs to keep herself from getting "bored."

25. A

Ambrose's plan to elope with Ermengarde is not very realistic, so we can immediately rule out alternative B. The contrast between "his integrity and her cynicism" (C) is also wrong because Ambrose's wish to sneak off to get married does not show very much integrity and Mrs. Levi's plans for people's futures shows that she is not cynical at all. Finally, alternative D is incorrect because the opposite is true. Mrs. Levi seems to be more worldly than Ambrose and he seems more naive than she. The most reasonable answer is alternative A, "his doubt and her assurance."

26. B

In this question, each of the alternatives describes something about Mrs. Levi, but only alternative B describes her role in this scene because it specifically states what she does.

"The Hard Life" – Synopsis

In "The Hard Life" by James Fallows, the author argues that Japanese life is needlessly "hard" (line 1). He supports this thesis by stating how he believes the Japanese to be essentially "content" with the way their government manages their economy. Because they are content, they do not apply pressure on their government to open markets to cheaper imports (lines 11 to 21). Fallows argues further that Japanese also live needlessly hard lives because of the crowded housing conditions in their neighbourhoods and because of crowded public transport systems that take commuters from their homes to work and back. He concludes that these aspects of Japanese culture are unlikely to change in the near future because the government is unwilling to alter its policies when its people do not want it to.

27. D

Every essay needs to have a thesis sentence that explains the purpose of the essay. In this essay, we can identify the thesis sentence in the opening question, "Why is life in Japan so hard?" To support this thesis sentence, the author lists the inconveniences experienced by the average Japanese. Although this list of inconveniences does "organize the essay" (**A**), and does "provide support for a personal point of view" (**C**), these statements are not as specific as alternative **D** and thus not as successful. Alternative **B**, "summarize the essay," is incorrect because the essay offers more than a list of the inconveniences experienced by the Japanese.

28. C

The best evidence that alternative **C** is the correct answer is offered at the end of the essay, which was written from the perspective of an American when Fallows states that the Japanese "might behave more like consumers in the rest of the world" (line 85). Alternative **B** states the opposite of the point Fallows tries to make, since he says that the Japanese already willingly make too many sacrifices (line 40). Alternative **A** implies that the Japanese should spend their money carefully, again not one of the points Fallows is trying to make. Alternative **D** is incorrect because the essay encourages a change in government policies, not a complete overthrow of the government.

29. D

Since the author is stating that friction already exists between Japan and its trading partners, the best answer would reflect his belief that things will not change in Japan. Only Alternative **D** implies that things will remain the same because "the Japanese public is already quite content" (lines 22 to 23).

30. A

The key to this answer is found in lines 20 and 21: "by using their ever increasing wealth to live in ever more comfortable style"; that is, by using their increasing wealth to increase their consumption. The idea presented in alternative **B** could be true for personal finances, but in the essay, this idea is not connected to market theory. The essay does not reflect the idea presented in alternative **D** nor does it express the idea stated in alternative **C**.

31. B

In both cases, the point preceding the dashes is very general. The information offered between the dashes helps explain this general point. Alternative **C** can be ruled out immediately because the information assists the flow of the argument rather than interrupting it. Alternative **D** can be eliminated because the information on either side of the dashes is part of the same thought, not of two different ones. Finally, alternative **A** could be correct because the use of dashes lends an informal tone to the writing. However, since the question asks for the primary function of the phrases between the dashes, you should select alternative **B** over alternative **A**.

32. C

Since the main purpose of the author's argument is to show how the Japanese are content living beneath the level of prosperity they could afford, the answer should reflect this purpose. With this in mind, alternative **A** "cultural traditions," alternative **B** "the uniqueness of the culture," and alternative **D** "social mores that prevent the country from maintaining a world presence" can be eliminated. Alternative **C**, "sacrifices made by the citizens in order to foster national prosperity" is the only possible right answer.

33. C

The "vivid details" of the subway ride include "digging" heels, "immobilized" arms, a "jammed" hip, and the "odd appendages" that are pressed into his body as he gets stuffed onto the subway during rush hour. Alternative **B**, "suspense," is not correct because the reader is not left waiting for something to happen. The writer does not use "figures of speech" (**D**) to convey his meaning in these lines. Alternative **A** has some merit since it does seem that the strength of this writing is its contrasting of conditions in Tokyo with conditions in the "uncrowded" West. But since the writer does not make this comparison himself, we would have to select alternative **C** as the better response.

34. B

The clearest hint that the writer offers as to the meaning behind his conclusion is in lines 40 to 44. The "social contract" of under-consumption that has allowed Japan to succeed as a nation is reflected in the contentment of the two friends with their houses. The writer does not give any information that would lead us to believe that the Japanese attitude toward houses was part of a "cultural tradition" (**D**). Both alternatives **A** and **C** are contrary to the position taken by the writer and so could not be correct responses to the question.

35. A

The "acceptance of the status quo" is correct because the writer states that his impression is that "the Japanese public is already quite content" (lines 22 to 23). Although one of our impressions of living without material goods is that it can lead to a simpler lifestyle (**D**), the essay does not indicate that this is the lifestyle he observes in Tokyo. Similarly, the average citizen does not seem ambitious to improve his or her "material status" (**B**), and also does not feel "frustrated" at "foreign criticism" (**C**), so these answers are incorrect.

Tender Mercies – Synopsis

Rosellen Brown's story Tender Mercies *describes the experiences of growing up as a working-class adolescent, as told from the viewpoint of a guy who is falling in love with a girl from a wealthier family. Instead of just telling the reader about Laura from a third person point of view, the description is given through the eyes of Dan. The things that he notices about her, such as the "delicacy and force in her, and that serious listening quality" (line 21), tell us about him, as well, and the qualities that he considers important in a person. If we compare these early descriptions of his character with the perceptions of others around him, we are able to arrive at a more balanced assessment of his character. So when Mrs. Hurley gives the "annual lecture to the Society of Future Felons of N.H.," directing her comments especially at Dan (lines 59 to 60), we recognize his trouble-making more as a result of his adolescence than as a tendency toward outright criminal activity. Dan and his friends were, as the excerpt concludes, "puppies growing into their feet" (line 87).*

36. B

The clearest hint that Dan perceives himself to have undiscovered possibilities comes shortly after the line that is quoted in the question. When he devotes himself to "mastering the signs of her uniqueness" (lines 4 to 5), he is discovering some of his own power to be charming and attractive to Laura. Thus, he is not simply realizing that he cannot stop himself from "lying" (**A**) and is also not confused about "falling in love with a rich girl" (**D**). Although he is highly competitive, since he wants to "win" Laura (**C**), his way of approaching her does not indicate that he is competing with either her or anyone else.

37. A

The description of the Hyland girls that Dan offers makes use of the metaphor of "background music" to describe the constant chatter that he finds unappealing. The girls' talk sounds like a radio that is always turned on. The fact that they cannot feel comfortable with a silent moment in the conversation contrasts with Laura's not caring about such things. Alternative **B** would be a close second to alternative **A** because Dan probably does dislike their tendency to gossip. But alternative **A** is a better answer because it describes why these girls gossip all the time. Alternatives **C** and **D**, on the other hand, are not correct because they take the "background music" to be literally referring to music. Instead, this "music" is more like noise, because of all their empty talk.

38. C

The "survivors and holdouts" are those friends of Dan's who have either not fallen for the empty charms of the Hyland girls or who have returned from relationships with one of them. In the line just above this one, the narrator states that "his friends had begun to marry and to run from [the Hyland girls]" (lines 25 to 26). Because "survivors and holdouts" refers to this group of his friends, alternatives **A**, **B**, and **D** are incorrect.

39. A

Since a "paradox" is a statement that combines elements usually considered to be opposites, the phrase "trying to be alone in their old familiar company" is an example of paradox because it combines "alone" with "company." An "allusion" (**B**) is a statement that refers to something else without discussing it in detail. An "analogy" (**C**) is an illustration of an idea by means of an example that is similar or parallel to it in some significant feature. A "pun" (**D**) refers to the double meaning that some words have and is usually intended as a joke.

40. C

Dan likes dogs because they "wouldn't laugh or push him away" (line 39), which indicates his feelings of vulnerability. These feelings of vulnerability are the opposite of "confidence" (**A**) or of "masculinity" (**B**). The final choice, "sentimentality" (**D**), would refer to someone who shows more feeling than might usually be considered appropriate for a situation, something that Dan does not do.

41. A

Since he states in the next sentence that he "fell asleep on uplifting music," we can infer that "dulcimers" play "uplifting music" and that, together with artichokes, they represent Dan's idea of sophistication. He does not indicate that he thinks people who enjoy such things are "arrogant," thus ruling out alternative **B**. Although these preferences for different forms of entertainment may seem trivial, or unimportant, Dan does not indicate that he himself thinks of them as "petty," so we must also rule out alternative **C**. Alternative **D**, as well, is incorrect, because Dan does not state that he thinks he needs these things to improve himself or his chances with Laura.

42. B

Even if you are not certain what "prepossessing" means, by the process of elimination, you can arrive at the correct answer. None of the other options applies to this phrase. Since we know that he does not work hard at school (**A**), does not fear consequences at home (**C**), and does not have friends who take the blame (**D**), the only possible response left is the one referring to his "charm," (**B**).

43. A

The description of Dan as having "ordinary tastes" (**B**) does not reflect the idea of "glamor"; in fact, it does just the opposite. The quotation in alternative **C** and that in alternative **D** actually reinforce the idea of "ordinary tastes" not "glamor," so they can be eliminated also. Someone who is "flamboyant" is outgoing and enjoys being with people. This quality, combined with being "mysterious and foreign sounding" would lend him an aura of "glamor."

44. D

Since his mother's struggles are described in relation to her having pieced together a set of china dishes from other sets, we could infer that Dan resents wealthy people because of their "extravagance." "Extravagance" refers to the habit of spending more than is necessary. Neither "sloppiness" (**B**) nor "selfishness" (**C**) are mentioned in the passage, so we must rule out them as correct answers. Likewise, "gentility" (**A**), which means having well-cultivated manners, is not mentioned in the passage, and thus could not be the correct alternative.

Troilus and Cressida, Act III, Scene iii – Synopsis

The introduction to the scene that is excerpted here provides a key to understanding the conversation between Achilles and Ulysses that follows. Simply put, Achilles complains to Ulysses that he has been unfairly overlooked by the other military leaders to lead the battle against Troy: "What, are my deeds forgot?" (line 56). Ulysses responds by telling him not to quit: "Perseverance .../ Keeps honor bright; to have done, is to hang/ Quite out of fashion ...." (lines 62 to 64). Ulysses continues by telling Achilles that he has been overlooked because he has been spending much time in his "tent" (line 98), and that he is in love with Polyxena, one of Priam's daughters (lines 106 to 107, 121 to 122). A courageous soldier such as Achilles, Ulysses states, should rather focus on his duty in battle and thus save his reputation as a heroic warrior (lines 123 to 127).

45. B

At this early point in the text, we have not been given very much information about Achilles, so we have to select that answer that is the most general. Even if you have never heard of "Thetis," you can infer that she is of some importance because she is called "great" (line 4). By welcoming Achilles with this reference, Ulysses is obviously reminding Achilles of his mother's good name and implying that Achilles should behave as his mother would.

46. B

To suggest that someone's attitude is "dismissive" about something indicates that they are downplaying the significance of that thing. This answer is more specific than alternative **D**, "disrespectful." If someone is speaking sarcastically (**A**), they might also be "dismissive," but they are doing so by saying the opposite of what they mean, probably sneering while they do so. Since alternative **C**, "conciliatory," refers to an action that attempts to mend differences and reconcile people, this cannot be the correct response.

47. B

The word "erratic" refers to someone who is very unpredictable, as Fortune is conventionally described. This would be a difficult answer to infer from the text unless you have some prior knowledge of how Fortune is usually portrayed.

48. A

Alternative A is the correct response because in the context of the speech, Ulysses is complaining about "what some men do …" (line 44). In lines 50 to 53, these men congratulate Ajax as if he had already beaten Hector, when in fact, their fight is still to come. Each of the other alternatives requires more information than we are given in the passage, and so could not be correct. We are not told whether Ajax and Hector harbour a "personal hostility" (**B**), nor whether the "Trojans will surrender once Hector is slain" (**C**), nor whether "Hector is the only Trojan left for Ajax to overcome" (**D**). By the process of elimination, we can arrive at the only correct response, **A**.

49. D

Since Achilles worries that his deeds are already "forgotten," the best answer to select would be the last one in this list. Although he may be "ready to do battle" (**A**), he is actually talking about the responses of others toward him. In this apparently petty concern for others' opinions about his reputation, he does not demonstrate wisdom nor understanding (**C**). As well, his speech shows that he is really "chastizing" others—not himself—for forgetting his great deeds, so alternative **B** cannot be the right answer.

Not for Reproduction

50. D

If you selected **D** as the correct answer for question 49, you probably correctly selected it as the correct answer here as well. Since "time," according to Ulysses, collects money ("alms") to prevent people from being forgotten (disappearing into "oblivion"), the "great-sized monster of ingratitudes" would logically refer to "forgetfulness" and not to "war," "wealth," or "charity."

51. A

Personification describes the giving of personal, human qualities to non-human things. Since emulation (**A**) is described as having "a thousand sons," this is the only phrase that exemplifies the use of personification.

52. D

The only clue required to establish alternative **D** as the correct answer is found early in Ulysses' second major speech to Achilles: "Perseverance, dear my lord,/ Keeps honor bright; to have done, is to hang/ Quite out of fashion, like a rusty mail/ In monumental mock'ry" (lines 62 to 65). If we keep in mind this central idea of Ulysses' speech—that only perseverance "keeps honor bright"—then alternative **D** is the best answer. Alternative **C** may seem correct since it refers to Achilles' reputation; however, we are not given any indication that it has been "besmirched," only that it has been forgotten. Therefore, alternative **C** would not be the best answer. The other two responses, that "the gods will protect Achilles" (**A**), and that "the Greeks will fail without Achilles" (**B**), are not supported by Ulysses actual speech, so they should be ruled out.

53. D

Ulysses' many references to the gods in relation to the experiences of the Greek hero Achilles make alternative **D** the answer. He does make use of each of the other three responses, "praise," "criticism," and "anecdote," but not as much as he does of "analogy."

"Dance at Santo Domingo" – Synopsis

In this informal essay, "Dance at Santo Domingo" by J. B. Priestley and J. Hawkes, the narrator tells of a primitive tribal ceremony in which he participated in a village outside of Santo Domingo. Instead of dismissing this ritual as a merely superstitious appeasement of the gods, the narrator is deeply moved by the ceremony, calling it a "poetry [that] offer[s] us visions for which science has no eyes ..." (line 80). If we recall that the narrator himself is a scientist, working as an anthropologist at the New Mexico Museum of Anthropology (line 3), his unscientific conclusion— that this tribal ritual represented pre-historic life "before the Fall" (line 86)—may demonstrate how intense his experience of this dance had been (lines 76 to 80).

54. D

The key to getting this answer right is in the word "adopts." The fact that the narrator has to put on a mindset to prepare himself for the dance is only reflected in one of the statements. The three other statements express his feelings of "delight" (**A**), "delight/shame" (**B**), "greed" (**C**), but none of them mentions his having to prepare himself for the dance. Therefore, alternative **D** is the only correct response.

55. A

The expression "bush telegraph" is an informal way of describing the word-of-mouth manner in which information would be passed along from one anthropologist to another. Alternative **D**, "primitive telecommunication system" is correct as well because the "grapevine" must be one of the earliest ways of passing messages along from one person to the next; however, because the phrase is more general than alternative **A**, it is a less satisfactory response to the question.

A "field telephone" (**B**) is an early mobile telephone that allowed a person to maintain contact with civilization if he/she was working in remote areas. Since the story does not mention any details about an actual telephone like this, alternative **B** would not be correct. Neither would alternative **C**, "extrasensory perception," for the reasons stated above.

56. C

Since "heart-rendering" is a phrase that is often used to indicate an experience that is deeply moving, the word "rending," on its own, is the correct answer. "Chanters" (**A**) are singers, not rattles. "Fourfold" (**B**) simply means "four times" and so does not indicate the "heart-affecting sound of the rattles." "Tripped" (**D**) does not refer to the effect these sounds have on his heart, and therefore would have to be ruled out.

57. D

The key to this answer comes in lines 45 to 47:"it meant that an intricate ritual which had passed from generation to generation through the centuries was to reach yet another." Although the children do provide a sense of "gaiety" (**A**) and of "charm" (**C**), and they do display an "impressive master of their skills" (**B**), none of these choices is as significant as the one indicating the continuity of the traditional ritual.

58. B

Since the word "regalia" refers to uniforms or costumes, alternative **B** is the most correct definition of "accoutrement." Even if you did not know what either of those words meant, from the context of sentence, you might determine that "accoutrement" referred to some kind of clothing. Of the four choices offered, you would also know that neither "paint," "discipline," nor "happiness" refers to clothing, leaving you with only alternative **B** to select.

59. C

Probably the easiest way to identify this answer (although this is a more difficult question than many of the others we have looked at) is by trying to find only one phrase that "suggests his inability to cross the boundary." This way, you do not have to figure out the meaning of each set of words, but you can eliminate them if they do not relate specifically to this phrase. From this perspective, the only set of words that are relevant to the question are those in alternative **C** because they suggest that the anthropologist remains aware that he attending a performance. In this performance, he is always an audience member, not a performer (or "actor"), and thus is able to maintain his stance as a "critical observer."

60. D

This question is made simpler once we take a moment to read the lines that are offered as answers in their context in this essay. When we do this, we realize that the "colours" of the speaker's "memory" could only refer to the insight that he states in the paragraph just above, that "their poetry … offer[s] us visions for which science has no eyes …" (line 80). The other statements occur too far away from his first waking memories to be relevant.

61. D

The word "punctuate" in this context means "to emphasize." So, emphasizing the "boundary between two … realms of experience" would be the most relevant response to the difference between the car and drums. The term "cultural alienation" (A) describes the sense that there is no way to establish contact across the two cultures. Since the narrator looks forward to being able to make contact with "a primitive people" (lines 12 to 13), alternative **A** would not be a satisfactory response. Alternative **B**, as well, is incorrect because the essay indicates that these people benefited from spiritual wealth. Although the narrator states that his hopes of seeing a primitive ritual are "fulfilled" when he hears the drumming, we are not given indications that connect a feeling of "uncertainty" with the narrator's car, and so must rule out this answer as well.

"The Stones" – Synopsis

The speaker in Suzanne Gardinier's "The Stones" tells of a time when she was caught briefly on the mountain by "fog" (line 3). The "terror" (line 2) and "fear" (line 7) of having to spend a night on the mountain with "nothing ... [that] would burn to warm a night" (lines 5 to 6) is set aside temporarily as she imagines what it might take to become one with the mountain instead of threatened by it. The speaker recognizes both the fragility of human existence (line 20) and the apparent stability and timelessness of the "streambeds" (line 14), "insects" (line 15), "gentians" (line 15), and "stones" (line 17). Finally, the fog clears and the speaker acknowledges how huge the gap is between humans and nature, "Language ... as useless as your eyes/ until the fog blew higher and withdrew" (lines 21 to 22).

62. A

The answer to this question is found in the first stanza, ("when … fog reached between the mountains and hid the painted stripes that marked the path") and at the bottom of the poem, in the last verse: "Language was as useless as your eyes/ until the fog blew higher and withdrew" (lines 21 to 22). The "snow," "glaciers," and "mountains" all become elements of her desire to become as ancient as them: "taught the measurement of time in eras" (line 19).

63. C

Since "ambivalence" means to feel two or more things at once, this is the answer you should have chosen. We find these contradictory feelings expressed in the speaker's feelings of "terror" (line 2) and her "wild wish" (line 8) to stay where she was and try to become like the mountain. Her sense of "confidence" (**A**) is complicated by the powerful feelings of fear she experiences when she thinks of spending the night on the mountain in the fog (lines 5 and 6). Both alternatives **B** and **D** are incorrect because no evidence is offered in the poem to support her having these feelings. Since we must base our interpretations on what the poem itself actually says, we have to rule out both of these possibilities as well.

64. D

Alternative **D** is the best answer because it refers to the speaker's way of establishing a sense of well-being despite being in a life-threatening situation. The "imaginary fears" (**A**) of the first choice are incorrect since the fears she experiences on the mountain in the fog are justified, and not imaginary at all. That "human isolation" (**B**) is not correct is explained in the phrase that follows: "over the borders/ you'd drawn for safety" (lines 7 to 8). Since the speaker has in effect "drawn" these borders herself, "human isolation" does not make sense as a response. After all, her isolation is imposed on her by the incoming fog. Similarly, "physical barriers" (**C**) could not be correct. As soon as the fog lifts, so too do the "physical barriers" and she is able to "climb down" (line 24).

65. C

Given the selections we are offered, the speaker's "wild wish" is best expressed as a desire to "shed the predictability of humanness." Since she wants to spend time with "forms [she] couldn't make resemble faces" (line 13), alternative **A**, "return to the crowded shelter" would not be a satisfactory answer. Her wish to "persuade" the stones to accept her as one of them (lines 17 and 18), makes alternative **B** a weak response, because she wishes to become "one" with the mountain, instead of "mastering" it. For the same reason, alternative **D** is also incorrect because, despite her initial feelings of "terror" (line 2), she chooses to accept staying "where there was no sign of the human" (line 9).

66. C

Since "galloped" and "leaped" are words that have a lot of energy in them, words that are full of exuberance, the best response would be to say that they emphasize a sense of "excitement." The other terms all emphasize a different feeling and are therefore not satisfactory responses.

67. C

The question that the speaker asks herself, or us, is a rhetorical question because it is one that cannot be answered literally. A sense of futility is not conveyed by any of the other statements that are offered. The feeling conveyed in alternative **A**, "there was no sign of the human," is something the speaker welcomes at this point. Alternative **B**, "forms you couldn't make resemble faces," acknowledges a condition of nature that the speaker appreciates and does not want to change. Finally, alternative **D**, "the fog blew higher and withdrew," does not show a sense of futility but of hope for reunion with the others in the camp below.

68. A

Since each of the phrases refer to "landmarks" used for her own sense of safety and comfort, the only answer that expresses this sense is alternative **A**. Although these boundaries are "unnatural" to the natural landscape in which she is temporarily trapped, they are "natural" to her, therefore ruling out alternative **D**. Neither "spiritual challenge" (**B**) nor "physical limitations" (**C**) are relevant to the items that are listed and are therefore incorrect answers.

69. C

The word "inscrutability" means difficult to understand. The speaker realizes that asking nature questions "was as useless as your eyes/ until the fog withdrew" (lines 21 to 22), since nature does not respond, of course, and does not expose any of its "secrets." The "other side," therefore, that the speaker wishes to tell in this poem, is nature's side, partly because it is "indifferent" and "inscrutable" (**C**). The first two responses, therefore, are incorrect because they refer to noble human actions such as "human sacrifice" and "heroic endeavours," but not from the perspective of nature. Alternative **D** would be a weak response because it refers to general difficulties instead of specific aspects of nature.

70. D

We notice that for all the speaker's hopefulness of becoming more closely united with nature (the "wild wish" of line 8), in the end she "climbed down" (line 24) once the fog withdrew. Her climbing down from the mountain to the safety of the "cramped shelter" (line 12) indicates that her "wish" must be unfulfilled because humans could never live in the "eras,/ infinite" (lines 19 to 20) of mountains. Again, each of the other answers could be correct in a different context, but we need to be careful to limit our responses to only the evidence that is offered by the text itself.

JANUARY 2004 DIPLOMA EXAMINATION

I. Questions 1 to 8 are based on this excerpt from a personal essay.

from THE COUNTRY OF ILLUSION

Journal

May 17, Athabasca Glacier: I park the car, button up my coat and step out into snow falling on snow.

A white world, blue-shadowed, hushed. Above, a smear of more luminous whiteness
5   where the sun might be. The low whine of wind off the barely visible glacier, its upper reaches lost in a haze of snow and ice fog. The season is officially spring, yet here that fact is still a month and a valley away.

We, on the other hand, have arrived too soon. Cars and busloads of us, all making an early pilgrimage to the ice. I pass an older couple sipping coffee on the steps of their
10   motorhome. A young man with a baby in a carrier on his back. I take my place in the slow, meandering procession, across the footbridge and up the rising path to the terminus.[1] With a nod and smile for those who pass me on their way back down, their faces flushed and wind-bitten, their eyes glistening with tears. Faces that register both weather and dissatisfaction. I struggle over the icy gravel of the path, lowering my head against the
15   wind, raising it every now and again to keep my bearings. Reading the dates on the few stone recession markers that are not blanketed in snow. 1967. 1979. 1984. And ignoring, like everyone else, the posted signs that advise me to stay off the ice.

Eventually gravel disappears under snow and I realize I have climbed from the terminal moraine[2] onto the glacier itself.

20   Ahead of me is a group of Japanese tourists, five men in business suits and dress shoes, scrambling, slipping and laughing their way upward. I pass a family—a boy skipping on ahead, a smaller child riding piggyback on dad, mom bringing up the rear and calling above the wind: *I think we should turn back.* A young couple huddled together on an outcrop of rock, sharing sips from a juice box. I squint into the falling snow and see the
25   hazy shapes of the foolhardy few who have hiked far out onto the ice. One of the Japanese businessmen pans a video camera across the blank whiteness.

What are we doing here? What will the businessman see when he takes that tape home and plays it back for his family?

Some uncertain distance ahead I can make out a stretch of the glacier's slope which the
30   wind has almost cleared of snow. The pale blue of ice suggests itself there, and it is to that possibility of revelation that most of us are heading, intrigued, determined, but perhaps, bitten by the unrelenting wind and numbed by a shrouded, featureless world, already disillusioned.

Moving through the flurrying stillness of falling snow, I wonder about the desire to turn the
35   world of substance into words. About the unforeseeable events that create that desire or at least make one aware of its dormant presence. I remember a moment, years ago, when instead of a slow and chosen ascent like this one, I made a swift and unforeseen descent.

This is the field the Canadian writer walks onto, with no stick to prod for snow pockets, no gauge for the solidity of the earth. The open field of snow, the page, the white space of the
40   Canadian voice, whatever that is.

Aritha van Herk, "A Frozen Tongue/Crevasse"
in A Frozen Tongue

Memory

One Saturday in late winter, two of my high-school friends invited me to go ice-scrambling
45   with them in Maligne Canyon. Or I may have talked them into letting me come along. I'm no longer certain on that particular point, but there is no doubt that among many ignorances, I could claim a complete absence of experience in ice-scrambling. My friends were not professional climbers, but they had explored the canyon in winter before. They knew enough to bring rope, as well as ice axes and crampons[3] for themselves, and they
50   were also thoughtful enough to suggest that I take along a stick.

We headed upstream along the frozen floor of the canyon, but soon found our way blocked by a towering icefall and so had to turn around and be content with exploring the lower reaches. Despite my lack of appropriate gear, I managed to keep up with my friends and consequently felt pleased with myself, conveniently forgetting that we had so far avoided
55   any of the canyon's real difficulties. Then we reached a narrow spot where the gentle slope of snow and ice we were inching down dropped at a suddenly precipitous angle and out of sight around a curve in the canyon walls. Confronted by the unknown, we stopped. There might be an icefall or, on a warm day like this, a pool of open water just around the bend. My friends decided to go on ahead and explore, leaving me to wait either for their return or
60   for a signal that it was safe to join them.

I resented being left behind. The three of us had worked as a team up to this point, I thought, and I felt I'd earned the right to share in the adventure of discovery. I crouched, leaning on my stick, and listened impatiently as the voices of my friends gradually receded. Finally I called out, "Is it safe to come down?"

65   I thought I heard a muffled yeah, although my friends later denied they'd replied to, or even heard my question. I stood up. I set aside the stick because at the entrance to the curve, the canyon walls were narrow enough that with arms outspread I could brace myself against them. Somehow I imagined this would be enough to keep me from falling, and so I stepped eagerly forward.

70   I like to think now that it was during those next few frozen seconds, as I lost my footing, crashed down and slid around the curve, that I entered the country of illusion. There was the brief image of my friends turning in shock as I shot toward them. A gloved hand reaching out to grab me and only giving me a clout on the nose as I swept helplessly past. And then the slope ended and I soared off the edge into the unknown.

75   Some years later, I wrote a short story about that lesson in the unforgiving character of mountain landscape. I tried to capture in words the moment before I went over the edge, and what happened afterwards, because I could not remember the fall itself. As it turned out, beyond the edge of the ice slope was a mere ten- or twelve-foot drop to a lower and more level section of the canyon. In the story, I described how I landed and sat there,
80   stunned, as my mind tried to catch up with what had happened to the rest of me. My only injuries were a bruised backside and a bloody nose from my friend's attempt to catch hold

of me. The story ended with something that happened after the fall: I looked up and saw the contrail of a jet cross the narrow strip of blue sky between the dark canyon walls. I suppose, with an epiphany like that, I had decided this mishap could be read as the myth of Icarus.[4]

85 I was never happy with that story. And now, wondering about the events that brought me to writing, I see that it was the instant before the fall that really mattered. That was the scene that I would replay over and over again in memory. Entertaining other possibilities of its ending. Wondering how I could have been so uncharacteristically reckless. Somehow I had been tricked, or more likely I had tricked myself, and the rest was left up
90 to the capricious recalcitrance[5] of ice. At that moment, sliding toward the edge, watching the unknowable future rush ineluctably[6] toward me, I knew that there was no way out of this story, however it might end. At that moment, perhaps, began my obsession with narrative. And with landscape.

Journal

95 May 30, Mt. Edith Cavell. Today the sun is fierce in a cloudless sky. Climbing the path alongside the wall of the lateral moraine, I hear the trickle and clunk of meltwater gently nudging the stones.

I move in and out of the range of sounds: an endless, intermittent conversation going on among the elements. And I wonder what I think I'm doing here, an interloper who cannot
100 understand the language.

A distant crash. I turn too late and glimpse only the tumbling fragments of the serac[7] that has just detached itself from the foot of Angel Glacier.

As I descend toward the meltwater tarn[8] at the base of Cavell, the tiny dark specks I had glimpsed from high up on the path have become massive boulders. I climb a huge table
105 rock near the shore of the tarn, sip steaming tea from a thermos and take out my notebook. Cloud shadows ghost across the valley floor.

As I write, I remember why I've come here, again.

Crack and rumble of an avalanche. I search Cavell's face. There. Smaller than the sound led me to imagine. Powdery spume over a lip of rock. Dull succuss[9] of thunder. Distance
110 collapses in vertigo:[10] it seems for a moment as if the avalanche might pour across the tarn and engulf me. I look and look until I am exhausted.

June 16, Sunwapta Lake near Athabasca Glacier:

Rock. Clay. Water. Flap of a page in the wind.

The difficulty: how to write about this landscape? How to write beyond the familiar
115 words that obscure the world in a white-out of cliché? Rugged grandeur. Brooding majesty. Monarchs. Mountains as heads of an outmoded body politic.

Sometimes a mountain is too familiar to look at. Sometimes an entire mountain is too insignificant for words.

Better to pick up one of the morainal fragments of rock at my feet. To describe the cool,
120 pitted, secretive age of it in my palm. An immensity of time and pressure within its light heft. The play of surface: streaks and filaments of copper, nacre,[11] ebony. Delicate striations,[12] scratches. Tiny craters. Satellite of the mountain.

Reading the surface of the rock, I know that I am reading a fragment of a larger story.
I set the rock down in a different place from where I picked it up and turn a page in my
125 notebook.

Thomas Wharton (1963–)
Wharton was born in Grande Prairie.

He has published two novels: Icefields *and* Salamander.

[1] terminus—end point

[2] terminal moraine—an accumulation of stone and other debris deposited at the edge of a glacier

[3] crampons—sets of spikes attached to shoes to prevent slipping when walking on ice or climbing

[4] Icarus—in Greek mythology, Icarus and his father, Daedalus, escaped imprisonment in a labyrinth by using wings that Daedalus constructed. Despite his father's warning that flying too close to the sun would melt the wax holding his wings together, Icarus flew too close to the sun. The wax melted, and he fell into the sea and drowned.

[5] capricious recalcitrance—unpredictable stubbornness

[6] ineluctably—inevitably

[7] serac—a large, pointed mass of ice in a glacier

1. In lines 8 to 15, the writer uses sentence fragments to emphasize

   A. his fleeting impressions

   B. his temporary discomfort

   C. the monotony of the landscape

   D. the difficulty of remaining optimistic in a harsh climate

2. The rhetorical questions asked in lines 25 to 26 reveal the writer's

   A. pessimism regarding the future

   B. intention to retain the moment in memory

   C. displeasure with the behaviour of the other tourists

   D. desire to understand the significance of the experience

3. In the quotation from "A Frozen Tongue/Crevasse" (lines 35 to 37), Aritha van Herk suggests that the Canadian writer's challenge in discovering a Canadian voice can be likened to a journey across ice in that both "fields" are

   A. cold and bleak

   B. hostile and disillusioning

   C. featureless and uncertain

   D. prescriptive and confining

Read the quotations below and answer the question that follows.

> "there is no doubt that among many ignorances, I could claim a complete absence of experience in ice-scrambling" (lines 43 to 44)
>
> "Despite my lack of appropriate gear, I managed to keep up with my friends and consequently felt pleased with myself, conveniently forgetting that we had so far avoided any of the canyon's real difficulties" (lines 50 to 52)

4. In the excerpt, the quotations above serve to
    A. convey the writer's fear of falling
    B. foreshadow the writer's unexpected fall
    C. reinforce the writer's feelings of reluctance
    D. emphasize the writer's lack of independence

5. That the writer feels responsible for his unanticipated descent is revealed in the quotation
    A. "I resented being left behind" (line 57)
    B. "I thought I heard a muffled *yeah*, although my friends later denied they'd replied to, or even heard, my question" (lines 61 to 62)
    C. "Somehow I imagined this would be enough to keep me from falling, and so I stepped eagerly forward" (lines 63 to 64)
    D. "I like to think now that it was during those next few frozen seconds, as I lost my footing, crashed down and slid around the curve, that I entered the country of illusion" (lines 65 to 66)

6. The description "Cloud shadows ghost across the valley floor" (lines 97 to 98) reinforces an impression of the
    A. harshness of the environment
    B. stillness of the mountain scene
    C. inhospitable nature of the glacier
    D. mysterious quality of the landscape

7. The writer's immersion in what he observes is **most clearly** revealed in the quotation
    A. "As I write, I remember why I've come here, again" (line 99)
    B. "Smaller than the sound led me to imagine" (lines 100 to 101)
    C. "I look and look until I am exhausted" (line 103)
    D. "The difficulty: how to write about this landscape?" (line 106)

8. When contemplating how to describe the landscape, the writer rejects the words "Rugged grandeur. Brooding majesty. Monarchs" (lines 107 to 108) because

    A. their meaning has been trivialized by overuse

    B. their connotations are unfamiliar to modern audiences

    C. they establish a metaphor between people and mountains

    D. they personify mountains as being arrogant and imperious

II. Questions 9 to 11 are based on this poster.

This is a campaign poster for the Green Party, the German environmental political party that currently forms part of the German government. The caption reads: Green breaks through! Show your colours.

Holger Matthies

Eng30_03 Art posters - Green Breaks Through
(Persuasive Images, Princeton University Press, NJ.1992)

9. An idea communicated by this poster is that the Green Party

    A. adheres to a single issue

    B. is making slow, steady progress

    C. has a small but dedicated membership

    D. lacks the resources to create a large political impact

10. Which of the following artistic choices most emphatically support the main idea of this poster?

    A. Bright colour and verbal irony

    B. Clever slogans and honest claims

    C. Implied understatement and subtle paradox

    D. Powerful symbolism and dramatic contrast

11. The details of this poster suggest that the political party advertised in the poster would **most strongly** appeal to people who

    A. lack political sophistication

    B. are knowledgeable about party politics in Germany

    C. desire a rapid, sweeping change in the political scene

    D. seek a principled political alternative to the status quo

III. Questions 12 to 21 are based on this poem.

This found poem is developed by using direct quotations from the Bible, political speeches, newspaper and magazine articles, and books.

BLESSED IS THE MAN

who does not sit in the seat of the scoffer—

the man who does not denigrate, depreciate, denunciate;

who is not "characteristically intemperate,"

who does not "excuse, retreat, equivocate; and will be heard."

5 (Ah, Giorgione![1] there are those who mongrelize and those who heighten

anything they touch; although it may well be that if Giorgione's self-portrait

were not said to be he, it might not take my fancy. Blessed the geniuses who

know that egomania is not a duty.)

"Diversity, controversy; tolerance"—in that "citadel

10 of learning" we have a fort that ought to armor us well.

Blessed is the man who "takes the risk of a decision"—asks

himself the question: "Would it solve the problem?

Is it right as I see it? Is it in the best interests of all?"

Alas. Ulysses' companions[2] are now political—

15 living self-indulgently until the moral sense is drowned,

having lost all power of comparison,

thinking license emancipates one, "slaves whom they

themselves have bound."

Brazen authors, downright soiled and downright spoiled, as

20 if sound and exceptional, are the old quasi-modish counterfeit,

mitin-proofing[3] conscience against character.

Affronted by "private lies and public shame," blessed is the

author who favors what the supercilious[4] do *not* favor—

who will not comply. Blessed, the unaccommodating man.

25 Blessed the man whose faith is different from possessiveness—of a kind not framed by
"things which do appear"[5]—who will not visualize defeat, too intent to cower; whose

illumined eye has seen the shaft that gilds[6] the sultan's tower.

Marianne Moore (1887–1972)
American poet

[1] Giorgione—15th-century Italian painter

[2] Ulysses' companions—Ulysses' shipwrecked companions were transformed into animals and chose to remain that way despite having the opportunity to be restored to human form

[3] mitin-proofing—applying a protective coating

[4] supercilious—contemptuous, disdainful

[5] faith is … not framed by "things which do appear"—an allusion to the Bible, meaning that faith is not based on the concrete appearance of things

[6] gilds—covers with a layer of gold

13. By enclosing lines 5 to 8 in parentheses, the **main** impression that the writer creates is one of

A. a personal aside

B. an act of reverence

C. a humorous interjection

D. an expression of excitement

14. In lines 9 to 10, "that 'citadel /of learning' " refers to an environment that is

    A. military

    B. political

    C. religious

    D. academic

15. The word "armor" (line 10) suggests that " 'Diversity, controversy; tolerance' " will

    A. guarantee future success

    B. create a reliance on change

    C. provide protection against ignorance

    D. cause aggression toward threatening forces

16. In the context of line 11, the person who " 'takes the risk of a decision' " is described as admirable because he

    A. seeks the advice of peers

    B. commits to a higher purpose

    C. admits personal inadequacies

    D. commits to a dangerous choice

17. The word that signals a contrast to hope or expectation is

    A. "Ah" (line 5)

    B. "Alas" (line 14)

    C. "self-indulgently" (line 15)

    D. "counterfeit" (line 20)

18. In context, the statement "Ulysses' companions are now political" (line 14) suggests that

    A. ancient Greece set a fine example of leadership

    B. politics is now in the hands of the people

    C. politicians have become self-serving

    D. Greek citizens enjoyed conflict

19. In lines 22 to 24, "the author . . . /who will not comply" is an author who resists

    A. professional improvement

    B. private needs and demands

    C. traditional practices that are outdated

    D. complacent adherence to current trends

20. The diction on line 25 specifically celebrates "the man" who

   A. perseveres despite having nothing to show for his efforts

   B. appreciates artistic endeavour despite lacking talent

   C. judges others by the evidence of their actions

   D. gives generously to all who are in need

21. In the context of lines 26 to 27, the "illumined eye" is considered to be the result of

   A. inner conviction

   B. positive counsel

   C. spiritual cynicism

   D. materialistic longing

IV. Questions 22 to 30 are based on this excerpt from a Shakespearean play.
Question 34 requires you to consider this reading together with Reading V.

Shakespeare is believed to have written this play between the years 1593 and 1596, during the reign of Queen Elizabeth I.

from THE TRAGEDY OF KING RICHARD THE SECOND

CHARACTERS:

QUEEN—wife of King Richard
LADY—one of the Queen's ladies
GARDENER
[1.] **MAN**, [2.] **MAN**—Gardener's assistants

This excerpt is set in England in 1399, the last year of King Richard's reign. Shakespeare depicts Richard as a self-indulgent monarch whose chaotic reign has resulted in civil unrest. This excerpt takes place in a garden at the castle of the Duke of York.

   Enter the Queen with [two Ladies,] her Attendants.

   QUEEN: What sport shall we devise here in this garden

   To drive away the heavy thought of care?

   LADY: Madam, we'll play at bowls.   ⁴bowls—lawn bowling

5 **QUEEN:** 'Twill make me think the world is full of rubs   ⁵rubs—difficulties

   And that my fortune runs against the bias.   ⁶bias—tendency of a
                                                                        bowling ball to curve
   LADY: Madam, we'll dance.

   QUEEN: My legs can keep no measure in delight

   When my poor heart no measure keeps in grief.

10 Therefore no dancing, girl; some other sport.

LADY: Madam, we'll tell tales.

QUEEN: Of sorrow or of joy?

LADY: Of either, madam.

QUEEN: Of neither, girl;

15 For if of joy, being altogether wanting,

It doth remember me the more of sorrow;

Or if of grief, being altogether had,

It adds more sorrow to my want of joy;

For what I have I need not to repeat,

20 And what I want it boots not to complain.   [20]boots—helps

LADY: Madam, I'll sing.

QUEEN: 'Tis well that thou hast cause;

But thou shouldst please me better, wouldst thou weep.

LADY: I could weep, madam, would it do you good.

25 **QUEEN**: And I could sing, would weeping do me good,

And never borrow any tear of thee.

Enter Gardeners [one the Master, the other two his Men].

But stay, here come the gardeners.

Let's step into the shadow of these trees.   [30]My wretchedness unto
a row of pins—my
30 My wretchedness unto a row of pins,   misery against a
triviality
They will talk of state, for every one doth so

Against a change: woe is forerun with woe.   [32]Against—anticipating

[Queen and Ladies step aside.]

GARDENER: Go bind thou up yon dangling apricocks,   [34]apricocks—apricots

35 Which, like unruly children, make their sire

Stoop with oppression of their prodigal weight.   [36]prodigal—excessive

Give some supportance to the bending twigs.

Go thou and, like an executioner,

Cut off the heads of too-fast-growing sprays

40 That look too lofty in our commonwealth.

All must be even in our government.

You thus employed, I will go root away

The noisome weeds which without profit suck

The soil's fertility from wholesome flowers.

45 **[1.] MAN**: Why should we, in the compass of a pale,

Keep law and form and due proportion,

Showing, as in a model, our firm estate,

When our sea-wallèd garden, the whole land,

Is full of weeds, her fairest flowers choked up,

50 Her fruit trees all unpruned, her hedges ruined,

Her knots disordered, and her wholesome herbs

Swarming with caterpillars?

GARDENER: Hold thy peace.

He that hath suffered this disordered spring

55 Hath now himself met with the fall of leaf.

The weeds which his broad-spreading leaves did shelter,

That seemed in eating him to hold him up,

Are plucked up root and all by Bolingbroke—

I mean the Earl of Wiltshire, Bushy, Green.

60 **[2.] MAN**: What, are they dead?

GARDENER: They are; and Bolingbroke

Hath seized the wasteful king. O, what pity is it

That he had not so trimmed and dressed his land

As we this garden! We at time of year

65 Do wound the bark, the skin of our fruit trees,

Lest, being overproud in sap and blood,

With too much riches it confound itself.

Had he done so to great and growing men,

They might have lived to bear, and he to taste

70 Their fruits of duty. Superfluous branches

We lop away, that bearing boughs may live.

Had he done so, himself had borne the crown,

Which waste of idle hours hath quite thrown down.

[2.] MAN: What, think you the king shall be deposed?

75 **GARDENER**: Depressed he is already, and deposed

'Tis doubt he will be. Letters came last night

To a dear friend of the good Duke of York's

That tell black tidings.

---

[45] a pale—a walled or enclosed garden

[51] knots—intricately patterned flowerbeds

[58] Bolingbroke—the Duke of Hereford; he was Richard's cousin who later became King Henry IV. Bolingbroke has just taken Richard to London.

[67] confound—ruin

[75] Depressed—lowered in degree or authority

[76] 'Tis doubt—it is feared

QUEEN: O, I am pressed to death through want of speaking!

80   [*Comes forward.*]

Thou old Adam's likeness, set to dress this garden,

How dares thy harsh rude tongue sound this unpleasing news?

What Eve, what serpent, has suggested thee

To make a second fall of cursèd man?

85   Why dost thou say King Richard is deposed?

Dar'st thou, thou little better thing than earth,

Divine his downfall? Say, where, when, and how

Cam'st thou by this ill tidings? Speak, thou wretch!

GARDENER: Pardon me, madam. Little joy have I

90   To breathe this news; yet what I say is true.

King Richard, he is in the mighty hold

Of Bolingbroke. Their fortunes both are weighed.

In your lord's scale is nothing but himself,

And some few vanities that make him light;

95   But in the balance of great Bolingbroke,

Besides himself, are all the English peers,

And with that odds he weighs King Richard down.

Post you to London, and you will find it so.

I speak no more than every one doth know.

100   **QUEEN**: Nimble mischance, that art so light of foot,

Doth not thy embassage belong to me,

And am I last that knows it? O, thou thinkest

To serve me last, that I may longest keep

Thy sorrow in my breast. Come, ladies, go

105   To meet at London London's king in woe.

What, was I born to this, that my sad look

Should grace the triumph of great Bolingbroke?

Gard'ner, for telling me these news of woe,

Pray God the plants thou graft'st may never grow.

110   *Exit [with Ladies].*

[81]Adam's likeness—a reference to the biblical Adam, the first man

[83]Eve—a reference to the biblical Eve, the first woman, Adam's wife

[101]embassage—message

> **GARDENER**: Poor queen, so that thy state might be no worse,
>
> I would my skill were subject to thy curse!
>
> Here did she fall a tear; here in this place
>
> I'll set a bank of rue, sour herb of grace.
>
> *115* Rue, even for ruth, here shortly shall be seen,   [115]ruth—compassion
>
> In the remembrance of a weeping queen.
> *Exeunt.*
>
> *William Shakespeare (1564–1616)*

22. By hiding from the gardeners (line 29), the queen is able to

  A. seek refuge from further grief

  B. maintain the dignity of her role

  C. learn the latest political developments

  D. cover her embarrassment at her husband's downfall

23. In lines 38 to 39, the gardener's reference to "an executioner" metaphorically suggests that overly ambitious growth is regarded as

  A. treachery

  B. cowardice

  C. foolishness

  D. wastefulness

24. The phrase "our sea-wallèd garden" (line 48) refers to

  A. York

  B. London

  C. Wiltshire

  D. England

25. In lines 45 to 52, compared with the efforts of the gardeners, Richard's rule is depicted as

  A. indulgent and nurturing

  B. neglectful and irresponsible

  C. disrespectful and inconsiderate

  D. considerate and forward-thinking

26. In his speeches in lines 53 to 73, the gardener suggests that Richard's impending downfall could have been avoided if Richard had

   A. curtailed the powers of men such as Bushy and Green

   B. demonstrated greater understanding of Bolingbroke

   C. defeated Bolingbroke when Bolingbroke was weak

   D. encouraged greater support from the Duke of York

27. In lines 82 to 88, the queen confronts the gardener's news of her husband's impending downfall with

   A. painful humility

   B. bitter acceptance

   C. mournful despair

   D. righteous indignation

28. The queen's curse upon the garden and gardener (lines 108 to 109) **mainly** reinforces her

   A. dismissive treatment of commoners

   B. animosity toward those who gossip

   C. lack of respect for the gardener's lack of sympathy

   D. anger about the news the gardener has revealed to her

29. In lines 112 to 115, the gardener responds to the queen's curse by vowing to

   A. reveal his resentment

   B. plant a symbol of bitter rejection and anger

   C. plant a symbol of forgiveness and sympathy

   D. ensure broad knowledge of the queen's emotional suffering

30. The **main** literary device used throughout this excerpt is

   A. irony

   B. parody

   C. allusion

   D. metaphor

V. Questions 31 to 33 are based on this excerpt from an essay.
Question 34 requires you to consider this reading together with Reading IV.

This excerpt is taken from an essay written as an introduction to the play *The Tragedy of King Richard the Second*.

from INTRODUCTION TO THE TRAGEDY OF KING RICHARD THE SECOND

It[1] came at a time when the aged Elizabeth I and her councillors were extremely sensitive to the possible political repercussions of stage plays. Consequently when it appeared in print in 1597 the actual dethronement (IV, i, 154–318) had been excised.[2] It had almost certainly been included in the stage performances and may well have been banned by
5 the censor of books for that very reason. It was not printed until 1608, when Elizabeth's successor, James I, was firmly seated on the English throne.

As for the queen's anxiety, the perspective of three and a half centuries makes clear that while, like every re-enactment of history, the play had political meaning, it can have had no political purpose, and that, in supposing it could be useful as propaganda, both her
10 majesty's government and the opposition were deceived. It is a vivid, impartial re-creation of a political impasse which brought death to a tyrant, but to a usurper a troublesome reign, and to the realm eventually some thirty years of civil war. It is full of conflicting political ideas: the divine right of kings, the subject's duty of passive obedience, the dangers of irresponsible despotism, the complex qualities of an ideal ruler. But which of these ideas
15 were Shakespeare's own is impossible to discern. On politics as on religion he preserves as always "the taciturnity of nature." What can be said of this aspect of Richard II is that here, as in all the histories, Shakespeare wrote as a true patriot and that England was the heroine. The continuing power of the play to interest audiences in England and elsewhere can come only from its universal human appeal as drama.

Matthew W. Black
University of Pennsylvania

[1] It—refers to the play The Tragedy of King Richard the Second

[2] excised—removed

31. The writer suggests that portions of the play that were performed in stage productions of *Richard II* were not included in the early print version because

A. Elizabeth I was descended from Bolingbroke

B. Elizabeth I feared their impact on her uneasy reign

C. Elizabethan audiences preferred short dramas that held their attention

D. Elizabethan audiences neither appreciated nor understood the play's historical context

32. The writer implies that in *Richard II*, "as in all the histories" (line 16), Shakespeare's work **mainly** reflects

    A. the complexities associated with historical accuracy and political idealism

    B. the complexities associated with faithfully transferring an English historical event into a drama

    C. a lack of attention to political or historical accuracy but reveals instead his affection for England

    D. a lack of detail about England's many conflicts but reveals instead its extended history of despotism

33. The writer suggests that a dramatization of history can serve to

    A. provide a human perspective to distant historical events

    B. bring public attention to long-ignored historical facts

    C. diffuse public discontent with current political actions

    D. force audiences to question their personal beliefs

34. Reading IV and Reading V could be used together as supporting evidence for a response to which of the following research questions?

    A. To what extent was Richard II an effective monarch?

    B. To what extent is censorship an effective measure to counteract political activism?

    C. How has Shakespeare depicted the role of the commoner in Elizabethan society?

    D. How has Shakespeare used the history of monarchies to develop significant ideas in his plays?

VI. Questions 35 to 44 are based on this excerpt from a novel.

This is the opening chapter of the novel.

from FLESH AND BLOOD

1935 / Constantine, eight years old, was working in his father's garden and thinking about his own garden, a square of powdered granite he had staked out and combed into rows at the top of his family's land. First he weeded his father's bean rows and then he crawled among the gnarls and snags of his father's vineyard, tying errant tendrils back
5   to the stakes with rough brown cord that was to his mind the exact color and texture of righteous, doomed effort. When his father talked about "working ourselves to death to keep ourselves alive," Constantine imagined this cord, coarse and strong and drab, electric with stray hairs of its own, wrapping the world up into an awkward parcel that would not submit or stay tied, just as the grapevines kept working themselves loose and shooting out
10 at ecstatic, skyward angles. It was one of his jobs to train the vines, and he had come to despise and respect them for their wild insistence. The vines had a secret, tangled life, a slumbering will, but it was he, Constantine, who would suffer if they weren't kept staked and orderly. His father had a merciless eye that could find one bad straw in ten bales of good intentions.
15 As he worked he thought of his garden, hidden away in the blare of the hilltop sun, three square feet so useless to his father's tightly bound future that they were given over as a toy to Constantine, the youngest. The earth in his garden was little more than a quarter inch

of dust caught in a declivity of rock, but he would draw fruit from it by determination and work, the push of his own will. From his mother's kitchen he had spirited dozens of seeds,

20 the odd ones that stuck to the knife or fell on the floor no matter how carefully she checked herself for the sin of waste. His garden lay high on a crown of scorched rock where no one bothered to go; if it produced he could tend the crop without telling anyone. He could wait until harvest time and descend triumphantly, carrying an eggplant or a pepper, perhaps a tomato. He could walk through the autumn dusk to the house where his mother

25 would be laying out supper for his father and brothers. The light would be at his back, hammered[1] and golden. It would cut into the dimness of the kitchen as he threw open the door. His mother and father and brothers would look at him, the runt, of whom so little was expected. When he stood in the vineyard looking down at the world—the ruins of the Papandreous' farm, the Kalamata Company's olive groves, the remote shimmer of town—

30 he thought of climbing the rocks one day to find green shoots pushing through his patch of dust. The priest counseled that miracles were the result of diligence and blind faith. He was faithful.

And he was diligent. Every day he took his ration of water, drank half, and sprinkled half over his seeds. That was easy, but he needed better soil as well. The pants sewn by

35 his mother had no pockets, and it would be impossible to steal handfuls of dirt from his father's garden and climb with them past the goats' shed and across the curving face of the rock without being detected. So he stole the only way he could, by bending over every evening at the end of the workday, as if tying down one last low vine, and filling his mouth with earth. The soil had a heady, fecal taste; a darkness on his tongue that was at once

40 revolting and strangely, dangerously delicious. With his mouth full he made his way up the steep yard to the rocks. There was not much risk, even if he passed his father or one of his brothers. They were used to him not speaking. They believed he was silent because his thoughts were simple. In fact, he kept quiet because he feared mistakes. The world was made of mistakes, a thorny tangle, and no amount of cord, however fastidiously tied,

45 could bind them all down. Punishment waited everywhere. It was wiser not to speak. Every evening he walked in his customary silence past whatever brothers might still be at work among the goats, holding his cheeks in so no one would guess his mouth was full. As he crossed the yard and ascended the rocks he struggled not to swallow but inevitably he did, and some of the dirt sifted down his throat, reinfecting him with its pungent black

50 taste. The dirt was threaded with goat dung, and his eyes watered. Still, by the time he reached the top, there remained a fair-sized ball of wet earth to spit into his palm. Quickly then, fearful that one of his brothers might have followed to tease him, he worked the handful of soil into his miniature garden. It was drenched with his saliva. He massaged it in and thought of his mother, who forgot to look at him because her own life held too

55 many troubles for her to watch. He thought of her carrying food to his ravenous, shouting brothers. He thought of how her face would look as he came through the door one harvest evening. He would stand in the bent, dusty light before his surprised family. Then he would walk up to the table and lay out what he'd brought: a pepper, an eggplant, a tomato.

Michael Cunningham (1952–)
Cunningham is an American writer who received the
Pulitzer Prize for Fiction for The Hours.
He lives in New York City

[1] hammered—shaped or marked by hammer blows

35. Constantine's impression of the cord being "the exact color and texture of righteous, doomed effort" (line 5) conveys a sense of

    A. futility

    B. remorse

    C. uniformity

    D. uncertainty

36. The paradoxical aspect of the family's existence on the vineyard is **best** demonstrated in the phrase

    A. "working in his father's garden and thinking about his own garden" (lines 1 to 2)

    B. " 'working ourselves to death to keep ourselves alive' " (line 6)

    C. "wrapping the world up into an awkward parcel that would not submit or stay tied" (lines 7 to 8)

    D. "he had come to despise and respect them for their wild insistence" (lines 9 to 10)

37. The description of the vines as having "a secret, tangled life, a slumbering will" (lines 10 to 11) provides an image of Constantine's

    A. opinion of his brothers

    B. personal characteristics

    C. relationship with his mother

    D. curiosity regarding his father

38. The quotation "He could wait until harvest time and descend triumphantly" (line 20) reveals Constantine's

    A. passion for the vineyard

    B. illusion of his family's neediness

    C. motivation for growing a garden

    D. lack of concern for practical matters

39. The father's impact on Constantine's behaviour is **most strongly** revealed in the quotation

    A. "His father had a merciless eye that could find one bad straw in ten bales of good intentions" (line 12)

    B. "he thought of his garden, hidden away in the blare of the hilltop sun, three square feet so useless to his father's tightly bound future that they were given over as a toy to Constantine" (lines 13 to 14)

    C. "He could walk through the autumn dusk to the house where his mother would be laying out supper for his father and brothers" (lines 21 to 22)

    D. "it would be impossible to steal handfuls of dirt from his father's garden" (line 31)

40. Constantine's efforts to obtain water and soil for his garden demonstrate his

    A. superstition and cunning

    B. confidence and sympathy

    C. sophistication and certainty

    D. perseverance and conviction

41. The meaning of the word "fastidiously" (line 39) is

    A. quickly

    B. carefully

    C. roughly

    D. temporarily

42. The statement that provides an explanation for Constantine's quiet nature is

    A. "With his mouth full he made his way up the steep yard to the rocks" (lines 35 to 36)

    B. "They believed he was silent because his thoughts were simple" (lines 37 to 38)

    C. "Punishment waited everywhere" (line 40)

    D. "Every evening he walked in his customary silence past whatever brothers might still be at work" (lines 40 to 41)

43. The mother's behaviour that **most strongly** influences Constantine's feelings toward her is conveyed in the quotation

    A. "From his mother's kitchen he had spirited dozens of seeds, the odd ones that stuck to the knife or fell on the floor no matter how carefully she checked herself for the sin of waste" (lines 16 to 18)

    B. "His mother and father and brothers would look at him, the runt, of whom so little was expected" (lines 23 to 24)

    C. "his mother, who forgot to look at him because her own life held too many troubles for her to watch" (lines 48 to 49)

    D. "He thought of her carrying food to his ravenous, shouting brothers" (line 49)

44. The **main** idea presented in this excerpt is most clearly captured in the quotation

    A. "it was he, Constantine, who would suffer if they weren't kept staked and orderly" (lines 11 to 12)

    B. "miracles were the result of diligence and blind faith" (lines 27 to 28)

    C. "It was wiser not to speak" (line 40)

    D. "He thought of how her face would look as he came through the door" (line 50)

VII. Questions 45 and 46 are based on this photograph and commentary.

ONE THAT ALMOST GOT AWAY

Final Edit

PUERTO RICO

Why We Pulled the Taffeta

Early one morning, deep in Puerto Rico's rural heartland, photographer Amy Toensing found a freshly washed harvest—of formal wear. "I was driving around Utuado and saw these little dresses hanging on a clothesline. I just had to stop the car," she remembers. "There was something about those colors that really said 'Puerto Rico' to me."

But not to illustrations editor Susan Welchman. "Every photograph we use has to help tell the story about that particular place," she says. "This picture is beautiful, but it didn't do the job."

The dreamlike image did do a job on several female staffers, however. "You either had dresses like these when you were a girl, or wanted them," sighed one writer. "Not me," says Toensing, a child of the seventies. "I wore pants."

[1] Taffeta—a crisp, woven fabric of silk, rayon, or nylon; often used to make girls' clothing

45. The commentary reveals that the editorial policy of this magazine regarding visual texts (lines 5 to 6) favours communication that

A. is gender neutral

B. presents a consistent interpretation

C. prioritizes written texts over visual texts

D. includes interactions among the people in the featured area

46. That this photograph was "one that almost got away" and that it prompted several different opinions among "female staffers" (line 7) suggests that

A. women respond to this photograph in a predictably similar manner

B. Welchman has a limited appreciation and understanding of what appeals to women

C. this photograph elicits responses that vary according to perception and personal experience

D. this photograph, which was intended to suggest the Puerto Rican experience, instead captures a singularly universal experience

VIII. Questions 47 to 51 are based on this excerpt from an essay.
Question 70 requires you to consider this reading together with readings IX and X.

from INTRODUCTION to the COMPLETE ANNOTATED
GILBERT AND SULLIVAN

Sir William Schwenk Gilbert (1836–1911), an English playwright and humourist, is best known for his collaborations with Sir Arthur Seymour Sullivan (1842–1900) in writing comic operettas. This excerpt is from the introduction to a complete collection of Gilbert and Sullivan operettas published in 1996.

On the morning after the opening night of The Gondoliers in December 1889 W. S. Gilbert wrote to Sir Arthur Sullivan thanking him for all the work that he had put into the piece. He added with rare magnanimity:[1] "It gives one the chance of shining right through the twentieth century with a reflected light."

5 The works of Gilbert and Sullivan have, indeed, continued to shine right through the twentieth century. In fact, they are almost certainly more widely known and enjoyed as it draws to a close than they were in its early years. This is in large part due to modern technology which has made them available on records and compact discs, audio and video tapes, television, film and radio as well as through the more traditional medium of stage
10 performances by both amateur and professional companies.

What are the reasons for the enduring popularity of the Savoy Operas?[2] Undoubtedly the nostalgia factor is an important one. At a time of shifting values and rapid change, roots and tradition have come to assume considerable importance. The burgeoning heritage industry, which seems to be turning just about every other derelict industrial site into a
15 working museum or theme park, testifies to the appeal of the past, and especially of the Victorian era which seems to stand for so much that we have lost in the way of reassuring solidity and self-confidence. The operas of Gilbert and Sullivan undoubtedly appeal to many people today because they are a genuine piece of Victoriana, as authentic as William Morris wallpaper, the Albert Memorial or a Penny Black stamp.

20 Half the charm of the Savoy Operas is that they are so dated. They seem to breathe the innocence, the naïvety and the fun of a long-vanished age. Even when they were written, of course, they had a strong element of pure escapism with their fantastic topsy-turvy[3] settings and plots. Now, a hundred years on, their mannered dialogue and topical references to themes and personalities that have long passed into the realms of history give
25 them an added quaintness as period pieces.

There are those who feel that our strong attachment to the works of Gilbert and Sullivan is part of the British disease of always looking backwards and never looking forwards. In a letter to The Times in December 1990 Sir Graham Hills, Principal of the University of Strathclyde and member of the Board of Governors of the BBC, proposed, apparently in all
30 seriousness, a moratorium[4] for at least five years on performances of the Savoy Operas. He wrote:

They engender in the British (and especially in the English) nostalgic fondness for Britain's imperial past which is a serious obstacle to change and reform. Everything associated with that past, from lord chancellors and the like in fancy
35 dress to light-hearted, bone-headed military men in scarlet, gives credence to the idea that great wealth flows effortlessly and unceasingly from such cultivated minds. The facts are that our wealth-creating apparatus, in the form of business and industry, continues to decline almost monotonically, and has done so since those operas were first performed.

40 There is clearly room for someone to do a doctoral thesis (perhaps under Sir Graham's supervision?) on the relationship between Gilbert and Sullivan and Britain's economic decline. Perhaps he does have a point, although he would have to explain how the Savoy Operas have remained very popular in the United States in a culture which is much more forward-looking and enterprise-friendly. His call for a moratorium, I am relieved to

45 say, has not been taken up and as far as I am aware, no operatic group, either amateur or professional, has forsaken the works of Gilbert and Sullivan as their contribution to helping Britain's economic recovery.

Ian Bradley
Bradley is a clergyman, university lecturer,
writer, and broadcaster.
He lives in Scotland.

[1] magnanimity—generosity and forgiveness

[2] Savoy Operas—operettas of Gilbert and Sullivan are often referred to as the Savoy Operas. In 1881, D'Oyly Carte, a successful producer of theatrical works, built the Savoy Theatre for the performance of Gilbert and Sullivan's operettas.

[3] topsy-turvy—upside-down, confused

[4] moratorium—suspension of performance

---

47. In stating that "Half the charm of the Savoy Operas is that they are so dated" (line 19), the writer reinforces the idea that people

   A. consider the operas to be mindless entertainment

   B. do not appreciate the complexities of the operas

   C. promote the concept that history is fiction

   D. long for a past that they idealize

48. Sir Graham Hills' reason for suggesting a moratorium on the performance of the Savoy Operas (lines 29 to 33) is **best** revealed in his belief that the British

   A. people have failed to undertake serious social reforms in Britain

   B. preoccupation with past glories has stifled financial growth in Britain

   C. desire for progress has resulted in the maintenance of a stagnant status quo

   D. people have overestimated the sophistication and intelligence of the operetta dialogue

49. The writer refutes Sir Graham's argument by stating that

   A. Sir Graham should undertake the supervision of a student's doctoral thesis

   B. Sir Graham has overestimated the influence of amateur theatre groups in Britain

   C. Sir Graham's theories make further academic research crucial to defend the Savoy Operas

   D. Sir Graham's theories do not explain why the popularity of the Savoy Operas in the United States has not reduced American economic progress

50. In lines 37 to 39, the writer's understated tone emphasizes

   A. the illogical nature of Sir Graham's assumptions

   B. Sir Graham's hurtful intent in his pointed criticism

   C. the need for a careful restructuring of English expectations

   D. Sir Graham's undue preoccupation with monetary considerations

51. The writer's attitude toward the works of Gilbert and Sullivan is **best** summarized in the quotation

   A. "This is in large part due to modern technology which has made them available" (lines 7 to 8)

   B. "They seem to breathe the innocence, the naïvety and the fun of a long-vanished age" (lines 19 to 20)

   C. "references to themes and personalities that have long passed into the realms of history give them an added quaintness as period pieces" (lines 22 to 23)

   D. "no operatic group, either amateur or professional, has forsaken the works of Gilbert and Sullivan as their contribution to helping Britain's economic recovery" (lines 41 to 43)

IX. Questions 52 to 64 are based on this excerpt from a screenplay.
Question 70 requires you to consider this reading together with Readings VIII and X.

from TOPSY-TURVY

Gilbert and Sullivan collaborated on 14 operettas between 1871 and 1896. These 14 operettas, still popular today, are the most frequently performed operettas in history. None of the work produced individually by either man remained popular beyond his own time.

This excerpt from a screenplay about the lives of **GILBERT** *and* **SULLIVAN** *is set in London in 1885.*

CHARACTERS:

SULLIVAN—Sir Arthur Sullivan, musical composer

CARTE—D'Oyly Carte, producer

GILBERT—W. S. Gilbert, writer of plays and lyrics

HELEN—Miss Helen Lenoir, stage manager

> **SULLIVAN** *is in his study, late at night. He is in his shirtsleeves, working at the desk—writing (like many composers,* **SULLIVAN** *didn't compose at the piano). He has a cigarette in its holder.*
>
> 5 *He writes a couple of bars, stops, crosses something out, and lets his pen drop on to the page. He holds his head in his hands. He lets his monocle drop. Near by, Big Ben strikes the quarter. He looks helpless. He is not happy.*
>
> *In* **CARTE***'s office. Day. Footsteps. Until* **GILBERT** *and* **SULLIVAN** *sit, we see only a close shot of the desk: hands, cigars, etc.*

Sullivan as depicted in the film Topsy-Turvy

GILBERT: Good morning, Carte.

10 **CARTE**: Good morning, Gilbert. Cigar? (*He offers the cigar box.*)

GILBERT: Thank you very much (*He refers to* **CARTE***'s cigar-cutter.*)

SULLIVAN: Gilbert.

GILBERT: Sullivan. May I? (*He refers to* **CARTE***'s cigar-cutter.*)

CARTE: Certainly.

15 **SULLIVAN**: Good morning, D'Oyly.

CARTE: Hello, Arthur.

GILBERT: Good morning, Miss Lenoir.

HELEN: Good morning, everybody.

SULLIVAN: Good day, Helen.

20 (**GILBERT** *and* **SULLIVAN** *sit, side by side.* **GILBERT** *lights his cigar.* **CARTE** *sits on the ottoman by the wall.* **HELEN** *sits in* **CARTE***'s chair behind his desk.* **CARTE** *gives her a discreet nod.*)

HELEN: Now, gentlemen, we all know why we're here. We seem to have come to something of a standstill.

D'Oyly Carte and Helen Lenoir
as depicted in the film Topsy-Turvy What did he like? Tearing up trees on the bush hog.
Swimming in heartstopping water.

25 **SULLIVAN**: Indeed we have.

HELEN: Which, Arthur, is because …?

SULLIVAN: Oh. Because, Helen, I am unable to set the piece[1] that Gilbert persists in presenting.

GILBERT: The piece I persist in presenting, Sullivan, is substantially altered each time,
30 otherwise there'd be little point in my presenting it to you.

(**SULLIVAN** *lights a cigarette.*)

SULLIVAN: With great respect, old chap, it is not substantially altered at all. You seem merely to have grafted on to the first act the tantalizing suggestion that we are to be in the realms of human emotion and probability, only to disappoint us by reverting to your
35 familiar world of topsy-turvydom.

GILBERT: That which I have grafted on to Act One, Sullivan, has been specifically at your request. If you take exception to topsy-turvydom, you take exception to a great deal of my work over the past twenty-five years. Not to mention much of what you and I have written together since eighteen hundred and seventy-one.

40 **SULLIVAN**: Oh, that is patent balderdash!

GILBERT: Is it?

HELEN: Gentlemen, if we might keep things cordial, we may make some progress. Arthur, can you really not see your way to setting this new piece?

SULLIVAN: Alas, Helen, I cannot.

45 **HELEN**: Cannot, or will not?

SULLIVAN: I am truly unable to set any piece that is so profoundly uncongenial to me.

HELEN: Uncongenial though it may be to you, I must remind you that we here are conducting a business.

Eng30_02 Topsy-Turvy6

Gilbert and Sullivan as portrayed in the film Topsy-Turvy

SULLIVAN: And may I remind you, Helen, that I am not a machine.

50 **HELEN**: I would not suggest for one moment that you were.

SULLIVAN: You all seem to be treating me as a barrel-organ. You have but to turn my handle, and 'Hey Presto!'—out pops a tune!

(**GILBERT**, **CARTE** *and* **HELEN** *speak at once.*)

GILBERT: That's not strictly true.

55 **CARTE**: Arthur!

HELEN: Come now, that's unfair. (*She continues.*) You are both contractually obliged to supply a new work on request.

GILBERT: And the very act of signing a joint contract dictates that we must be businesslike.

60 **HELEN**: Yes, Mr Gilbert, and I was wondering whether you might not be able to solve our wee difficulty.

GILBERT: How, pray?

HELEN: By simply writing another libretto[2] (**SULLIVAN** *looks worried.*)

65 **GILBERT**: That's out of the question. I have spent many long months working at this play, which I have every confidence will be the best we have yet produced at the Savoy, and to abandon it would be not only criminal, but wasteful.

HELEN: I see.

GILBERT: Now, had Sullivan lodged his complaint at an earlier date, that might have been a different matter.

70 **SULLIVAN**: I made my complaint the moment you presented me with the libretto.

GILBERT: The point being that I was unable to present you with the libretto until you returned from your Grand Tour of Europe.[3]

SULLIVAN: That is neither here nor there.

GILBERT: No, Sullivan—indeed! I was here, and you were there! Ha!

75 **HELEN**: What I don't understand, Arthur, is why you cannot set this piece. You're our greatest composer—surely you can do anything.

SULLIVAN: How very kind you are, Helen; but I say again to you all, I am at the end of my tether. I have been repeating myself in this … class of work for too long, and I will not continue so to do.

80 **GILBERT**: Neither of us runs any risk of repeating himself, Sullivan. This is an entirely new story, quite unlike any other.

SULLIVAN: But, Gilbert, it bears a marked similarity to *The Sorcerer*. People are already saying we're repeating ourselves.

GILBERT: In what way is it similar to *The Sorcerer*?

85 **SULLIVAN**: Obviously, both involve characters who are transformed by the taking of a magic potion. A device which I continue to find utterly contrived.

GILBERT: Every theatrical performance is a contrivance, by its very nature.

SULLIVAN: Yes, but this piece consists entirely of an artificial and implausible situation.

GILBERT: If you wish to write a grand opera about a prostitute dying of consumption in
90 a garret, I suggest you contact Mr Ibsen[4] in Oslo. I am sure he will be able to furnish you with something suitably dull.

CARTE: Gilbert—please.

GILBERT: Hmm? I do beg your pardon, Miss Lenoir.

HELEN: Oh, no, granted.

SULLIVAN: The opportunity to treat a situation of tender, human and dramatic interest is
95 one I long for more than anything else in the world.

GILBERT: If that is your sincere desire, I would be willing, with Carte's permission, to withdraw my services for one turn, to allow you to write a grand opera with a collaborator with whom you have a closer affinity than myself.

SULLIVAN: No, Gilbert.

100 **GILBERT**: I am in earnest, Sullivan.

CARTE: No doubt that is something we shall be pursuing in the future.

GILBERT: Indeed? Well, that is your prerogative, Carte.

HELEN: However, we are concerned with the present. Arthur, will you or will you not set Mr Gilbert's new and original work?

105 **SULLIVAN**: *Ma belle Hélène, ce n'est pas possible.*[5]

HELEN: Truly?

SULLIVAN: I'm afraid so.

HELEN: That being the case … Mr Gilbert: would I be right in supposing that you remain unable to accommodate us?

110 **GILBERT**: Indeed, Miss Lenoir. I have had what I deem to be a good idea, and such ideas are not three a penny.

HELEN: What a pity. This will be a very sad day for many thousands of people.

(**CARTE** *takes out his pocket watch.*)

CARTE: Well, gentlemen . . . I don't know about you, but, speaking for myself, I could
115 murder a pork chop.

(*He snaps his watch shut. Very long pause.*)

GILBERT: If you'll excuse me, I shall retrieve my hat. (*He gets up, and goes through to* **HELEN***'s office. She watches him. Then* **CARTE** *gets up, and stands by* **HELEN***'s chair. Pause.* **SULLIVAN** *hesitates, then he too gets up and goes towards* **HELEN***'s office.*
120 **GILBERT** *is on his way back. They meet in the doorway.*)

SULLIVAN: Gilbert.

GILBERT: Sullivan. (*He puts on his hat, and addresses* **CARTE** *and* **HELEN**.) Good day to you both. No doubt we shall be in communication in the near future. (**CARTE** *and* **HELEN** *speak at once.*)

125 **CARTE**: Gilbert.

HELEN: Good day, Mr Gilbert.

GILBERT: Good day. (*He leaves the office.* **SULLIVAN** *returns from* **HELEN***'s office. He is wearing his top hat. Pause.*)

SULLIVAN: You know where to find me.

130 **HELEN**: Arthur. (*He leaves. Pause.* **HELEN** *sighs.*)

Mike Leigh (1943–)
Leigh was born in Lancashire, England.
He is an award-winning film maker who received the Michael Balcom Award
for Outstanding Contribution to British Cinema in 1995.

[1] Set the piece—compose music for the lyrics

[2] libretto—the text of a dramatic musical work, such as an opera

[3] Grand Tour of Europe—extended travel often undertaken by English gentlemen to gain experience and enlightenment

[4] Mr Ibsen—Henrik Ibsen (1828–1906) a Norwegian playwright who introduced to the European stage a new order of moral analysis that was placed against a realistic middle-class background

[5] *Ma belle Hélène, ce n'est possible.* "My dear Helen, that is not possible."

52. In context of the time period of the setting, the cigarette holder and monocle (lines 2 and 4 and shown in the photograph on page 132) suggest Sullivan's
    A. failing health

    B. cynical attitudes

    C. style and worldliness

    D. carelessness and stubbornness

53. The description in lines 6 to 7 creates an atmosphere of
    A. nostalgia

    B. animosity

    C. confusion

    D. anticipation

54. The irony of seating Gilbert and Sullivan "*side by side*" (line 19) in this scene lies in the fact that
    A. Gilbert writes the text and Sullivan writes the music

    B. the two collaborators are in complete disagreement

    C. the two collaborators leave the room at different times

    D. Gilbert smokes a cigar while Sullivan smokes a cigarette

55. The **main** reason that Sullivan is unhappy with Gilbert's revisions to the script (lines 31 to 34) is that in Sullivan's opinion, the revisions
    A. are impossible for Sullivan to set to music

    B. include only unnecessary changes to the original

    C. promise a story with human depth but quickly return to the frivolous

    D. are little compensation for Sullivan's boredom with their collaboration

56. When Sullivan calls Gilbert's libretto "profoundly uncongenial" (line 45), he means that he finds it
    A. unvaryingly gloomy

    B. completely unsuited to his tastes

    C. seriously flawed and unsuccessful

    D. inappropriately abstract for his intellect

57. The simultaneous responses of Gilbert, Carte, and Helen (lines 52 to 55) indicate their attempt to convince Sullivan that they regard him as
    A. a genuinely creative artist

    B. a skilled musical performer

    C. a truly cultured gentleman of the times

    D. an accomplished producer of popular tunes

58. In the context of lines 51 to 54, the description *"She continues"* (line 55) indicates

   A. an end to overlapping speech

   B. that Helen speaks these lines gently

   C. Helen's disinterest in their opinions

   D. that the men are ready to back down

59. Gilbert's mockery of Sullivan's "Grand Tour of Europe" in lines 70 and 71, and of Ibsen's plays (lines 88 to 90) shows Gilbert's

   A. self-centredness

   B. deceitfulness

   C. melancholy

   D. formality

60. When Gilbert exclaims "Ha!" (line 73), he believes that he has

   A. expressed his outrage at Sullivan's morals

   B. used Sullivan's excuses to justify his laughter

   C. pointed out the futility of working with Sullivan

   D. made a clever but telling point at Sullivan's expense

61. Sullivan takes his stance against Gilbert's libretto (lines 76 to 78) because Sullivan is no longer willing to

   A. please the public

   B. repeat his efforts

   C. be Gilbert's partner

   D. ignore Gilbert's hostility

62. When Carte agrees with Gilbert that they might indeed have to seek a new collaborator for Sullivan (line 101), Gilbert's response in line 102 reveals that Carte has

   A. called Gilbert's bluff

   B. tried to flatter Gilbert

   C. sided with Gilbert's feelings

   D. intended to insult Gilbert deeply

63. A synonym for the word "prerogative" as used in the context of line 102 is

   A. conclusion

   B. argument

   C. opinion

   D. right

64. The excerpt concludes in an atmosphere of

    A. strained uncertainty

    B. contented resolution

    C. cautious optimism

    D. irrevocable defeat

X. Questions 65 to 69 are based on this excerpt from an operetta.
Question 70 requires you to consider this reading together with readings VIII and IX.

from THE PIRATES OF PENZANCE

The setting of this operetta written by Gilbert and accompanied by the music of Sullivan is a seashore in Cornwall, England.

CHARACTERS:

KING—the pirate king

RUTH—a pirate maid

ALL—the pirate crew

FRED—Frederic, a young pirate

       SONG—PIRATE KING

       KING: Oh, better far to live and die

       Under the brave black flag I fly,

       Than play a sanctimonious[1] part,

5   With a pirate head and a pirate heart.

       Away to the cheating world go you,

       Where pirates all are well-to-do;

       But I'll be true to the song I sing,

       And live and die a Pirate King.

10   For I am a Pirate King.

       ALL: You are!

       Hurrah for the Pirate King!

       KING: And it is, it is a glorious thing

       To be a Pirate King.

15   **ALL**: It is!

       Hurrah for our Pirate King!

KING: When I sally forth to seek my prey

I help myself in a royal way:

I sink a few more ships, it's true,

20 Than a well-bred monarch ought to do;

But many a king on a first-class throne,

If he wants to call his crown his own,

Must manage somehow to get through

More dirty work than ever *I* do,

25 For I am a Pirate King.

ALL: You are!

Hurrah for the Pirate King!

KING: And it is, it is a glorious thing

To be a Pirate King!

30 **ALL**: It is!

Hurrah for our Pirate King!

    (*Exeunt all except* **FREDERIC**.)

    (Enter **RUTH**.)

RUTH: Oh, take me with you! I cannot live if I am left behind.

35 **FRED**: Ruth, I will be quite candid with you. You are very dear to me, as you know, but I must be circumspect. You see, you are considerably older than I. A lad of twenty-one usually looks for a wife of seventeen.

RUTH: A wife of seventeen! You will find me a wife of a thousand!

FRED: No, but I shall find you a wife of forty-seven, and that is quite enough. Ruth, tell

40 me candidly, and without reserve: compared with other women—how are *you*?

RUTH: I will answer you truthfully, master—I have a slight cold, but otherwise I am quite well.

FRED: I am sorry for your cold, but I was referring rather to your personal appearance. Compared with other women, are you beautiful?

45 **RUTH** (*bashfully*): I have been told so, dear master.

FRED: Ah, but lately?

RUTH: Oh, no, years and years ago.

FRED: What do you think of yourself?

RUTH: It is a delicate question to answer, but I think I am a fine woman.

50 **FRED**: That is your candid opinion?

RUTH: Yes, I should be deceiving you if I told you otherwise.

FRED: Thank you, Ruth, I believe you, for I am sure you would not practise on my inexperience; I wish to do the right thing, and if—I say if—you are really a fine woman, your age shall be no obstacle to our union! (*Chorus of Girls heard in the distance*.) Hark!
55 Surely I hear voices! Who has ventured to approach our all but inaccessible lair? Can it be Custom House?[2] No, it does not sound like Custom House.

RUTH (*aside*): Confusion! it is the voices of young girls! If he should see them I am lost.

FRED (*looking off*): By all that's marvellous, a bevy of beautiful maidens!

RUTH (*aside*): Lost! lost! lost!

60 FRED: How lovely! how surpassingly lovely is the plainest of them! What grace—what delicacy—what refinement! And Ruth—Ruth told me she was beautiful!

W. S. Gilbert (1836–1911).

[1] sanctimonious—hypocritical or falsely righteous

[2] Custom House—officers from Customs and Excise, a government office that collects import duties

---

65. The Pirate King justifies the fact that he sinks "a few more ships, it's true, / Than a well-bred monarch ought to do" (lines 19 to 20) by implying that

A. he has not been taught civility and fairness

B. his being a pirate alleviates his need for fairness

C. even a royal king is forced to commit devious acts to keep his crown

D. even though he performs heinous acts, he remains happy in his pirate's life

66. In line 41, Ruth's reply to Fred's question "how are *you*?" evokes

A. concern since Ruth is unwell

B. doubt since he questions Ruth's sincerity

C. humour because Ruth's response is literal

D. drama because Ruth's position is threatened

67. In the context of lines 42 to 50, Ruth's statement "I should be deceiving you if I told you otherwise" (line 50) is an example of the use of

A. irony

B. metaphor

C. hyperbole

D. oxymoron

68. In line 56, Ruth's asides reveal that the stage direction "*bashfully*" in line 44 is intended to demonstrate Ruth's

A. embarrassment as a result of Fred's questions about her beauty

B. reluctance to discuss the compliments she received in the past

C. attempt to manipulate Fred's affections

D. sensitivity about her age

69. Fred's statement "And Ruth—Ruth told me she was beautiful!" (line 60) characterizes him as

A. trusting and generous

B. innocent and gullible

C. intuitive and discerning

D. vulnerable and demanding

Refer to Reading VIII, Reading IX, and Reading X to answer question 70.

70. Readings VIII, IX, and X could be used as support for a response to which of the following research topics?

A. The influence of literature and music on a nation's economy

B. The role of the United States in popularizing musical theatre

C. The longstanding appeal of the lives and collaborative works of Gilbert and Sullivan

D. The role of film in preserving the traditions and variety of the musical operas of Gilbert and Sullivan

JANUARY 2004 DIPLOMA EXAMINATION
WRITTEN RESPONSE

DESCRIPTION

Time: 2½ hours. This examination was developed to be completed in 2½ hours; however, you may take an additional ½ hour to complete the examination.

Plan your time carefully.

Part A: Written Response contributes 50% of the total English Language Arts 30–1 Diploma Examination mark and consists of two assignments.

• Personal Response to Texts Assignment: Value 20% of total examination mark

• Critical/Analytical Response to Literary Texts Assignment: Value 30% of total examination mark

> Recommendation: Read and reflect upon the whole examination before you begin to write. Time spent in planning may result in better writing.

Do not write your name anywhere in this booklet. Feel free to make corrections and revisions directly on your written work.

Instructions

Complete the Personal Response to Texts Assignment first. The Personal Response to Texts Assignment is designed to allow you time to think and reflect upon the ideas that you may also explore in the Critical/Analytical Response to Literary Texts Assignment.

• Complete both assignments.

• You may use the following print or electronic references:

   – an English and/or bilingual dictionary

   – a thesaurus

   – an authorized writing handbook

• Space is provided in this booklet for planning and for your written work.

• Use blue or black ink for your written work.

Additional Instructions for Students Using Word Processors

• Format your work using an easy-to-read
12-point or larger font such as Times.

• Double-space your final copy.

• Staple your final printed work to the pages indicated for word-processed work for each assignment. Hand in all work.

• Indicate in the space provided on the back cover that you have attached word-processed pages.

PERSONAL RESPONSE TO TEXTS ASSIGNMENT

Suggested time: approximately 45 to 60 minutes

Carefully read and consider the texts on pages 248 to 250, and then complete the assignment that follows. The photographs and commentaries on pages 248 and 249 are from a brochure from the City of Edmonton Archives.

Eng30_03 City of Edmonton
(brochure,City of Edmonton Archives)

Public concern over the growing loss of historically significant information led to creation of an Archives Committee by the City of Edmonton in 1938. Documents and photographs recording Edmonton's early history were acquired and preserved in liaison with the Northern Alberta Pioneers and Old Timers Association (N.A.P.O.T.A.).

Twenty years later the City opened the Historical Exhibits Building in cooperation with N.A.P.O.T.A. Essentially a museum, one room was devoted to archival materials. The City assumed control over the facility in 1966, and by 1971 had established the City of Edmonton Archives as the official repository for civic government records. Two years later, the building was devoted entirely to documents and photographs relating to Edmonton's history.

In 1992 the Archives moved to the renovated Prince of Wales Armouries. Modern techniques of storage and preservation ensure the availability of our documentary heritage for future generations.

Still and Moving Images

Over 100,000 historical photographs, dating from the 1880s, are kept in the Archives. Of these, approximately 3,200 were inherited from N.A.P.O.T.A. The more than 70,000 slides currently housed here are of a more contemporary nature. Much of our collection consists of negatives, slides, moving images, and prints.

Newspapers

We provide a large collection of local newspapers including the Edmonton Bulletin, from 1880 to 1951, the Edmonton Journal, from 1903 to the present, as well as editions of the Strathcona Plaindealer and the Edmonton Capital on microfilm. An extensive collection of newspaper clipping files, dating from the late 1920s, is also available.

Maps and Architectural Drawings

Over 300 current and historical maps of the Edmonton area, dating from 1882, provide a unique geographical guide to Edmonton's development.

More than 25,000 plans and architectural drawings of significant buildings and bridges from the City Architect's Department and other sources are accessible to researchers.

Oral Histories

A series of oral histories of prominent local citizens is available to augment the researcher's understanding of Edmonton's past.

Current and Historical Publications

Our non-circulating library of current and historical books and periodicals supplements our clients' needs.

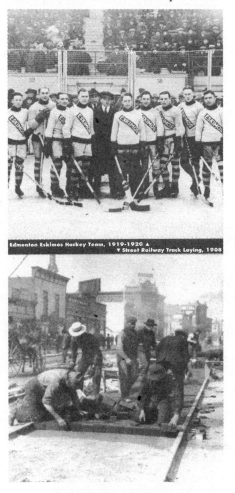

Eng30_03 City of Edmonton photos
(City of Edmonton brochure)

This excerpt is set in Ireland.

from FOUR LETTERS OF LOVE

At twelve, then, the world changed. My father came home in his grey suit one evening, sat to tea and listened to my mother tell how all day she had waited for the man to come to repair the leak in the back kitchen roof, how I'd come home from school with a tear in the knee of my pants, how Mrs Fitzgerald had called to say she couldn't play bridge this Thursday. He sat in that rumpled, angular quietness of his and listened. Was there a special glimmering of light in his eyes? I have long since told myself I remember there was. It cannot have been as simple and understated as I see it now, my father swallowing a second cup of milky tea, a slice of fruit loaf, and saying, "Bette, I'm going to paint."

At first, of course, she didn't understand. She thought he meant that evening and said, "Grand, William," and that she would tidy up after the tea and let him go along now and get changed.

"No," he said quietly, firmly, speaking the way he always spoke, making the words seem larger, fuller than himself, as if the amplitude of their meaning was directly related to the thinness of himself, as if he were all mind. "I'm finished working in the office," he said.

My mother had stood up and was already putting on her apron for the dishes. She was a petite woman with quick brown eyes. She stopped and looked at him and felt it register, and with electric speed then crossed the kitchen, squeezed my upper arm unintentionally hard and led me from the table to go upstairs and do my lessons. I carried the unexploded fury of her response from the kitchen into the cool darkness of the hall and felt that gathering of blood and pain that was the bruise…coming. I climbed six steps and sat down. I fingered the tear in the knee of my trousers, pushed the two sides of frayed corduroy back together as if they could mend. Then, my head resting on fists, I sat and listened to the end of my childhood.

Niall Williams (1958–)
Williams lives in Kiltumper, Ireland, with his wife Christine
and their two children. Four Letters of Love, *Williams' first novel, is being made into a film.*

THE ASSIGNMENT

In the excerpt from the novel *Four Letters of Love*, the narrator recalls a vivid memory of a significant event that was clearly fixed forever in his mind. The photographs and commentaries from the City of Edmonton Archives brochure recount some of the formal ways that we preserve memories of the past.

What do these texts suggest to you about the significance of our memory of the past? Support your idea(s) with reference to one or more of the texts presented and to your previous knowledge and/or experience.

In your writing, you should

- select a *prose form* that is appropriate to the ideas you wish to express and that will enable you to effectively communicate to the reader

- discuss ideas and/or impressions that are meaningful to you

Personal Response to Texts Assignment

Initial Planning

You may respond from a personal, critical, and/or creative perspective. Keep in mind that regardless of the form you choose, you must communicate clearly to the reader.

Briefly identify your choice of prose form, your reason(s) for choosing this prose form, and what you intend to communicate.

CRITICAL/ANALYTICAL RESPONSE TO LITERARY TEXTS ASSIGNMENT

Suggested time: approximately 1½ to 2 hours

Reflect on the ideas and impressions that you discussed in the Personal Response to Texts Assignment concerning the significance of our memory of the past.

The Assignment

> Consider how the significance of memory of the past has been reflected and developed in a literary text or texts you have studied. Discuss the idea(s) developed by the author(s) about the significance of our memory of the past.

In your planning and writing, consider the following instructions.

• You must focus your discussion on a literary text or texts *other than* the texts provided in this examination booklet.

• When considering the work(s) that you know well, select a literary text or texts meaningful to you and relevant to this assignment. Choose from short stories, novels, plays, screenplays, poetry, films, or other literary texts that you have studied in your English Language Arts 30–1 class.

• Carefully consider your *controlling idea* or how you will create a strong, *unifying effect* in your response.

• As you develop your ideas, support them with appropriate, relevant, and meaningful examples from literary text(s).

Critical/Analytical Response to Literary Texts Assignment

Initial Planning

You may use this space for your initial planning. This information assists markers in identifying the text(s) you have chosen to support your ideas. The markers who read your composition will be very familiar with the literary texts you have chosen.

Literary Text(s) and Author(s)

_____

_____

PERSONAL REFLECTION ON CHOICE OF LITERARY TEXT(S)

Suggested time: 10 to 15 minutes

Briefly identify your reasons for choosing this literature as support for your response. What strategies did you use when making your choice? You may respond in point form, using a diagram such as a mind map, or in another format of your choice. Markers will consider the information you provide here when considering the effectiveness of your supporting evidence.

ANSWERS AND SOLUTIONS—JANUARY 2004
DIPLOMA EXAMINATION

1. A	13. A	25. B	37. B	49. D	61. B
2. D	14. D	26. A	38. C	50. A	62. A
3. C	15. C	27. D	39. A	51. B	63. D
4. B	16. B	28. D	40. D	52. C	64. A
5. C	17. B	29. C	41. B	53. D	65. C
6. D	18. C	30. D	42. C	54. B	66. C
7. C	19. D	31. B	43. C	55. C	67. A
8. A	20. A	32. C	44. B	56. B	68. C
9. B	21. A	33. A	45. B	57. A	69. B
10. D	22. C	34. D	46. C	58. A	70. C
11. D	23. A	35. A	47. D	59. A	
12. B	24. D	36. B	48. B	60. D	

The Country of Illusion

1. A

A journal is a daily record. The journal sections of this excerpt are written as though they are a record of impressions as they happen. The sentence fragments suggest fleeting impressions jotted down during a walk on the glacier. In several places (for example, in line 108), the writer describes himself adding his immediate impressions to his notebook.

B. Some sentences in lines 10 to 16 do suggest discomfort: the writer struggles over the icy gravel and lowers his head against the wind, and other tourists are wind-bitten and dissatisfied. However, the sentence fragments are used throughout the journal entries, so it unlikely that their purpose is limited to emphasizing something that appears in only a few lines.

C. Lines 3 to 5 suggest a monotonous landscape, but the question is about lines 8 to 15. These lines describe not the landscape but only what the writer can see close to him.

D. This journal entry describes one particular day in early spring. It may be windy and blowing snow, but the Japanese businessmen (line 19) are enjoying themselves in their suits and dress shoes. The climate (*weather* would be a better word) does not seem that harsh.

2. D

A rhetorical question is asked only for effect—no answer is expected. In fact, a rhetorical question may actually be a statement disguised as a question.

The first question is plain: what are we doing here? The second question is an observation hidden in a question: the tourist is recording what he sees, but his videotape record will show only blank whiteness. In other words, what is this experience all about? What is the tourist—and by extension, everyone—going to remember?

A. One rhetorical question does ask what will there be to see when the tape is played back in the future. However, the point of the question is that there is nothing to be seen, which is neither pessimistic nor optimistic.

B. The tourist with the video camera intends to remember the moment, but he is only one of the crowd of tourists on the glacier. The question is about all those present. "What are we doing here?"

C. The questions themselves do not express displeasure with the tourists' behaviour. Nor does the description of the tourists suggest that there is anything to complain about in their behaviour, even if the businessmen in their suits and dress shoes might seem a little odd.

3. C

Aritha van Herk uses a metaphor, a figure of speech used to compare two things by describing one thing as the other thing, to compare writing with venturing onto an ice field: "This is the field the Canadian writer walks onto, . . . The open field of snow, the page." Thus anything true of the ice field could be metaphorically true of writing—unless the metaphor is limited. And, the metaphor *is* limited: there "is no stick to prod for snow pockets, no gauge for the solidity of the earth." In other words, the snow-covered ice and the writer's page are both featureless and uncertain.

A. Both the ice field and the writer's blank page might be described as cold and bleak. However, although both terms might be appropriate to the metaphor, they are not used in the metaphor.

B. An ice field is a hostile place, and it could be disillusioning if the walker discovers a deep crevasse under the smooth, unbroken snow. Similar words might describe a writer's struggle. However, although both terms might be appropriate to the metaphor, they are not used in the metaphor.

D. Both prescriptive, which means imposing rules, and confining might be suitable to the metaphor, for you must follow the rules of ice-field walking or suffer the consequences. Similar words might describe a writer's attitude to writing. However, although both terms might be appropriate to the metaphor, they are not used in the metaphor.

4. B

Line references are given after each quotation. Although in this case the answer is contained in the quotations, it is always a good idea to review the context of all line references.

The second quotation makes it clear that the writer is overconfident since he and his friends had not so far encountered any real trouble. The words "so far" set up an expectation of trouble to come. Since the first quotation makes it clear that the writer does not know what he is doing, we can guess that he will not be prepared for trouble or be able to handle the trouble when it comes.

This is an example of foreshadowing, the literary technique of hinting at some future event so that it later seems to be a natural and inevitable part of the story.

A. There is no mention of fear of falling. On the contrary, the writer is overconfident and is not thinking of trouble.

C. The writer is not at all reluctant. He is pleased with himself and overconfident. This attitude helps to foreshadow the later recklessness that causes the fall.

D. It is true that the writer is dependent on the knowledge and skill of his friends even though he does not know it. However, that fact is not emphasized. It is the future trouble caused by his ignorance and overconfidence that is emphasized.

5. C

Even though this particular question can be answered by considering the quotations that are supplied, it is always a good idea to check the context of all line references.

The words "Somehow I imagined" show clearly that the writer is accepting responsibility. He does not know what he is doing, but without any reason at all ("**Somehow** I imagined"), he imagines he does know.

A. The words "I resented" suggest that at that moment the writer felt that he was not being treated properly. This might suggest that he is shifting blame.

B. The word "deny" is sometimes used to mean refusing to admit the truth. The quotation might suggest that the writer does not believe his friends.

D. Do not be misled by the fact that this quotation contains a reference to "the country of illusion," which is the name of the book that this extract was taken from. Although this fact suggests that the quotation would be important in understanding the theme of the book, it is not significant in determining who is responsible for the fall.

6. D

Refer to line 109 and to lines 107 to 108.

Writers pick images carefully, choosing each one for a purpose. The words "ghost" and "shadows" suggest mystery. The image reinforces an impression of the mysterious quality of the landscape.

A. Clouds, shadows, and ghosts might suggest the harsh environment. However, the image is insubstantial, for there is no danger in a daytime image of ghost-like cloud shadows. The writer's impression of the avalanche (lines 111 to 114) is what reinforces the impression of a harsh environment.

B. The mountain scene may be still, but the image is one of movement.

C. The shadows are on the valley floor, not on the glacier.

7. **C**

The bolded words *most clearly* indicate that each of the responses is true to some degree. Take extra care. It might be useful to reread each quotation in context.

All the quotations describe the writer's thinking and imagining—his immersion in what he observes. The words "look and look" suggest a long time spent looking, and the word "exhausted" clearly shows the degree of mental effort expended in looking.

A. His remembering might take up only a moment, and the writer is actually thinking of why he came, not looking at what is around him.

B. Here is a quotation that should be reread in context. The "sound" is the sound of a distant avalanche (line 91). The writer stares until dizziness makes the avalanche seem close and threatening. Everything connected to this quotation is part of the build-up to the looking until exhausted.

D. Everyone who has written knows the degree of immersion into the problem of "how to write." But notice that the writer has withdrawn from what he is observing so that he can think about how to write about it.

8. **A**

The answer to the question is found in lines 106 to 108 in the question "How to write beyond the familiar words that obscure the world in a white-out of cliché?" Clichés, or words that have lost their meaning through overuse, are compared with a "whiteout," or blizzard that reduces visibility to zero. In other words, clichéd words like "Monarch" and "grandeur" would not only have no real meaning, they would actually obscure meaning.

Notice the value of checking quotations in context.

B. The biographical note at the end of the extract tells us that the writer is a Canadian. Athabasca Glacier and Mt. Edith Cavell establish the Canadian setting. Since Canada's head of state is a monarch, the connotations can hardly be unfamiliar, at least to Canadian readers.

C. The words would indeed establish a metaphor between people and mountains. That is the function of metaphor, to describe what is unfamiliar in terms of what is familiar. The writer rejects them not because they are a metaphor but because the metaphor has become clichéd.

D. The words "grandeur," "Brooding," and "majesty" do not necessarily connote, or suggest, arrogance or imperiousness. The word "Monarch" can have that connotation, but such connotations are part of the "white-out of cliché" that obscures meaning.

The Green Party Poster

9. **B**

The poster is an advertisement for the German Green Party, and both the growing plants and the caption are a play on words. However, when interpreting a visual that works by suggesting associations, be careful not to read into the image everything that you may know about those associations.

The image of plant growth suggests slow steady progress. The plants breaking through the hard-packed, stony soil and the caption, which reads "Green breaks through," reinforce this idea.

A. No information about issues is contained or suggested by the poster. A person unfamiliar with the Green Party would have no idea of its adherence to any issue.

C. The Green Party does have a small membership and the members seem to be dedicated, but the poster does not indicate that at all.

D. The Green Party does lack the resources to strongly affect German politics—it gains a small percentage of the vote and has few members in the *Bundestag*, or German parliament—but you would have to know that already.

10. D

To answer this question, you have to understand some literary terms and techniques. Although you will not be asked about dramatic contrast by name, you must be able to understand what it is and to identify it.

Dramatic contrast is the deliberate juxtaposition of very different things for dramatic effect. This poster contains a contrast between the green, growing plants and the hard-packed, stony soil.

A symbol is something that is used to stand for something else. In this poster, green plants are used as a symbol for the Green Party (a party of environmentalists).

A. The bright green supports the idea of the poster (see question 9), but there is no verbal irony. The caption is a play on words because green plants breaking through the stony ground suggest that the Green Party is breaking into political influence. Irony, on the other hand, is the use of words in such a way that their true meaning is the opposite of their literal meaning. Irony is used in sarcasm and satire. There is no irony intended in the poster.

B. Since the slogan contains two plays on words ("Green breaks through" and "Show your colours"), it can be considered clever. However, although there are claims implied in the image, they may or may not be honest claims. The Green Party presents itself as good (whatever is green and growing is good), as growing vigorously, and as breaking through the sterile, stony ground of politics and public life—but the party might be self-deluded or merely lying. We cannot tell.

C. Understatement is the use of deliberately restrained or incomplete statements. Understatement emphasizes by pretending not to. Since the poster makes no direct claims, but instead suggests life and growth, it might be said to be using understatement.

Paradox is a combination of two seemingly contradictory statements that actually contain some true observation about life. On one level, a paradox is self-contradictory and nonsensical. Properly understood, a paradox expresses truth. "You never know what you've got 'til it's gone" is a paradox.

The growing plants and the stony soil do not present an example of paradox, but of contrast used for effect. Our own observations can tell us that there is no contradiction in plants growing in bad soil. Plants do that all the time.

11. D

This question must be answered by interpreting the images. The green plants are pushing up through a packed, stony surface. The plants are breaking through a crust, and there appears to be better soil beneath. The symbolism is clear. Green plants = good. Stony soil = bad. For *good*, we are meant to infer reference to the Green Party and its policies. For *bad*, we are meant to infer reference to the established parties and policies—the status quo.

A. Since the poster is intended to appeal through symbols and suggestion rather than through ideas and thought, it may well appeal to voters who lack political sophistication. However, the poster is suggesting something through its symbolism, and that something is described in response D.

B. The idea of "party politics" is suggested by the image of the stony, crusted ground. The plant is breaking through the ground. Someone knowledgeable about party politics would likely think, "It's not that simple."

C. The image of a plant growing suggests slow and steady change, not rapid and sweeping change.

Blessed is the Man

12. B

The words *in context* always indicate that you must check how the words are used. Even if you know the meanings of the given words, any word can have unusual meanings and some writers—especially poets—give words meanings that are idiosyncratic, or personal.

As it happens, there are no clear context clues on line 5. Any of the pairs of antonyms, or words that have opposite meanings, could fit in the original sentence without producing nonsense. It is also fair to say that the writer's syntax, vocabulary, allusions, and meaning are not the clearest. Without further information, any of the pairs of responses could fit.

What about other clues? The words "scoffer," "denigrate," "depreciate," and "denunciate" (line 2) might suggest *criticize* (response **C**) as one of the meanings. The words "excuse," "retreat," and "equivocate" (line 4) might suggest *neglect* (response **D**). The words "diversity" and "tolerance" (line 9) might suggest *accept* (response **A**). Since three clues are linked to three different responses, it is safe to say that there are no useful context clues in the poem.

The context clues, then, must be found in the words and responses themselves. Here is a way of extracting clues. First, examine the words themselves and see if suffixes, prefixes, and word roots supply any clues. Observe that adding the suffix *-ize* to the noun *mongrel* gives the verb *mongrelize*. Unfortunately, anyone who does not know the word *mongrel* can go no further. (Anyone who knows that a mongrel is a dog of mixed breed, and that mongrel dogs are less valuable than purebreds, can easily go from *mongrel* to *mix* to *contaminate* to *taint*.) What about the word *heighten*? *Height* plus the suffix *-en* means *add height*—or *increase* or even *make more intense*.

Second, compare the words themselves with the responses given. (Sometimes it may be necessary to examine the roots, prefixes, and suffixes of some or all of the responses.) Compare the second word, *heighten*, with second word of each response: *accept, enhance, praise, preserve*. The best fit is *heighten = enhance*. (In fact, *heighten* is one of the meanings of *enhance*.) Then, *mongrelize* must mean *taint*.

A. *exclude*: leave out; *accept*: take in

B. *taint*: contaminate; *enhance*: improve, increase

C. *criticize*: point out flaws; *praise*: express approval (*Criticize* also means *assess, give a considered opinion*. But *expressing disapproval* is the meaning that fits in the context of the other pairs of antonyms.)

D. *neglect*: fail to care for; *preserve*: care for, maintain

13. A

Parentheses enclose explanations, supplements, afterthoughts, and asides. These parentheses produce the impression of a personal aside. Of course, the entire poem is a personal comment. The parenthetical addition is a poetic effect within the overall effect of the poem.

B. The praise for the Renaissance painter Giorgione might seem to be reverence. However it is first of all an aside. Parentheses mark asides; that is their function.

Also, although the aside seems to begin by praising the painter, the writer goes on to say that if the Giorgione's self-portrait were of someone else, she might not like it. The next sentence explains her ambivalence: "Blessed the geniuses/who know that egomania is not a duty." It seems that Giorgione displays unhealthy ego in his self-portrait. As a matter of fact, the self-portrait does seem to show excessive ego. Giorgione painted himself as David, the famous biblical hero, and he presented himself as remarkably handsome. Of course, you could not know this on an exam. Thus, the aside is not an example of reverence.

C. The aside begins with an interjection—"Ah, Giorgione!"—and if everything inside the parentheses is meant to be humorous, then the aside might be described as a humorous interjection. However, the aside does not appear to be humorous (unless the whole thing is ironical—see response B) and it is first of all an aside. Again, parentheses mark asides.

D. One function of the exclamation mark is to mark a sentence that expresses some excitement. The other function is to mark some strong emotion in an interjection. The first two words function as an interjection. There is no need to read excitement into them, only strong feeling. There is no excitement apparent in the rest of the aside.

14. D

The quotation spans two lines, so the **virgule**, or slant (/), is used to mark the break between the lines of poetry.

A citadel is a fortress, but a "citadel of learning" is a fortress devoted to learning. The image is academic, with suggestions of conflict.

A. The words "of learning" modify "citadel" in such a way that the image is not military.

B. The words "citadel" and "learning" do not suggest anything political.

C. The words "citadel" and "learning" do not suggest anything religious.

15. C

Refer to line 10 and also to line 9. "Armor" is used for protection. Together with "diversity," "controversy," "tolerance," and "citadel of learning," the word "armor" suggests protection against ignorance. (In Canada, *armour* is the preferred spelling. The *-or* spelling is used to match the reading.)

A. The word "ought" in the phrase "ought to armor us well" includes the possibility of *not armoring well*. There is no guarantee.

B. The words "citadel" and "armor" suggest permanence, not change.

D. Armor is used for defence. Weapons are used for offence. Armor is defensive, not aggressive.

16. B

Refer to lines 11 and 13 and to lines 14 and 15.

The words "right" and "best interests of all" suggest a higher purpose. The lines that follow these describe the opposite sort of people—those who, like Ulysses' companions, choose animal self-indulgence, the opposite of higher purpose.

A. The one who risks a decision does not seek the advice of others, instead he asks himself. The writer was born in 1887 and died in 1972. She used the words *man* and *he* when speaking of human beings in general—a usage that was customary.

C. The one who risks a decision asks three questions. None of the questions includes an admission of inadequacy.

D. Risk may mean danger, but it need not. The one who makes an unpopular decision may risk danger, but may also merely risk unpopularity, discomfort, or the loss of promotion.

17. B

Always check the context.

Since *alas* means *unfortunately*, the word likely signals a contrast to hope. The word's context makes this certain. Just before "Alas" is the description of the "blessed man"; just after is the description of the present reality, the "animal man" in whom the moral sense is drowned.

A. "Ah" is an interjection that can express anything from disgust to delight. Thus, it could be used to signal a contrast to hope or expectation. In this case, however, it is used to express something like approval: "Ah, Giorgione!"

C. The word "self-indulgently" refers to the giving in to appetites and desires. This word is used in line 14 to contrast with the proper behaviour described in lines 9 to 11. The word does not signal contrast; it is used to describe the contrast.

D. The word "counterfeit" means *false imitation*. In the right context, the word might signal a contrast to hope. In the context of lines 19 to 21, the word is actually one more way of describing dishonest writers.

18. C

The phrases "living self-indulgently" and "the moral sense is drowned" show that the writer is saying that politics has become self-serving.

A. Ulysses' leadership in the *Iliad* and the *Odyssey* make him a useful example of leadership, especially when he is contrasted with those of his men who chose to remain animals. However, he does not stand for ancient Greece as a whole. In fact, Ulysses is a literary character, not part of the real history of Greece.

B. The word *political* is used to describe a certain kind of behaviour. We know this from the literary allusion to Ulysses and his companions, and also from the phrase "living self-indulgently until the moral sense is drowned." The quotation has nothing to do with the political system called democracy. The writer almost certainly knows that political life has always been tainted to some degree by self-interest, so an allusion to a mythological rather than an historical figure is appropriate.

D. Conflict is not mentioned in lines 13 to 15, nor is any particular connection with Greek citizens. Ulysses' companions are characters in a story.

19. D

What does the "blessed" author not comply with? Look before, in, and after lines 20 to 24. This author is not "modish" (fashionable) or "counterfeit" (an imitation of the truth), is "Affronted" (offended) by lies, and has a faith that is not based on material possessions. All the bad things that this author rejects are presented as the way of the world, as current trends. The "blessed" author does not follow these trends.

A. Professional improvement, or the growth in professional skill, is a good thing. The "blessed" author does not reject good things.

B. The "blessed" author is not like Ulysses' companions, the ones who live self-indulgently, who give in to appetites and desires (lines 14 to 15). As a result, this is a very plausible response. We could say that he resists private needs and demands. However, in lines 22 to 24, the "blessed" author is clearly resisting evils in the world around him.

C. Traditional practices are not mentioned in lines 22 to 24. In addition, the past is said—at least as a poetic device—to be better than the present (see lines 11 to 15).

20. A

Refer to lines 25 to 28. Diction is the choice of words and the way those words are used. The last lines contain a good example of poetic diction, an allusion to the first stanza of Edward Fitzgerald's *The Rubaiyat of Omar Khayyam*. The words themselves are taken from the poem, and their imagery suggests the richness of the original.

However, this question is not about diction, even though the wording of the question does emphasize the diction of lines 25 to 28. Instead, this question requires the simple interpretation of the writer's words.

Since the right kind of man does not visualize defeat and is too busy "to cower," or show fear, it may seem that his efforts are not very successful. Of course, he perseveres.

B. The lines do not mention either artistic endeavour or lack of talent. Other lines in the poem do mention a painter and both good and bad authors, but a politician is also mentioned (lines 11 to 13).

C. There is no mention of judgement, although it may be implied by the fact of choosing better things and avoiding worse ones. However, any judgement is not of people.

D. Giving generously is not mentioned or implied.

21. A

Refer to lines 25 to 28. None of the ideas contained in the responses is mentioned directly. In such a case, reread carefully and look for clues.

The one with the "illumined eye" has a faith that is based on spiritual things, not material things (lines 25 to 28). He will not picture defeat (line 26) and is too intent on what he is doing to be afraid (line 27). He has seen light, not literally, but by means of his *illumined*, or enlightened, eye (lines 27 to 28). All these characteristics of the "blessed" man are related to spirit and thought. Inner conviction, although not mentioned directly, is what results in enlightenment.

B. *Counsel* is advice, but there is no hint of giving or receiving advice.

C. *Spiritual cynicism* is the doubting, the despising, or the mocking of spiritual things. The "blessed" man would not do any of these things. The illumined, or enlightened eye, cannot be cynical.

D. "Blessed the man whose faith is different from possessiveness" (line 25). The enlightened eye is definitely *not* the result of materialistic longing.

The Tragedy of King Richard the Second

22. C

Understanding the queen's action depends partly on thinking about possible motivations (see responses B and D especially) and partly on careful reading. Notice that the words in line 30 end with a comma, so the sentence continues.

Knowing that the words are an introductory sentence element, we can see that "my wretchedness unto a row of pins" must be understood in the context of the full sentence. A marginal note makes it clear that the phrase means *my misery against a triviality*. **Always read the notes and any other explanatory material**. When the queen says this, she cannot mean that her unhappiness is set up against some trifle. She is using a figure of speech that refers to a wager, or bet. She means something like *It's a hundred to one that they're going to talk politics*.

Then is she hiding because if the gardeners saw the queen, they would not talk freely? It must be her intent to overhear what they are saying. The last words of line 32 confirm this: "woe is forerun with woe" can easily be understood as *trouble is the forerunner of trouble*, or bad news warns us of worse news that is yet to come.

A. A first reading of line 30 might suggest that the queen is seeking refuge from further grief. However, the words are the first part of a longer sentence.

B. The queen says nothing about her dignity. Indeed, she is so miserable that we may guess she is not thinking of her dignity. As well, if dignity were on her mind, she should not be hiding, which is very undignified.

D. The queen does not speak of embarrassment, only of wretchedness. Since she later tells the gardener off for not showing enough respect for the king, we can guess that she is not embarrassed to be seen by a gardener. Anyway, she could have had one of her ladies-in-waiting send the gardeners away if she did not want to be seen.

23. A

If there is any doubt about the meaning of the metaphor, the question itself makes it clear. The faults in the responses are all human faults and have nothing to do with fruit trees.

Beheading (line 39) was the penalty for treason committed by noblemen. The suckers that the second gardener is told to prune are compared with men of high standing who have grown too high for the common good ("our commonwealth," line 40); that is, the good of the country. Their crime is treason.

B. The death penalty is not imposed for cowardice unless it occurs in battle. There is no mention of battle.

C. Foolishness does not merit the death penalty. The suckers that must be pruned are not being compared with a foolish man.

D. It is the weeds that the gardener himself is going to root up (lines 42 to 44) that are wasteful, not the branches.

24. D

The city of London, the Duke of York, the Duke of Wiltshire, and England are all named in the excerpt. The city of York and the county of Wiltshire are not. They are merely suggested by the mention of the two dukes who took their titles from the place names.

The answer can also be found in line 48, in the words "our sea-wallèd garden, the whole land." The noun phrase "the whole land" is in apposition to the noun phrase "sea-wallèd garden." An appositive is a noun or nominal that immediately follows another noun or nominal and that defines or restates it. The garden is the whole land—or England. Of course, a little geography is still needed.

Knowledge of geography would help identify York as a town. Wiltshire includes the word *shire*, which means an administrative area and not a town. Neither the towns nor the county could be reasonably called *sea-walled*, not even in a poetical device. Only England could be called sea-walled.

25. B

Refer to lines 45 to 52.

The gardeners "Keep law and form and due proportion," while the king has left the country "full of weeds, her fairest flowers choked up, / Her fruit trees all unpruned, her hedges ruined." The king has clearly been neglectful and irresponsible.

A. It is the gardeners who nurture their garden.

C. The king is said to have left the country full of weeds. This has nothing to do with respect.

D. A king who neglects the proper rule of a country is not forward-thinking.

26. A

The gardener says in lines 64, 69, and 73 that Richard should have acted like the gardeners who prune those branches that hinder the proper growth of fruit. In line 69, the gardeners say clearly that Richard should have pruned the powers of the "great and growing men," that is, men like Bushy and Green.

B. Greater understanding of Bolingbroke might have caused the king to understand his danger and to act, and do what Bolingbroke finally did—curtail the powers of Bushy and Green.

C. Defeating Bolingbroke might have solved the king's immediate problem, but it would have done nothing for the country that has been so neglected. The gardener is concerned for England, not the king's power.

D. Support from the Duke of York might have helped maintain the king, but the gardener is concerned for the country, not the king.

27. D

The queen tells the gardener that he is "old Adam's likeness." She says that he just like Adam, the archetype, or original model, of sinfulness. In other words, her attitude is one of righteous indignation, or justified anger. After all, the gardener, a low-born man, has dared to criticize her husband, the king. Both as a woman and a queen, she is angry.

A. *Humility* is the state of being humble. *Humble* means modest and unassuming, not proud or arrogant. The queen's attitude is not humble.

B. The queen comes to *bitter acceptance* in lines 102 to 108, not in this passage. She does not yet know that what the gardener says is true—or at least, she is not ready to believe it. That is why she demands, in lines 87 and 88, to know where the gardener heard the news.

C. *Despair* is complete lack of hope. Yet in lines 87 and 88, the queen demands to know how the gardener heard his news. She is still hoping the news is not true, even though she has heard in lines 76 to 78 that letters have arrived with the news.

28. D

The answer to this question is in line 107. The phrase "for telling me these news of woe" reveals that it is the news itself that has upset her. Earlier she has been upset at the gardener's words about the king, but now it is the truth of the news that causes her to vent her anger.

A. When she calls the gardener a "little better thing than earth," we might suspect that she dismisses commoners as unworthy of attention. Yet it is when she accepts, in lines 102 to 108, the truth of what he says that she curses his garden.

B. Overhearing what the gardener and his men have said certainly upsets the queen. However, it is not the fact that they are gossiping, it is the content of their gossip—the news—that has upset her.

C. In the context of this response, the word *respect* refers to tolerating someone else's opinion. The queen certainly shows that she does not think much of the gardener's opinion, and she tells him in so lines 82 to 88 and 100 to 109. However, it is not his opinion of the king that has really upset her, it is the news itself.

29. C

As a marginal note makes clear, *ruth* means compassion, and as the gardener says in line 115, the herb rue stands for ruth. In remembrance of the queen, he will plant rue on the spot where her tear fell. He clearly forgives her angry words and feels sympathy for her wretchedness.

A. The gardener is not resentful. On the contrary, in lines 112 and 113, he says that he would be ready to lose his skill if it would help the queen— "so that thy state might be no worse, / I would my skill were subject to thy curse!"

B. As the context shows, "sour" does not mean bitterness: rue is an "herb of grace," and it stands for "ruth," or compassion. In fact, sour herbs were valued for their medicinal qualities.

D. The planting of symbolic herbs in a walled garden is a private act of remembrance.

30. D

This question is based on the entire extract. The question is also a good example of choosing the best answer. Each of the literary devices is used in the extract, but one is the **main** device.

A metaphor is a way of comparing two unlike things. One thing is described in terms of the other. The walled garden, the gardener, his helpers, and much of the extract are part of an extended metaphor that compares the state of a garden with the state of a kingdom.

Notice that it is possible to overlook the other literary devices, but that the garden metaphor is impossible to miss.

A. One form of irony is found in the difference between expectations and reality. Shakespeare uses irony in having a gardener deliver wise judgements on the actions of the king and later responding to the queen's angry curse with understanding and magnanimity.

B. In general, a parody can be called a humorous imitation. The gardener and his helpers discuss affairs of state like men of the power and influence. This is a kind of parody. A parody is generally mocking and can be very cruel, but not always. This example is gentle one.

C. An allusion is an indirect reference to something. When used as a literary device, allusion is meant to bring to the audience's mind all the things connected with whatever is alluded to. When the queen compares the gardener with Adam, she reminds the audience of the biblical story, and thus of sin, judgement, and suffering.

Introduction to the Tragedy of King Richard the Second

31. B

No line references are given for this question. The whole excerpt must be considered.

Aged (line 1) means very old, so we know that the queen was nearing the end of her reign. In lines 1 to 3, the writer says that Queen Elizabeth and her councillors were nervous about the political effects of the representation of a monarch being dethroned.

In lines 5 to 6, the reference to the next king, James, being firmly seated on the throne by 1608 suggests that his first years as monarch were unsettled. In other words, Elizabeth feared the impact on her uneasy reign.

A. The queen's ancestors are not mentioned.

C. The preferences of Elizabethan audiences are not mentioned. In fact, classic plays and books are sometimes abridged to suit the short attention spans of modern audiences.

D. In lines 10 to 12, the writer says that the overthrow of Richard resulted in a troubled reign for the usurper who succeeded him and also that thirty years of civil war followed.
He is saying the Elizabeth and her counsellors were mistaken in thinking this picture of disaster following upon rebellion would encourage rebellion among Elizabethan audiences. What is implied here is that the audiences *did* understand the play's historical context.

32. C

The answer is in line 16 in the sentence that the words "as in all the histories" are taken from. The sentence continues, "Shakespeare wrote as a true patriot and . . . England was the heroine." In other words, he reveals his affection for England.

The first part of this alternative raises a question. It is true that Shakespeare's work shows a lack of attention to political or historical accuracy. We know that Shakespeare shaped his dramas from whatever sources came to hand and he invented whatever he needed.

However, in this excerpt, the writer does not say that. Instead, in line 10, the words "vivid" and "impartial" give the impression that Shakespeare was realistic and accurate. Then how do we know that response B is correct? We know because the second part is correct and all the other responses are incorrect.

A. In lines 10 to 18, the writer implies that the play is complex and he implies that there is historical accuracy (lines 11 to 12 and see response **B**, above) and also political idealism (line 13). However, all this is what the writer says about this play, *The Tragedy of Richard II*. When he writes "as in all the histories," he is connecting *all* the histories to *one* aspect of the current play. He does not imply that everything that is true of *Richard II* is true of all the histories.

B. In lines 8 to 11, the writer implies that the play is complex, but he does not mention the complexities of accurately representing a piece of history in a play. He does imply in line 10 that the play is accurate (see response A, above) but that is all.

D. The writer does not mention England's many conflicts or an extended history of despotism.

33. A

Observe how the writer develops the ideas in the two paragraphs of this excerpt. He starts with a detail about the censoring of Richard II, then goes on to discuss that detail and then to discuss the complexities of the play itself. Then he sums up the play's continuing power to interest audiences. The writer moves from the specific to the general, presenting a generalization at the end: "The continuing power of the play .... can come only from its universal human appeal as drama."

The question asks for a generalization. It is one of the questions that requires a consideration of reading as a whole. The writer's pattern of organization puts the generalization at the end. Since the *"continuing power of the play ... can come only from its universal human appeal as drama,"* then we can say that *a dramatization of history can serve to provide a human perspective to distant historical events*.

B. The writer says clearly that the "continuing power of the play ... can come only from its universal human appeal as drama." In other words, the play remains interesting as drama, not as a detailed record of history.

C. In line 8, the writer says clearly that the play had no political purpose. It would not diffuse public discontent.

D. Firstly, forcing audiences to question their personal beliefs is not mentioned. Secondly, it is not likely that the political ideas listed in lines 12 to 13 would cause soul-searching among modern audiences.

34. D

This question requires you to consider all of readings IV and V together.

One way to approach questions of this kind is to mentally turn each response into the topic sentence of a paragraph. Then consider which of the readings would supply details that could be used in developing that topic sentence into a paragraph. If both readings could supply details for more than one topic, choose the topic that would have the **most** supporting details. *Remember to consider each reading as a whole.*

In Reading IV, the gardener's extended metaphor comparing England with a garden contains significant ideas. In Reading V, the writer lists a number of the significant ideas contained in the play. Both readings could be used to support a discussion of how *Shakespeare used the history of monarchies to develop significant ideas in his plays*.

A. The gardener in the Reading IV has a lot to say about Richard's ineffectiveness as a monarch, but Reading V contains nothing on this topic. Richard is mentioned as a tyrant, but his effectiveness is not.

B. Censorship is discussed in the first paragraph of Reading V but not at all in Reading IV. When the gardener speaks of how Richard should have managed his nobles, he is not thinking of censorship. By pruning, he probably means the execution of treacherous nobles.

C. The role of the commoner is not mentioned in Reading V. The subject's duty of obedience applies to every subject of the crown, not just to commoners. The gardener in Reading VI seems to be an uncommon commoner, but possibly something about Shakespeare's depiction of the role of the commoner in Elizabethan society could be extracted from the gardener's role in the play.

Flesh and Blood

35. A

Since one of the meanings of "doomed" is certain to fail, and futility means uselessness, the quotation conveys a sense of futility. Lines 9 to 10 reinforce the sense of futility, since the vines "kept working themselves loose" (line 8).

Notice how the context of a quotation can supply further information. Always check references and quotations in context.

B. Remorse is sorrow or regret that results from wrongdoing. Since the effort is righteous, or morally justified, it cannot lead to remorse.

C. Uniformity means sameness, or regularity. Although it might suggest tying up one vine after another, careful reading of the quotation and its context shows that uniformity does not fit.

D. Uncertainty does not fit. There is nothing uncertain about what is happening in this passage.

36. B

Review the context of each quotation.

A paradox is a literary device, a statement that when taken literally contains a contradiction. However, the contradiction contains some truth.

Notice the word *best*. Two of the responses are paradoxical and thus fit the question. Two of the responses contain a contradiction and could seem to be paradoxes if they are not read carefully.

The expression "working ourselves to death to keep ourselves alive" is the best example of paradox. The words are literally contradictory, but they effectively express the father's frustration with the struggle to stay alive. In addition, if the working conditions are harsh enough, they may well result in an early death. The words "working ourselves to death" could be hyperbole, or exaggeration for effect. They could also be literally true. In the second case, they would express not just frustration, but a bitter truth.

A. The phrase "working in his father's garden and thinking about his own garden" contains a kind of contradiction, but the two phrases in the quotation do not contradict each other. Thus, the statement is not paradoxical.

C. The phrase "wrapping the world up into an awkward parcel that would not submit or stay tied" contains a kind contradiction, but it is better seen as a metaphor, a literary figure in which two things are compared by describing one of them as the other.

D. The quotation "he had come to despise and respect them for their wild insistence" contains a contradiction. However, although the words *despise* and *respect* contradict each other and are thus paradoxical in form, they are actually a literal description of contradictory emotions in the boy.

37. B

The words "a secret, tangled life, a slumbering will" must describe something living. Only living things have a life; only living things have a will. The words must describe Constantine. In other words, they describe his personal characteristics.

A. Constantine's opinion cannot have a life and will. Could an opinion be said figuratively to have life and will? Yes, but there is nothing in the context of the quotation to support such a figurative use. In addition, the brothers have not yet been mentioned.

C. A relationship cannot have a life and will. Could a relationship be said figuratively to have life and will? Yes, but there is nothing in the context of the quotation to support such a figurative use. In addition, the mother has not yet been mentioned.

D. Someone's curiosity cannot have a life and will. Could someone's curiosity be said figuratively to have life and will? Yes, but there is nothing in the context of the quotation to support such a figurative use. In addition, Constantine has shown no curiosity about his father.

38. C

Constantine looks forward to the triumph of producing food from his garden. He is thinking of his goal. The words clearly describe his motivation.

A. Constantine will "descend triumphantly" from his garden, not from the vineyard.

B. His family's neediness does not seem to be an illusion. Lines 6, 14, and 15 suggest a struggle for existence.

D. Lines 19 to 21 make it clear that his garden will not produce very much. However, line 24 makes it clear that the quantity of food is not the point. Constantine is "the runt, of whom so little was expected." His goal is as much proving himself as it is producing food. Also, the boy is only eight; he can hardly be called impractical at that age.

39. A

Check the context of each quotation. The whole of the first paragraph shows that Constantine works hard in the family garden and vineyard. Since Constantine's father "had a merciless eye that could find one bad straw in ten bales of good intentions" and since the boy "would suffer if [the vines] weren't kept staked and orderly," the father's effect on the boy's behaviour is shown very strongly.

B. The father gives the scrap of land to Constantine because it is useless except as toy for his youngest. That is the end of the father's effect on his son's gardening. All the rest of Constantine's hard work on the garden is the result of the entire family's attitude (see response **C**).

C. In lines 20 to 24, it is clear that Constantine is thinking about proving himself to the whole family. All the careful, secret work on the garden is the result of the attitudes of everyone, not just of his father.

D. Taking handfuls of earth would be regarded as stealing. It would also be impossible, meaning that Constantine would not be allowed. He is therefore reduced to taking mouthfuls of earth. This does show how the father affects Constantine's behaviour. However, hours of careful attention to hard and frustrating work (response **A**) more strongly show the effect of the father on his son's behaviour.

40. D

Constantine's efforts to obtain water and soil are described in lines 29 to 36.

When considering the paired words in each response, be careful. Notice that in three of the responses, one word fits the story and one does not. It would thus be easy to choose the wrong response.

Perseverance, or determined continuation, and *conviction*, or firm belief, both describe the boy's actions in obtaining water and soil for his garden. His daily use of half his water and his carrying earth in his mouth both demonstrate perseverance and conviction.

A. *Superstition* is irrational belief in the magical effects of objects or actions and *cunning is* clever skill or clever deceit. Cunning describes the boy's actions, but he is not superstitious. The counsel of the priest is mentioned in lines 27 and 28, but do not make the mistake of confusing superstition and religious belief.

B. *Confidence* refers to certainty and belief and *sympathy* to sharing or entering into another's feelings. Confidence does describe the boy's actions. He is certain that he will get results. However, there is no mention of sympathy. Indeed, sympathy seems to be lacking in everyone in the family.

C. *Sophistication* refers to worldliness and self-confidence and *certainty* to confidence. The boy is not sophisticated, even if he has confidence in what will happen when seeds have soil and water.

41. B

Fastidious usually means fussy, demanding, or hard to please. None of these meanings fits any of the responses. It can also mean *meticulous*, a word that means careful. However, you many not know all or even any of the meanings of fastidious.

Vocabulary questions can often be answered by using context clues. In lines 38 to 40, "fastidiously" is used in the clause "the world was made of mistakes, a thorny tangle, and no amount of cord, however fastidiously tied, could bind them all down." The context strongly suggests care and attention to detail: the boy does not want the thorny tangle to come undone. "Carefully" fits the sentence perfectly. The writer chose to use "fastidiously" because of the connotations suggested by its primary meanings—not even fussy, excessive care is enough to avoid making mistakes.

A. A *quickly* tied cord would likely be a carelessly tied cord. The word does not fit the context.

C. Here *roughly* would have to mean barely adequate. The word does not fit the context.

D. A cord *temporarily* tied would not stay tied very long. The word actually contradicts the meaning.

42. C

Review all the quotations in context.

In context, the answer is very clear. The statement "Punishment waited everywhere" is immediately followed by "It was wiser not to speak." In other words, *because punishment waited everywhere, it was wiser not to speak*.

A. Constantine is certainly quiet when his mouth is full of earth. However, the silence of a few minutes does not explain his nature. *Quiet nature* means that he is habitually quiet.

B. "They believed he was silent because his thoughts were simple. In fact, he kept quiet because …" The words that begin the sentence after the quotation show that he is quiet not because he is simple, but for another reason.

D. The words "customary silence" may refer to his silence whenever he has a mouthful of earth. If that is the case, see response **A**. On the other hand, "customary silence" may refer to his quiet nature. In this case, the quotation merely describes his quiet nature; it does not explain why he is customarily quiet.

43. C

Check each quotation in context. Note the words *most strongly*, and expect to find at least two responses that are correct to some degree.

When Constantine is working in his garden, he thinks of his mother, "who forgot to look at him because her own life held too many troubles for her to watch." Then he thinks "how her face would look as he came through the door one harvest evening." The context of the quotation shows that Constantine feels neglected and is trying to win her attention. That his mother forgets to look at him—forgets him—is the best example of how her behaviour affects his feelings.

A. The mother's care not to waste makes it harder for Constantine to take seeds from the kitchen, but there is nothing to suggest that this affects his feelings for her.

B. His mother regards Constantine as the runt and expects little of him, just as the others do. He knows it, and it is part of the reason for his plan to prove himself. This response is partly correct, yet it is not the best example.

D. When Constantine is working in his garden he thinks of his mother "carrying food to his ravenous, shouting brothers." Then he thinks "how her face would look as he came through the door one harvest evening." The context of the quotation shows that Constantine feels neglected and is trying to win her attention. However, although his brothers force their mother's attention, this response is not the one that shows most strongly how Constantine's feelings are influenced.

44. B

Note that the question asks about the main idea presented in the excerpt. Check each quotation in context, but also think about the excerpt as a whole. The main idea is the theme.

Note the words *most clearly*. Even though the words are not bolded, expect to find at least two responses that are correct to some degree.

The entire excerpt describes Constantine's actions and the thoughts and emotions that are the cause of his actions. He lives a hard life, he is neglected, and he wants to prove himself to his family, especially to his mother. The words "he thought of how her face would look as he came through the door one harvest evening" most clearly capture this main idea.

A. This quotation helps establish part of the reason for Constantine's efforts with his garden. The word *suffer* makes it clear that his father is harsh and unloving. This is a supporting detail.

C. Constantine's attitude to miracles is used to help explain his perseverance. It is a supporting detail.

D. Constantine's silence is another example of what is described in response A. Again, this is a supporting detail.

Final Edit

45. B

Refer to the photograph and to lines 5 to 6.

The only information about the editorial policy of the magazine is found in the words of Welchman, the illustrations editor: "'Every photograph we use has to help tell the story about that particular place.'" In other words, the photograph has to match the story that it illustrates or present a consistent interpretation.

A. The editorial policy of the magazine can found in the words of the illustrations editor. She does not speak of gender at all.

C. The policy is not based on what appeals to women. It is based on a consistent way of telling stories with both words and pictures. In fact, a glance at the credits at the end of the exam will show that the magazine is *National Geographic,* which is not a women's magazine.

D. Nothing is said about people and their interactions.

46. C

Some women did respond emotionally to the photograph ("sighed one writer", line 8), but the photographer herself did not. The editor's response was "'beautiful, but it doesn't do the job.'" Clearly, this photograph elicits responses that vary according to perception and personal experience.

A. Since the excerpt contains different responses, women do not respond to this photograph in a predictably similar manner.

B. Welchman, the editor, makes her decision based not on what appeals to women but on what fits the editorial policy.

D. The experience is not universal because the photographer herself does not share it. Although word *singular* means one of a kind, in this response it is used as an intensifier to emphasize *universal*. Given the emphasis, any exception disproves the statement.

Introduction to the complete annotated Gilbert and Sullivan

47. D

In line 20, the author goes on to say that the Savoy operas "seem to breathe the innocence, the naïvety and the fun of a long-vanished age." This suggests longing for an idealized past.

A. The fact that something that is *dated*, or from the past, has nothing to do with whether or not the thing is mindless. For example, Shakespeare's plays are dated, but few would argue that they are mindless. The Savoy operas, although they are light entertainment, are very clever.

B. There is no connection between being dated and being either simple or complex (compare response A).

C. Something that is dated is necessarily part of history. However, the fact that some dated fiction is charming cannot suggest that history itself is fiction.

48. B

In line 30, Sir Graham says that nostalgia for the past "is a serious obstacle to change and reform." Financial growth is not mentioned in these lines; however, on line 33, he mentions "creating wealth."

A. Reform is indeed mentioned, but social reform is not. It may be inferred that serious reforms must include social reform, but this inference does not provide the best answer.

C. The writer clearly believes that it is nostalgia for the past, not desire for progress, that has maintained the status quo.

D. The quality of the operettas is not the question. It is nostalgia for the past that disturbs Sir Graham.

49. D

Lines 37 to 43 contain the writer's response to Sir Gilbert.

To refute is to prove wrong. The writer does not actually prove Sir Gilbert wrong. In fact, he says that "Perhaps he does have a point." However, the writer does say that Sir Gilbert's thesis does not cover the case of the economically successful United States, where the Savoy operas are very popular. Unless the thesis can account for the case of the United States, it is at best incomplete.

A. The mention of a doctoral thesis suggests that someone should look for real evidence to support Sir Graham's thesis, but it does not refute the thesis.

B. When the writer mentions amateur groups, he is saying that he is glad that they have not stopped performing Gilbert and Sullivan.

C. *Crucial* means very important, essential, vital. Yet the writer merely says that "There is clearly room for someone to do a doctoral thesis." In addition he does not mention defending the Savoy operas, merely investigating the relationship between them and Britain's economic decline.

50. A

Understatement is a literary technique that emphasizes by deliberately saying less than could be said. The writer could have used Sir Graham's own words to point out that "lord chancellors...in fancy dress" and "bone-headed military men" are hardly examples of cultivated minds. He could have pointed out that Sir Graham's own words are illogical.

Instead, the author makes fun of Sir Graham through understatement. For example, the mention of a doctoral thesis suggests that no evidence exists and it also suggests that the whole question is merely student work. The suggestion that Sir Graham might supervise the study also suggests a demotion for the principal of a university.

B. We may take Sir Graham at his word and assume that he has no hurtful intent, but rather is concerned about his country.

C. Everything about the writer's comments shows that he does not agree with Sir Graham and does not take him seriously. It is Sir Graham, not the author, who thinks that English expectations need changing.

D. The writer does not mention monetary considerations. He simply disagrees with Sir Gilbert.

51. B

Check the context of each quotation.

In this context, the word *attitude* refers to an overall opinion about something. This is reinforced by the word *summarized*. Which quotation best shows what the writer thinks about the plays?

The writer thinks that the plays seem to "breathe the innocence, the naïvety and the fun of a long-vanished age." That is a statement of what he thinks about the plays.

A. What the author says about modern technology tells how the work of Gilbert and Sullivan has become well-known. It does not tell his attitude to the plays themselves.

C. This response supports the attitude clearly expressed in response B; therefore, response **B** is a better answer.

D. The statement simply makes it clear that the Gilbert and Sullivan operettas are still produced. It does not summarize an attitude.

Topsy-Turvy

52. C

A monocle and cigarette holder are elements of fashion, of style. Since a monocle corrects the vision in only one eye, it is not as useful as glasses. A man who wears a monocle is obviously very concerned about style and appearance—he is worldly.

A. A cigarette suggests bad health only in the modern world. The question specifically mentions the time period of the setting, when cigarettes were not commonly thought unhealthy.

B. Monocles and cigarette holders are not of themselves associated with cynical attitudes. Of course, cynicism often goes along with style and worldliness, but that is response **C**.

D. The expression on Sullivan's face might suggest stubbornness, and in an age that valued proper dress, his open collar might suggest carelessness, but the question is about the cigarette and monocle.

53. D

In these lines, we are kept from seeing everything. We cannot see people's faces or bodies. We cannot even see whose office the scene takes place in. Why? We must wait to find out. The result is *anticipation*, or expectation.

A. A description of the period setting of the room would be required to produce *nostalgia*, or longing for the past.

B. The directions include the time of day, the fact that we hear footsteps, and instructions to show only what can be seen above the desk. There is no *animosity*, or hostility.

C. The camera is fixed on the desk. We hear people enter. Then we hear and see all the dialogue and actions contained in lines 8 to 18. Everything is perfectly clear. There is no *confusion*.

54. B

Irony exists when there is a difference between what is expected and what is real. It does not exist just because there is a difference. Three of the responses contain a difference of some kind, but no irony.

Gilbert and Sullivan are sitting side by side like old friends, but they are in complete disagreement. Appearance and reality are different.

A. Irony does not exist whenever there is a difference. We *expect* a composer to compose and a writer to write.

C. The two do leave the room at different times— at the end of the scene. The irony exists while they are seated throughout the scene.

D. The difference in cigar and cigarette is not ironical. Notice that Sullivan is not offered a cigar. We can guess from the earlier photograph that he prefers cigarettes. The difference is a matter of taste.

55. C

When looking for the main reason, expect to find partial reasons or at least reasons that seem plausible.

In lines 31 to 34, Sullivan complains that Gilbert has added the "tantalizing suggestion that we are to be in the realms of human emotion and probability," but that Gilbert then continues with his "familiar world of topsy-turvydom." In other words, the revisions promise a story with human depth but quickly return to the frivolous.

A. Sullivan does say (lines 26 to 27) that he cannot set the music, but he is talking about the entire piece, not about the revisions that are not mentioned until line 28.

B. In lines 31 to 34, Sullivan makes it clear that the changes are necessary but that they have not been taken far enough.

D. Sullivan does not say that he is bored with their collaboration. He does not mention boredom at all. He does say that he does not like the kind of story that Gilbert likes to write. He objects to frivolity.

56. B

That the libretto is "profoundly uncongenial to me" suggests that it does not suit Sullivan; it is not to his taste. If neither the meaning of the word "congenial" (compatible with one's taste) nor the context are helpful, proceed by elimination.

A. We know that Gilbert and Sullivan operettas are not gloomy.

C. Sullivan does think Gilbert's work is flawed— he does not like topsy-turvydom—but he also knows that the work has been successful.

D. Gilbert's light-hearted topsy-turvydom can hardly be called *abstract*, a word that suggests intellectual.

57. A

Sullivan has said that they regard him as a tune-making machine. Gilbert, Carte, and Helen quickly disagree. They are saying that he is a genuinely creative artist.

B. Sullivan is not a performer of music. He is a composer.

C. The topic of discussion is his creativity, not his culture.

D. Sullivan's image of turning a barrel-organ suggests a producer of popular tunes. That is exactly what Gilbert, Carte, and Helen are *not* trying to say to him.

58. A

First, there is the instruction "**GILBERT**, **CARTE** *and* **HELEN** *speak at once*." Then in line 55, there is the instruction "*She continues*." Helen is the last to be listed, and as she continues, it is clear that she has changed the topic. The overlapping speech has ended.

B. "*She continues*" does not mean she speaks gently. It is more likely that she speaks briskly as she gets the conversation back to business and away from artistic feelings.

C. Helen has just expressed the same opinion as Gilbert and Carte. She continues because she has something else to say.

D. Gilbert, Carte, and Helen have just disagreed with Sullivan. It is Sullivan that Helen would like to back down, not all three men.

59. A

Gilbert is mocking, or making fun of, Sullivan. His later mockery of Ibsen is actually directed at Sullivan. Since he is not merely disagreeing, but making fun of Sullivan, he is showing himself to be self-centred.

Of course, if Sullivan actually went on an extended trip, left Gilbert working on the libretto, and later complained about what Gilbert had produced, we might think that Gilbert has been provoked and is justified in making fun of Sullivan. However, in lines 88 to 90, he is sufficiently offensive to provoke a protest from Carte (line 91).

B. Deceitfulness means untruthfulness. If Gilbert is lying about Sullivan and Ibsen, then he would be deceitful. However, no one corrects him, and there is nothing else in the extract to suggest that he is a liar.

C. Gilbert is not melancholy, or sad. He is annoyed, even angry.

D. In line 73, Gilbert's words "No, Sullivan—indeed! I was here, and you were there! Ha!" are definitely not formal.

60. D

The context explains the meaning. Gilbert says "No, Sullivan—indeed! I was here, and you were there! Ha!" In the context, "Ha!" means *so there!* Gilbert thinks he has made a clever and telling point at Sullivan's expense.

A. Gilbert is not talking about Sullivan's morals. He is talking about Sullivan being away at the wrong time.

B. Neither line 72 nor Gilbert's earlier remark in lines 70 to 72 are examples of laughter. Gilbert is wittily mocking, but he is not actually laughing.

C. In certain contexts, "Ha!" might be used to point out futility. However, when the exclamation comes right after a witticism, it more likely expresses satisfaction.

61. B

Sullivan says "I have been repeating myself . . . for too long, and I will not continue." In other words, he will not *repeat his efforts*.

A. Sullivan does not mention the public.

C. Sullivan is not willing to continue working with Gilbert on the same kind of libretto, but he is still willing to work with Gilbert, as he makes clear in line 99, in his response to Gilbert's offer to stand aside.

D. The phrase "this … class of work" is a clear reference to Gilbert's libretto. Sullivan is not talking about Gilbert himself.

62. A

Gilbert has offered to stand aside for one turn. When Carte says that is a possibility, Gilbert does not respond as though he had made an offer that he really wanted to have accepted. "Well, that is your prerogative" means *well, I cannot stop you*. In other words, he had never meant that his offer should be taken seriously.

B. It would hardly be flattering to Gilbert to suggest that he might be replaced.

C. Carte might be siding with Gilbert's feelings if Gilbert really felt that he wanted to be replaced—but in that case, Gilbert would probably respond with thanks.

D. Suggesting that Gilbert could be replaced might be insulting to Gilbert's feelings. After all, he probably thinks himself irreplaceable. However, although Gilbert responds coolly, he does not seem to think that he has been deeply and intentionally insulted.

63. D

Look carefully at the context. Gilbert offers to step aside. Carte agrees that is possible. Gilbert immediately drops the subject. Gilbert knows that Carte has the contractual right, the power, to have him replaced.

A. If Gilbert says "I suggest X," and Carte replies, "That is a possibility," then Gilbert is not going to reply, "Well, that is your conclusion." That would be nonsense.

B. Carte is not arguing with Gilbert, he is agreeing with him.

C. If Gilbert says "I suggest Ẋ," and Carte replies, "That is a possibility," then Gilbert is not going to reply, "Well, that is your opinion." That would be nonsense.

64. A

The conclusion contains four directions to pause (lines 116, 119, 130, and 133). Combined with the curt, name-only goodbyes (lines 121, 122, 126, and 132) the pauses indicate strain and uncertainty.

B. There is no resolution and no one is content.

C. No one is optimistic. Sullivan has said he cannot write and Gilbert has said that he cannot rewrite.

D. They are not irrevocably defeated. They have reached an impasse, but the contract is still in force and neither the operetta nor the collaboration has been called off.

The Pirates of Penzance

65. C

Read the whole of lines 17 to 25. The pirate king justifies himself quite plainly. He says that he behaves like a king, helping himself in a royal way, and that although he sinks a few more ships than he ought to, any first-class king "must manage somehow to get through / More dirty work than ever *I* do." So, compared with many "respectable" kings, he is not a bad fellow.

A. He does not mention his background, so there is no way of knowing what he has been taught.

B. He justifies himself by comparison, not by saying that piracy cancels standards of right and wrong.

D. It is true that he is happy as a pirate, but that is not how he justifies his actions. In fact, he does not say that he is happy. We infer that fact from what he says in lines 17 to 25 and also in lines 2 to 10.

66. C

Refer to line 41. When Frederic asks, "compared with other women—how are *you*?" he is asking about her person. She answers "I have a slight cold, but otherwise I am quite well." One of the humorist's standards is to have one party to a conversation respond literally to something. The intent is humour (and on stage, properly delivered, this line *is* funny).

A. A slight cold is nothing to be concerned about—but she is probably quite well.

B. Frederic does not question Ruth's sincerity. Until line 59, after he has seen the bevy of beautiful maidens, he believes Ruth when she claims to be beautiful.

D. This is an *operetta*. There is no drama and no real threat.

67. A

Dramatic irony exists when a character does not know something that the audience and other characters know. Since the audience knows that Ruth is not telling the truth, this is an example of dramatic irony.

B. Metaphor is a figure of speech used to compare two unlike things by describing one of them as the other.

C. Hyperbole is exaggeration for effect. Ruth is not exaggerating, she is lying.

D. Oxymoron is a figure of speech similar to paradox. It is a short phrase that contains two contradictory terms. The contradiction is only apparent.

68. **C**

Ruth acts *bashfully*; she pretends to be self-conscious or modest. Her bashfulness might be the result of embarrassment, reluctance, sensitivity, or an attempt to manipulate—any of the responses. However, her asides show that she intends to marry Frederic before he sees any woman of his own age. She is attempting to manipulate Frederic's affections.

A. A woman might be embarrassed by a direct question about her looks, but the asides show that Ruth has tried to deceive Frederic while he still knows little about the world away from the pirates.

B. A woman might be reluctant to discuss past compliments, but the asides show that she has mentioned them in order to deceive Frederic.

D. At 47, Ruth might be sensitive about her age, but the asides show that she has tried to deceive Frederic while he still knows little about the world away from the pirates.

69. **B**

Frederic has already been characterized as *innocent*, or inexperienced, and *gullible*, or easily deceived. This line reinforces his innocence and gullibility.

A. It is fair to say that Frederic is trusting and generous; however, innocent and gullible describe him even better.

C. Since Ruth has deceived him very easily, Frederic can hardly be called intuitive, able to know things as though by instinct, or discerning, having good judgement.

D. Since Frederic is easily deceived, he could be called vulnerable, or easily manipulated. However, he is not very demanding. On the contrary, he wishes to do the right thing (line 52) and seems to have a generous nature.

70. **C**

Consider readings VIII, IX, and X in their entirety.

The question asks which topic could be researched by using all three readings. In other words, each reading must supply useful information that could be used in a research paper on one of the topics.

Reading VIII gives reasons for the longstanding appeal of Gilbert and Sullivan. Reading IX gives a loosely historical picture of the two artists disagreeing about the quality of their work. Reading X is an example of their work. All three could be used in researching the longstanding appeal of Gilbert and Sullivan's works.

A. Only Reading VIII has any information about literature, music, and the economy. The other two readings are literature, but they contain no information about music or the economy.

B. Reading VIII contains a brief mention of the popularity in the United States of Gilbert and Sullivan's musical theatre, but nothing about the role of the United States in popularizing musical theatre in general. The other two readings have nothing to do with the United States.

D. Reading VIII mentions the role of film in preserving Gilbert and Sullivan's musical operas. Reading IX could be used as an example of how a film has helped preserve the operas. However, Reading X is an excerpt from one of Gilbert's librettos, and has nothing to do with film.

Appendices

SOME COMMON LITERARY TERMS

Abstract	Abstract terms and concepts name things that are not knowable through the senses; examples are love, justice, guilt, and honour. See CONCRETE.
Allegory	A story or visual image with a second distinct meaning partially hidden. It involves a continuous parallel between two or more levels of meaning so that its persons and events correspond to their equivalents in a system of ideas or chain of events external to the story.
Alliteration	Repetition of initial consonant sounds
Allusion	Indirect or passing reference to some person, place, or event; or to a piece of literature or art. The nature of the reference is not explained because the writer relies on the reader's familiarity with it.
Analogy	A comparison that is made to explain something that is unfamiliar by presenting an example that is similar or parallel to it in some significant way
Anecdote	A brief story of an interesting incident
Antecedent Action	Action that takes place before the story opens
Antithesis	A contrast or opposition of ideas; the second part of a statement that contrasts opposite ideas
Apathy	Lack of interest
Apostrophe	A speech addressed to a dead or absent person or to an inanimate object (Do not confuse this use of apostrophe with the punctuation mark.)
Archaic	Belonging to an earlier time; words or expressions that have passed out of use are said to be archaic
Aside	Comment made by an actor and supposedly not heard by other actors
Assonance	Repetition of similar or identical vowel sounds
Ballad	A narrative poem that tells a story, often in a straightforward and dramatic manner, and often about such universals as love, honour, and courage. Ballads were once songs. Literary ballads often have the strong rhythm and the plain rhyme schemes of songs. Songs are still written in ballad form, some old ballads are still sung, and some literary ballads have been set to music. Samuel Taylor Coleridge's "The Rime of the Ancient Mariner" is an example of a literary ballad.
Blank Verse	Poetry written in unrhymed iambic pentameters
Caricature	A distorted representation to produce a comic or ridiculous effect
Chronological	In order of time
Cliché	An overused expression; one that has become stale through overuse
Colloquial	Informal, suitable for everyday speech but not for formal writing
Concrete	A concrete thing exists in a solid, physical; and is knowable through the senses; trees, copper, and kangaroos are all examples of concrete things. See ABSTRACT.
Connotation	Implied or additional meaning that a word or phrase imparts. Such meaning is often subjective. See also DENOTATION.
Deduction	A conclusion reached by logic or reasoning, or by examining all the available information
Denotation	The explicit or direct meaning of a word or expression, aside from the impressions it creates. These are the meanings listed in dictionaries. See also CONNOTATION.
Discrepancy	Distinct difference between two things that should not be different, or that should correspond
Dissonance	Harsh sound or discordance; in poetry, a harsh jarring combination of sounds
Epic	A long poem that is often about a heroic character. The style is elevated and the poetry often represents religious or cultural ideals; the *Iliad* and the *Odyssey* are examples of epics
Epilogue	A final address to the audience, often delivered by a character in a drama
Fantasy	A literary genre; generally contains events, characters, or settings that would not be possible in real life
Foreshadowing	A storytelling technique; something early in the story hints at later events

Free Verse	Is usually written in variable rhythmic cadences; it may be rhymed or unrhymed, but the rhymes are likely to be irregular and may not occur at the end of lines
Hyperbole	A figure of speech that uses exaggeration for effect
Imagery	Language that evokes sensory impressions
Imitative Harmony	Words that seem to imitate the sounds to which they refer; *buzz* and *whisper* are examples of imitative harmony; also called ONOMATOPOEIA.
Interior Monologue	Conversation-like thoughts of a character
Irony	The difference—in actions or words—between reality and appearance. Authors use irony for both serious and humorous effects. Irony can also be a technique for indicating, through character or plot development, the writer's own attitude toward some element of the story.
Jargon	Special vocabulary of a particular group or activity; sometimes used to refer to confusing or unintelligible language
Justification	The giving of reasons or support; for example, giving an argument or reason that shows that an action or belief is reasonable or true
Juxtaposition (or contrast)	The deliberate contrast of characters, settings, or situations for effect; the effect may be a demonstration of character or heightening of mood
Lyric	A poem that expresses the private emotions or thoughts of the writer; sonnets, odes, and elegies are examples of lyrics
Metamorphosis	An alteration in appearance or character
Metaphor	Comparison without using the words *like* or *as*
Metrical poetry	Is written in regular, repeating rhythms and may be rhymed or unrhymed; when rhymes are used, they are generally regular, like the rhythm, and are often found at the end of the line
Monologue	A literary form; an oral or written composition in which only one person speaks
Mood	In a story, the atmosphere; when a writer orders the setting, action, and characters of a story so as to suggest a dominant emotion or patterns of emotions, this emotional pattern is the mood of the story. Also a person's state of mind or complex of emotions at any given time.
Motif	A recurring theme, situation, incident, idea, image, or character type that is found in literature
Ode	A poem expressing lofty emotion; odes often celebrate an event or are addressed to nature or to some admired person, place, or thing; an example is "Ode to a Grecian Urn" by John Keats
Onomatopoeia	Words that seem to imitate the sounds to which they refer.
Oxymoron	A combination of two usually contradictory terms in a compressed paradox; for example, "the living dead." An oxymoron is like a metaphor in that it expresses in words some truth that cannot be understood literally; *truthful lies* is an oxymoron that describes metaphors
Parable	A short, often simple story that teaches or explains a lesson—often a moral or religious lesson
Paradox	An apparently self-contradictory statement that is, in fact, true
Parallelism	The arrangement of similarly constructed clauses, verses, or sentences
Parenthetical	A word, phrase, or passage (sometimes within parentheses) that explains or modifies a thought
Personification	The giving of human attributes to objects or to abstract ideas
Prologue	An introduction to a play, often delivered by the chorus (in ancient Greece, a group, but in modern plays, one actor) who plays no part in the following action
Pun	A humorous expression that depends on a double meaning, either between different senses of the same word or between two similar sounding words
Rhetoric	The art of speaking or writing

Rhetorical Question	A question for which a reply is not required or even wanted; the question is asked for effect. Often, a rhetorical question is a way of making a statement: *Is there anyone who does not believe in freedom?* really means *Everyone believes in freedom.*
Ridicule	Contemptuous laughter or derision (contempt and mockery); ridicule may be an element of satire
Satire	A form of writing that exposes the failings of individuals, institutions, or societies to ridicule or scorn in order to correct or expose some evil or wrongdoing
Simile	Comparison using the words *like* or *as*
Soliloquy	A speech by a character who is alone on stage, or whose presence is unrecognized by the other characters; the purpose is to make the audience aware of the character's thoughts or to give information concerning other characters or about the action
Sonnet	A lyric poem fourteen lines long and usually written in iambic pentameter. The Shakespearean sonnet consists of three quatrains (four-line stanzas) and a couplet (two lines), all written to a strict end-rhyme scheme (abab cdcd efef gg). The development of the poet's thoughts is also structured. There are several methods: one method is to use each quatrain for different points in an argument and the couplet for the resolution of the argument. Because of the complexity of the sonnet, poets sometimes find it a suitable form for expressing the complexity of thought and emotion.
Symbol	Anything that stands for or represents something other than itself. In literature, a symbol is a word or phrase referring to an object, scene, or action that also has some further significance associated with it. For example, a rose is a common symbol of love. Many symbols, such as flags, are universally recognized. Other symbols are not so universally defined. They do not acquire a meaning until they are defined by how they are used in a story. They may even suggest more than one meaning. For example, snow might be used to symbolize goodness because of its cleanness, or cruelty because of its coldness. Symbols are often contained in story titles; in character and place names; in classical, literary, and historical allusions and references; in images or figures that appear at important points in a story; and in images that either receive special emphasis or are repeated.
Thesis	A statement that is made as the first step in an argument or a demonstration
Tone	A particular way of speaking or writing. Tone may also describe the general feeling of a piece of work. It can demonstrate the writer's attitude toward characters, settings, conflicts, and so forth. The many kinds of tone include thoughtful, chatty, formal, tragic, or silly; tone can also be a complex mixture of attitudes. Different tones can cause readers to experience such varying emotions as pity, fear, horror, or humour.

DIRECTING WORDS

The following list of directory words and definitions may help you plan your writing. For example, a particular discussion might include assessment, description, illustrations, or an outline of how an extended argument could be developed.

Agree Or Disagree	Support or contradict a statement; give the positive or negative features; express an informed opinion one way or the other; list the advantages for or against
Assess	Estimate the value of something based on some criteria; present an informed judgement. The word "assess" strongly suggests that two schools of thought exist about a given subject. Assessing usually involves weighing the relative merit of conflicting points of view; e.g., negative vs. positive, strong vs. weak components, long-range vs. short-term
Compare	Point out similarities or differences; describe the relationship between two things; often used in conjunction with CONTRAST
Contrast	Show or emphasize differences when compared; see COMPARE
Describe	Give a detailed or graphic account of an object, event, or sequence of events
Discuss	Present the various points of view in a debate or argument; write at length about a given subject; engage in written discourse on a particular topic
Explain	Give an account of what the essence of something is, how something works, or why something is the way it is; may be accomplished by paraphrasing, providing reasons or examples, or by giving a step-by-step account
Identify	Establish the identity of something; establish the unique qualities of something; provide the name of something
Illustrate	Give concrete examples to clarify; provide explanatory or decorative features
List	Itemize names, ideas, or things that belong to a particular class or group
Outline	Give a written description of only the main features; summarize the principal parts of a thing, an idea, or an event
Show (that)	Give facts, reasons, illustrations or examples, to support an idea or proposition
State	Give the key points; declare
Suggest	Propose alternatives, options, or solutions
Support	Defend or agree with a particular point of view; give evidence, reasons, or examples
Trace	Outline the development of something; describe a specified sequence

CREDITS

Every effort has been made to provide proper acknowledgement of the original source and to comply with copyright law. However, some attempts to establish original copyright ownership may have been unsuccessful. If copyright ownership can be identified, please notify Castle Rock Research Corp so that appropriate corrective action can be taken.

Excerpt from "Sanctuary" from SPEAK by Laurie Halse Anderson. Copyright © 1999 by Laurie Halse Anderson. Reprinted by permission of Farrar, Straus and Giroux, LLC.

Excerpt from "The Firstborn" by Christopher Fry, Oxford University Press, 1958. Reprinted by permission of Oxford University Press

Excerpt from "Pygmalion" by George Bernard Shaw

Excerpt from "Macbeth" by William Shakespeare

Excerpt from "To Build a Fire" by Jack London

Excerpt from "Another Solution" by Gilbert Highet, published in Harper's Magazine, November 1951, p.45

"The Hymn of a Fat Woman" by Joyce Huff, From Gargoyle Magazine, Volume 44, Copyright Joyce Huff. All rights reserved.

"High Jump" from *Stalin's Carnival by* Steven Heighton, Quarry Press, 1989

"Anthem for the Doomed Youth" by Wilfred Owen

"Sea-Fever" from *Salt-Water Ballads,* by John Masefield, London, Elkins Mathews, 1913

Excerpt from "The Sniper" by Liam O'Flaherty, from *Liam O' Flaherty: the Collected Stories, Volume 1*, Palgrave MacMillan Publishers Limited, 2000

Excerpt from "Dance at Santo Domingo" by Jacquetta Hawkes and J.B. Priestley from *Journey Down a Rainbow* (© Jacquetta Hawkes and J.B. Priestley 1969) is reproduced by permission of PFD (www.pfd.co.uk) on behalf of The Estate of Jacquetta Hawkes and The Estate of J.B. Priestley.

"How Mr. Dewey Decimal Saved My Life" from HIGH TIDE IN TUSCON: ESSAYS FROM NOW OR NEVER by BARBARA KINGSOLVER. Copyright © 1995 by Barbara Kingsolver.

"A Defense of Detective Stories" by G.K. Chesterton

"i have found what you are like". Copyright 1923, 1925, 1951, 1953, © 1991 by the Trustees for the E.E. Cummings Trust. Copyright © 1976 by George James Firmage, from COMPLETE POEMS: 1904-1962 by E.E. Cummings, edited by George J. Firmage. Used by permission of Liveright Publishing Corporation.

"Morte D'Arthur" by Alfred Lord Tennyson

Excerpt from "Hamlet" by William Shakespeare

"Variation on the Word Sleep" by Margaret Atwood

"The Faith" by Leonard Cohen, © 2004 Old Ideas LLC (BMI)

Excerpts from "A Modest Proposal" by Jonathan Swift

"To His Coy Mistress" by Andrew Marvell

"Fog" from CHICAGO POEMS by Carl Sandburg, copyright 1916 by Holt, Rinehart and Winston and renewed 1944 by Carl Sandburg, reprinted by permission of Houghton Mifflin Harcourt Publishing Company.

"Mother to Son", from THE COLLECTED POEMS OF LANGSTON HUGHES by Langston Hughes, edited by Arnold Rampersad with David Roessel, Associate Editor, copyright © 1994 by The Estate of Langston Hughes. Used by permission of Alfred A. Knopf, a division of Random House, Inc.

"Stars" by Marjorie Pickthall

"Waldon; or, Life in the Woods" by Henry David Thoreau

Excerpt from "A Rose for Emily" by William Faulkner, published in Forum, April 30, 1930

"Swimmer's Moment" by Margaret Avison, From: *Winter Sun.* Toronto: University of Toronto Press, 1962. pp.36

Photograph by Amy Toensing, published in National Geographic Magazine, March 2003, © Amy Toensing, reprinted by permission of Getty Images

"Dragon Night" by Jane Yolen. Copyright © 1980 Jane Yolen. Currently appears in HERE THERE BE DRAGONS, published by Harcourt Brace and Company. Reprinted by permission of Curtis Brown, Ltd.

"For the Lost Adolescent" by Deborah Digges, form *The New Yorker*, November 23, 1992, © Deborah Digges

Excerpt from "A River Runs Through It" by Norman Maclean, The University of Chicago Press, © 1976 by The University of Chicago

Excerpt from "The Matchmaker" by Thornton Wilder, from *Masters of Modern Drama*, 1962, Random House

Excerpt from "The Hard Life" by James Fallows, Copyright 2009 The Atlantic Media Co., as first published in The Atlantic Magazine. Distributed by Tribune Media Services

Excerpt from "Tender Mercies" by Rosellen Brown, published in Canada by Random House of Canada Limited, © 1978 by Rosellen Brown

Excerpt from "The History of Troilus and Cressida" by William Shakespeare, from *William Shakespeare, The Complete Works*, Viking, 1969

"The Stones" by Suzanne Gardinier, from *The New Yorker*, February 13, 1989

Excerpt from "The Country of Illusion" by Thomas Wharton, from *Fresh Tracks: Writing the Western Landscape*, edited by Pamela Banting, Polestar Book Publishers, 1998

Poster by Hoger Matthies. In *Persuasive Images: Posters of War and Revolution*, by Peter Paret, Beth Irwin Lewis, and Paul Paret. Princeton University Press, 1992

"Blessed Is The Man", from THE POEMS OF MARIANNE MOORE by Marianne More, edited by Grace Schulman, copyright © 2003 by Marianne Craig Moore, Executor of the Estate of Marianne Moore. Used by permission of Viing Penguin, a division of Penguin Group (USA) Inc.

Excerpt from "The Tragedy of King Richard the Second" by William Shakespeare, from *William Shakespeare: The Complete Works*, edited by Alfred Harbage. New York, Viking, 1969

Excerpt from "Introduction to the Tragedy of King Richard the Second" by Matthew W. Black, from WILLIAM SHAKESPEARE: THE COMPLETE WORKS by William Shakespeare, edited by Alfred Harbage, copyright © 1969 by Penguin Books, Inc. Used by permission of Viking Penguin, a division of Penguin Group (USA) Inc.

Excerpt from "Flesh and Blood" by Michael Cunningham, Copyright © 1995 by Michael Cunningham. Reprinted by permission of Farrar, Straus and Giroux, LLC.

"Why We Pulled the Taffeta," published in *National Geographic*, March 2003

Excerpt from "Introduction to the Complete Annotated Gilbert and Sullivan," by Ian Bradley, 1996, Oxford University Press. Reprinted with permission of the author.

Excerpt from "Topsy-Turvy," by Mike Leigh, published by Faber and Faber Limited, © 1999 by Mike Leigh

Excerpt from "The Pirates of Penzance" by W.S. Gilbert, from *The Complete Annotated Gilbert and Sullivan*, introduced and edited by Ian Bradley, Oxford University Press, 1996

"Preserving Our Past for Our Future," Brochure content created by the City of Edmonton Reprinted with permission.

"Four Letters of Love" by Niall Williams, London, Picador, 1997

ORDERING INFORMATION

SCHOOL ORDERS

Please contact the Learning Resource Centre (LRC) for school discount and order information.

THE KEY **Study Guides** are specifically designed to assist students in preparing for unit tests, final exams, and provincial examinations.

THE KEY **Study Guides** – $29.95 each plus G.S.T.

SENIOR HIGH		JUNIOR HIGH	ELEMENTARY
Biology 30 Chemistry 30 English 30-1 English 30-2 Applied Math 30 Pure Math 30 Physics 30 Social Studies 30 Social Studies 33	Biology 20 Chemistry 20 English 20-1 Pure Math 20 Physics 20 Social Studies 20-1 English 10-1 Pure Math 10 Science 10 Social Studies 10-1	Language Arts 9 Math 9 Science 9 Social Studies 9 Math 8 Math 7	Language Arts 6 Math 6 Science 6 Social Studies 6 Math 4 Language Arts 3 Math 3

Student Notes and Problems (SNAP) Workbooks contain complete explanations of curriculum concepts, examples, and exercise questions.

SNAP Workbooks – $29.95 each plus G.S.T.

SENIOR HIGH		JUNIOR HIGH	ELEMENTARY
Biology 30 Chemistry 30 Applied Math 30 Pure Math 30 Math 31 Physics 30	Biology 20 Chemistry 20 Pure Math 20 Physics 20 Pure Math 10 Applied Math 10 Science 10	Math 9 Science 9 Math 8 Science 8 Math 7 Science 7	Math 6 Math 5 Math 4 Math 3

Visit our website for a tour of resource content and features or order resources online at
www.castlerockresearch.com

#2340, 10180 – 101 Street
Edmonton, AB Canada T5J 3S4
e-mail: learn@castlerockresearch.com

Phone: 780.448.9619
Toll-free: 1.800.840.6224
Fax: 780.426.3917

CASTLE ROCK
RESEARCH CORP

ORDER FORM

THE KEY	QUANTITY	STUDENT NOTES AND PROBLEMS WORKBOOKS	QUANTITY	
			SNAP Workbooks	Solution Manuals
Biology 30		Math 31		
Chemistry 30		Biology 30		
English 30-1		Chemistry 30		
English 30-2		Applied Math 30		
Applied Math 30		Pure Math 30		
Pure Math 30		Physics 30		
Physics 30		Biology 20		
Social 30		Chemistry 20		
Social Studies 33		Pure Math 20		
Biology 20		Physics 20		
Chemistry 20		Applied Math 10		
English 20-1		Pure Math 10		
Pure Math 20		Science 10		
Physics 20		Math 9		
Social Studies 20-1		Science 9		
English 10-1		Math 8		
Pure Math 10		Science 8		
Science 10		Math 7		
Social Studies 10-1		Science 7		
Language Arts 9		Math 6		
Math 9		Math 5		
Science 9		Math 4		
Social Studies 9		Math 3		
Math 8				
Math 7		**TOTALS**		
Language Arts 6		**KEYS**		
Math 6		**SNAP WORKBOOKS**		
Science 6		**SOLUTION MANUALS**		
Social Studies 6				
Math 4				
Language Arts 3				
Math 3				

Learning Resources Centre

Learning Resources Centre

Castle Rock Research is pleased to announce an exclusive distribution arrangement with the Learning Resources Centre (LRC). Under this agreement, schools can now place all their orders with LRC for order fulfillment. As well, these resources are eligible for applying the Learning Resource Credit Allocation (LRCA), which gives schools a 25% discount off LRC's selling price. Call LRC for details.

Orders may be placed with LRC by
Telephone: 780.427.2767
     Fax: 780.422.9750
Internet: www.lrc.education.gov.ab.ca
Or mail: 12360 – 142 Street NW
      Edmonton, AB T5L 4X9

PAYMENT AND SHIPPING INFORMATION

Name: _____

School Telephone: _____

SHIP TO

School: _____

Address: _____

City: _____ Postal Code: _____

PAYMENT
☐ by credit card
  VISA/MC Number: _____
Expiry Date: _____
Name on card: _____
☐ enclosed cheque
☐ invoice school   P.O. number: _____

CASTLE ROCK
RESEARCH CORP

#2340, 10180 – 101 Street, Edmonton, AB T5J 3S4   **Phone:** 780.448.9619 **Fax:** 780.426.3917
Email: learn@castlerockresearch.com   **Toll-free:** 1.800.840.6224
www.castlerockresearch.com